HOPE FOR THE LAND

HOPE
FOR THE
LAND

CHARLES E. LITTLE

RUTGERS UNIVERSITY PRESS

New Brunswick, New Jersey

For Dorothy, Charles, and Katharine;
and for Julia and David

Little, Charles E.
  Hope for the land / by Charles E. Little
  p.   cm.
  ISBN 0-8135-1802-4
  1. Land use—Government policy—United States. 2. Environmental policy—United States.
3. Land use—Environmental aspects—United States. I. Title.
HD205.L58   1991
333.73'13'0973—dc20
                                                                    91-33963
                                                                        CIP
British Cataloging-in-Publication information available

This book was acquired and developed for Rutgers University Press by the Center for American Places,
Harrisonburg, Virginia.

The essays in this book were originally published in different form by American Forests; American Land
Forum Magazine; the Conservation and Research Foundation; Dowden, Hutchison, and Ross, Inc.;
Harrowsmith-Country Life; Journal of Soil and Water Conservation; Sierra Club Books;
Smithsonian; U.S. Government Printing Office; University of Illinois Law Review, copyright ©
1986 by the Board of Trustees of the University of Illinois; and Wilderness. Permission, as appropri-
ate, to adapt material from these sources is gratefully acknowledged.
    The author also acknowledges with thanks permission to quote lines from Carl Sandburg (page 5),
"The People, Yes," Part 2, in Complete Poems, Harcourt, Brace and Company, copyright ©
1936 by Harcourt, Brace and Company, by permission of Harcourt Brace Jovanovitch, Inc.; and to
quote lines from Joe Paddock (pages 214–215), "Black Wind," in Handful of Thunder: A Prairie
Cycle, Anvil Press, copyright © 1983 by Joe Paddock, by permission of the author.

CONTENTS

ABOUT THIS BOOK

In the early 1970s, when I first came to Washington, D.C., to begin a new phase of my career—as an analyst and writer on environmental policy—there was a well-developed legislative move afoot in our government to enact a "national land-use bill." It was a bipartisan effort, championed by a congeries of middle-of-the-road politicians including President Richard Nixon and his aide, lawyer John Erlichmann; the late, revered senator from Washington state, Henry M. Jackson; and the equally revered congressman of Arizona, Morris Udall, now retired. The group was so well placed and powerful, with Jackson and Udall in charge of the appropriate committees in the Senate and the House, and the concept so seemingly logical, everyone thought such legislation could surely succeed, just as the National Environmental Policy Act had succeeded a few years before, becoming law in 1969.

The idea was that since there were certain kinds of land (such as, say, coastal wetlands) with environmental values of greater than local concern, and certain kinds of land uses (such as huge shopping malls whose construction would affect the use of land for m iles around), also of greater than local concern, there ought to be a way for the people who didn't happen to live nearby to have a stake in the planning for such areas or such uses. The approach of the legislation, which had various titles but was most often known as the National Land Use Policy and Planning Act, was simply to provide state governments with the money to assure that local jurisdictions would undertake adequate planning and in doing so would observe ordinary precautions about dealing with sensitive land areas and sensitive land uses.

The bill very nearly passed at one point, managing to get through the Senate, but failing in the House. As time went on during several reintroductions, however, opposing forces had a chance to coalesce—and succeeded finally in beating the bill right into the ground. At the end of this sorry process, after about three years of increasingly rancorous disputation, one would have thought the Bolsheviks had taken over the minds and hearts of the decidedly moderate political leadership that had put forward the idea of a national land-use policy. Everyone, it seemed, had an ox that would be gored, or at least wounded slightly. Real estate investors and developers, champions of "home rule," farm and ranch organizations, small-business proprietors, and those who make a living sniffing out opportunities to practice the politics of fear and loathing—all, and more, inveighed against the bill so energetically that the surprised sponsors finally had to give up the idea. By 1976 almost everyone agreed that there would be no such thing as a national land-use policy in the United States of America. And there isn't to this day—which makes us unlike virtually every other industrial democracy in the world.

Had the bill been enacted, those of us who worked for its passage might have wound up with jobs implementing the law in one way or another. But it didn't and we didn't. Instead, a good many of us hung on, trying to find other ways to produce an equivalent result—by *parsing* the issues of land use, breaking them down into more manageable units for public discourse and, we hoped, legislative action. In place of an integrated and unitary land-use policy for the nation, we would express our hope for land by approaching its most salient issues separately: the need to preserve the physical integrity of our urban and suburban neighborhoods and rural communities; the need for a viable agriculture and the prime cropland necessary to sustain it; the need to manage our remaining natural areas and wildernesses to keep them from being fragmented and thus rendered ecologically dysfunctional; the need to save landscapes with outstanding aesthetic and cultural values.

This book pulls together my efforts during and after the "policy years" to give life and substance to that parsing. Some of the work resulted in legislation—notably for farmland and for the preservation of outstanding landscapes—but most did not, and probably never will. Still, a larger objective is involved here, for slowly but surely I have come to understand that our "hope for the land" derives, not from the mere mechanics of a land-use policy, but from the development of a pervasive land ethic. It is the land ethic, after all, which necessarily precedes and produces policy. It doesn't work the other way around. And so the book both begins and ends by emphasizing the need for a land ethic, even though for the most part it deals with more "practical" matters.

Hope for the Land owes much to those editors, publishers, sponsors, and colleagues who have helped frame my research and writing over the years. Of the many, many wonderful people I worked with on land-use issues, let me herein acknowledge a special indebtedness to Malcolm Baldwin, Dick Beamish, Norm Berg, Peter Borrelli, Wallace Bowman, Robert Cahn, Ken Cook, Robert Coughlin, Kevin Coyle, Arthur Davis, George Davis, Norah Davis, Barbara Dean, William Duddleson, George Dunsmore, Sara Ebenreck, Robert Einsweiler, Glenn Eugster, Wendell Fletcher, Richard Gardner, Don Goldman,

Richard H. Goodwin, Joe Goodwin, Robert Gray, Robert Hagenhofer, Keith Hay, Tony Hiss, Sydney Howe, Don Humphrey, William Jolly, Cecily Kihn, Philip Lewis, David Loeks, Meg Maguire, John Mitchell, Rice Odell, Larry Orman, Jake Page, David Plowden, Frank Popper, Richard Pough, Paul Pritchard, Tom Rawls, the late Robert Rodale, Bill Rooney, David Sampson, Neil Sampson, Andrew Scheffey, Max Schnepf, James N. Smith, Frits Steiner, the late Stanley Tankel, William Toner, T. H. Watkins, and William H. Whyte. These are the people who not only encouraged and supported me, but taught me. To those I have inadvertently left off the list, my deepest apologies.

George F. Thompson, president of the Center for American Places, served as the project editor for this book, working closely with me throughout its writing. His organizational skills and enthusiasm for the project were invaluable. Alice Calaprice deftly edited the manuscript with restraint and uncommon skill. Karen Reeds of Rutgers University Press has been a delight to work with, as have Marilyn Campbell, managing editor, and Kenneth Arnold, director of the press. My wife, Ila Dawson Little, reviewed the manuscript of *Hope for the Land* with the trained eye of a book editor (Macmillan) turned professor of English (University of the District of Columbia). And lastly, I am indebted, as always, to my literary agent and friend of many years, Max Gartenberg.

I inhale great draughts of space.
The east and west are mine,
   and the north and south are mine.
I am larger, better than I thought,
I did not know I held so much goodness.

—WALT WHITMAN
"Song of the Open Road"

PROLOGUE

The state of the American land is much on our minds these days. Best sellers, feature films, television documentaries, and endless newspaper stories tell of farm failure, of 1930s-style soil erosion, of the metastasis of suburban sprawl into the pure countryside, and of the destruction of neighborhood and community values, which are, after all, American values. We should do something about all this, of course.

Yet, how do you apprehend the American land—its lay, its cover, its history, culture, economy—much less solve its problems? We're lucky if we know our own patch. It takes a generation to know a piece of farmland, a Minnesota farmer once told me, even on a small place like his. Where the spring sun first hits, where the land gullies out, or where water collects in low-lying pockets. Where the soil is rich and deep, or underlain by rock. Just how to set the plow, and where to turn. The best place for a new shed. What grows in the hedgerows. How the wind moves across a field, and what the field thinks of it. What soaring creatures keep surveillance from above, and what nocturnal mysteries obtain on warm summer evenings in the neighborhood of just a handful of acres.

You can drive across the land, of course, and I have done it myself—coast to coast—five times. But that makes me no expert. How much actual surface have I visited in that fifteen or twenty thousand miles of concrete and asphalt? The right-of-way of an interstate is some 50 acres a mile, with maybe 200 acres per mile coming into view, and whizzing by. Sixteen million acres in the aggregate, then. But out of the total of 2.3 *billion* acres of U.S. land, that's only .006 of America. What can anybody know with a lifetime .006 average?

Once in a while, out of sheer frustration, I like to stop the car, get out, and just walk *into* the land. Did some conquistador step here, I wonder, or earlier an Anasazi—an old one—who trembled at the mountains that spurted fire and, returning to his pueblo, led his people away to we know not where? Joe Garcia, a Southern California vegetable grower and childhood acquaintance, took his wife and infant son across the border between Sonora and Arizona in 1935, to walk into the blazing desert wilderness toward Los Angeles. After a time, the infant's breathing slowed, then stopped, and Garcia and his wife scooped out a shallow grave in the loose earth, covering it with stones—a gesture only, for the coyotes would come that evening and the little cairn would mean nothing to them. Joe and his wife walked on, into the slanting rays of the afternoon sun which put the cholla and mesquite into sharp relief as the air cooled. Then they stopped. Something stopped them.

"No está muerto," Joe's wife said to her husband. "He is not dead." And she said it with such certainty that they turned in their tracks without another word and at a half-trot hurried back the miles to the cairn. Pulling away the rocks, Joe Garcia lifted the tiny body, loosely swathed in cotton, and placed the infant's sandy mouth to his ear. A shallow breath. He was alive.

Automobiles now speed past this very spot. What miracles there are in the land!

And disappointments. The New York farm of my grandmother's grandmother's father (I think, a generation out of ken, in any event) bordered on a tidal creek that separated the farm from the northern tip of Manhattan Island. ("Mannahatta, my city," Whitman sang in a greener time of the metropolis, when it clung to the bottom quarter of the island, a day's wagon ride away.) The farm's fields are now under the rubble of the South Bronx. As they excavate for some foundation footing, or just to clear away the detritus of the blighted lives in that blighted place, will a workman find a statesman's—a landowner's— clay pipe? Or a cruddle that was turned by the grandmother of a grandmother after she had switched the cows into the barn for the hired man to milk? Did the statesman's son, my distant uncle, on a Sabbath secretly cast a baited hook into the marshy water at the edge of the fields that ran down to it? To tempt a bass that could be filleted and fried in homemade butter? The pan resting on the coals in a stone fireplace? The stones pulled from the fields to which the rubble has now returned?

I have stood in the South Bronx, in the shadows of empty buildings, and wondered about this, knowing that the rats were scuffling nearby wondering about me. One day, the father of the grandmother of my grandmother said, "I have sold the farm. We are moving to Connecticut." I believe I can just make out a child, head down, walking across a beloved pasture that is busy with the insects of summer brushing the tops of the clover. Coming to a hillock, surmounted by a tall white oak that could not be cleared from the land, the child, a girl, sinks to the earth, soft with the leaf mold of many seasons, and looks out across the ruffling waters of the marsh to the wild scarp of Manhattan. Hugging her knees, she tries to picture being in another place, but cannot.

So it is that we come to love the land.

"The land was ours before we were the land's," said Robert Frost at a presidential inauguration. He was a land lover. It is a reasonable thing for an American to be, if you think about it. After all, land was the whole idea of the New World. A place to start over, to start fresh, to leave behind the feudal remnants of Europe, with its land enclosures and bars to ownership. What other people could understand Carl Sandburg singing of the land as a place

> Of tall corn, of wide rivers, of big snakes,
> Of giants and dwarfs, heroes and clowns,
> Grown in the soil of the mass of the people?

Soil and people, these are central images: manifest destiny, homesteading, "grass, trees, and a good place for the kids to grow up," the Jeffersonian Democracy of the Land. Even the great interstate highway system expresses this fantastic idea: on the road, goin' down the road, hit the road, one for the road. One, hell. Everyone for the road. Lighting out for the territory ahead of all the rest, as Huck Finn said in the last lines of the greatest American novel ever written.

In search of . . . what? Why, in search of the land! Our *place:* deserts, marshes, mountains, waves of grass and grain. A lush dairy farm in Vermont, endless rows of corn in Iowa, wheatlands in the Dakotas, great cattle and sheep ranges in the High Plains, wilderness mountaintops, dusty vineyards on the dry hillsides of the Coast Range, stump farms in Oregon, unspurious fishing villages, fogbound fields of artichokes near Carmel in California, blackdirt fields of pineapple below the volcanos of Hawaii, sugarbeet fields in Colorado, spud fields in Idaho, historic towns and quaint neighborhoods, and melon patches, peanut farms, cotton plantations, rice fields in the Southeast, jumble streets in Brooklyn, skyscrapers in Chicago, citrus groves and tomato patches in Florida, with tomatoes tough as baseballs—all places with their indigenous agrarians, experts in abundance and in real estate.

Yet despite this richness, a permanent sense of impermanence has settled over America's landscape these days. Some parts of it are poisoned by industry, uglified by office buildings and shopping malls, encroached on by condos. Elsewhere, natural areas are fragmented, losing ecological function, becoming *simplified.* And in other parts there is worse news yet: the land has been deserted. Farms are abandoned where deep soils have become shoals of the Mississippi or where the center-pivot irrigation rigs have made their last, slow pirouette, engines rusting quietly. Going-out-of-business signs appear in the country towns, school windows are boarded up, broken street lights keep a black vigil on empty corners.

Outside the car windows speeding through the land, beneath the airliners flying coast to coast above it, the surface, as mere extent, remains, of course. As I have said, the land keeps its secrets unless you get very, very close to it. But those who do may hear a whisper, a plea, that we not lose our grip on the idea of the American land—as expressed, for example, in the observations of a farmer on the rural fringes of a metropolis trying to understand a few acres, or by the story of a Mexican American who grew vegetables and raised children, or even in the quest of the descendant of New England farmers who sought a heritage in the rubble of an urban tragedy.

The idea of the land has many forms and many meanings. And we had better hang on to them all, brothers and sisters. For they are the idea of *America.* Of tall corn, of wide rivers, of big snakes, of giants and dwarfs, heroes and clowns, grown in the soil of the mass of the people.

I

LAND AND COMMUNITY

Most Americans tend to have a terrifically wrong-headed notion that somehow the community of land has nothing to do with the community of people when in fact the exact opposite is true. Land is not just a surface on which a settlement is built, like a Monopoly board where little green houses and red hotels are cleverly set out. Land is the origin of community—of the community of people every bit as much as it is the community of nature, as Aldo Leopold has so persuasively instructed us.

Our failure to connect land and community has led to the loss of both—in cities, suburbs, and rural areas. During the 1970s I had the opportunity to study citizen attitudes about land and community in a collection of cities, towns, villages, and settlements around the country where a "sense of place" was strongly felt in the face of intense development pressures. Such communities stand in extraordinary contrast to the rural areas now losing population. Reports from the field about both kinds of places—those with too many people arriving and those with too many people leaving—follow an introductory essay about Aldo Leopold's notion of the land ethic and its importance to the integrity of community.

The concluding section treats our environmental preferences as I discovered them in a series of "focus group interviews" in various communities of the Minneapolis–St. Paul metropolitan region. Of all the research I have ever done in behalf of land-use policy, this was the most significant, at least to me. I had hoped to continue this work—"Expectations of the American Land"—but could get no funding. "We don't care about policy," one foundation executive told me. I said that in America not to care about policy is to give up on democracy. To which he responded with a shrug. So it goes.

LETTING
LEOPOLD DOWN

In 1933 a forestry professor named Aldo Leopold published an article in the *Journal of Forestry* which set forth a proposition that today has become something of a growth industry among the intellectuals of the out-of-doors: the land ethic. "That land is a community," said Leopold in a later description of the idea, "is the basic concept of ecology, but that land is to be loved and respected is an extension of ethics." Professor Leopold's idea was published again as the last chapter of *A Sand County Almanac* in 1949, the very year that he died while fighting a brushfire near his summer home in Wisconsin. The book lives on, and through many editions has sold in the millions, especially to the "greening of America" youth who are now professors themselves.

Leopold suggested caution and deferred rewards in our use of land resources as an ethical proposition, rather than an economic one. Land is a community, he said, not a commodity. We would do well to use it with "love and respect." In time Aldo Leopold became the most-quoted author in conservation circles, with the possible exception of Thoreau. And yet, despite his noble and compelling idea—the land ethic—we have not heeded his advice. In this matter, the evidence of the senses is compelling. Just when we thought we had soil erosion licked, Texas dust started appearing again on cars parked in Ohio cities. Just as soon as we invented all manner of planning devices to control suburban sprawl, a new urban form arose—the "outer city"—and its metastasis appears to be unstoppable. As for the inner city, the downward spiral of environmental degradation persists, despite assurances that the bottom has been reached and there is no place to go but up. Finally, even our precious wildernesses and natural areas seem hopelessly beset, public ownership notwithstanding.

Although new generations rediscover the land ethic and tend to proclaim it as their own contribution to the conservation debate, the notion is, after nearly sixty years, getting gray around the temples, even a bit paunchy, endlessly (so it would seem) waiting for the bus. Nevertheless, the land ethic is, in my view, one of the most important ideas of the century, ranking (for a variety of reasons) with the concept of a congress of nations, as in the League of Nations, the United Nations, and the World Court; or with labor unionism, collective bargaining, and limitations on the exploitation of children as industrial workers.

The idea of ethical evolution, as Leopold expressed it, is simple enough. He tells of Odysseus returning from the Trojan wars and hanging "all on one rope some dozen slave girls of his household whom he suspected of misbehavior." Leopold states that for Odysseus this was simply a matter of the disposition of property, not of right and wrong. The ethic—which is a *social* concept—of not summarily executing the girls belowstairs had not yet caught up to history. After a while, perhaps with the emergence of the Christian concept of souls being equal before God, it did become antisocial to do away with one's servants in such a manner. And in further developments, society extended ethical behavior to cover quite complex human relationships— between and among families, tribes, communities, even nation-states.

Our currently sophisticated extension of social ethics reaches into a variety of institutional relationships, but not, finally, to the "land-relationship," as Leopold called it in 1933. "There is, as yet," he wrote, "no ethic dealing with man's relationship to land. . . . Land, like Odysseus' slave-girls, is still property, the land-relation is still strictly economic, entailing privileges but not obligations."

What is so terribly poignant about reading the 1933 version of Leopold's essay is that he thought the land ethic was on the eve of actually coming into being. "The extension of ethics to this third element in the human environment is, if we read evolution correctly, an ecological possibility. It is the third step in a sequence; the first two have already been taken," he wrote. He suggested that the conservation movement was the "embryo" of a fully realized land ethic to come—the third step in ethical evolution, after the ethics governing the relations of individual to individual and the relations of the individual to society.

But the beginnings of this third step, which would govern the ethical relations between people and land, were not revealed in that decade, or the next. By the late 1940s, just before he died, Leopold wrote in *A Sand County Almanac* that "no important change of ethics was ever accomplished without an internal change in our intellectual emphasis, loyalties, affections, and convictions. The proof that conservation has not yet touched these foundations of conduct lies in the fact that philosophy and religion have not yet heard of it." The statement does, however, hold out a glimmer of hope, for it implies that when philosophy and religion *do* hear of conservation—and the ethical imperatives such knowledge implies—*then* the embryo will grow.

So we have come to the heart of the matter. What can one say now, now that philosophy and religion *have* heard of conservation, and not only heard of it, but from the late 1960s onward made it one of their basic themes? During the "conservation decade," as former Secretary of the Interior Stewart Udall called the 1960s, through and beyond Earth Day in 1970 with its "teach-ins," philosophers and preachers, on campus and off, have commended the land ethic to their listeners. Their counsel was not always in the precise terms set forth by Aldo Leopold, but close enough to create a consciousness that the "land-relation" in the evolution of ethics was not only possible, but urgent. Today, there are academic chairs and journals of environmental ethics, including the ethics of land use; there are pronouncements by the clergy, such as those by the so-called heartland Catholic bishops, calling for a new stewardship of the land; there are nonsectarian organizations across the country, such as the Land Stewardship Project in Minnesota. All these philosophers and preachers carry the message that land is a community, not a commodity, and that society must use the land with love and respect.

But to what effect? The despoliation of land—Leopold's word—cannot be gainsaid. Everywhere, *everywhere*, the rate of despoliation increases: strip-mine gashes, kudzu-covered junkyards, billboards, antennas sprouting like asparagus; Stygian mill towns; clear-felled forests, dams imprisoning free rivers, festoons of electrical spaghetti, six-laners knifing through the land; natural beauty destroyed as recreational opportunity is enhanced: "condomania" on the coastlines from New Jersey to the Keys, asphalted national parks, national forests, national recreation areas, national wildlife refuges, monuments, and historic places—all of which make up the leisure-world trailer hook-up that has become America; the so-called gray suburbs of Archie Bunkerland in the Rust Belt, the ticky-tacky of "the Valley" in southern California; the sad, swaybacked shotgun houses of Southern fields, empty now, where occupants fled with the coming of giant machines that crawl monstrously on the land like battle tanks; the farm-belt fields washing down to become shoals in the Mississippi, farmsteads deserted, a handful of dust in the high plains; the outer-city high-rises commingling with the cows; and in one place near where I live, a new office building with primrose-colored windows that looks for all the world as if it had been filled to the top with pink cold cream.

Despite the sixty years of exposure—with some special emphasis during the last thirty, courtesy of organized religion and academic philosophy—the land ethic has not really made a dent nationally. Had policymakers caught some glimmer of it, we might have some significant national legislation. But we do not. And that failure, to my mind, is at least prima facie evidence that a land ethic simply does not now exist in the United States of America. There are "pockets of hope," to borrow the phrase of a colleague, but not many.

My question is, how come? How come America still lacks a land ethic, especially in view of the fact that so many other countries—without anywhere near the richness, diversity, cultural importance, or sheer size our land possesses—have managed to create permanent national policies for land conservation and landscape preservation? For example, Britain's Town and Country Planning Act, passed by a postwar socialist government in 1947, effectively nationalized the right to change the use of land. Despite its left-wing origins, the act has nevertheless survived a series of conservative governments, including the most conservative in Britain for over half a century. By contrast, on this side of the Atlantic, our effort to promote coastal zone planning is now virtually defunct after twenty years of trying; schemes to support state-level planning in accordance with national guidelines, regularly introduced during the early 1970s, failed so often that finally even conservationists got bored with them. Even a pusillanimous effort of a few years ago to protect farmland from urbanization (the Farmland Protection Policy Act) languishes largely unimplemented. Such is our ethical progress in sixty years. Is the fault in the stars, as Shakespeare's Cassius put it to Brutus, or in ourselves?

Many people make a case for the stars, especially those whose financial or political positions might be affected under a land ethic actually implemented rather than just talked about. The vastness of the continent suggests to them the irrelevance of conservation policy nationally applied. A social ethic that would govern behavior between people and land is too refined, they say, and runs counter to the individualistic spirit of the pioneers that made this country great. Democracy, by their definition, requires a free market economy untrammeled by regulation. So the arguments run, full of received truths, each asserting that "it's my land and I can do with it what I want."

Ignoring Leopold, the national conservation organizations respond with poor imitations of their adversaries, proposing that saving the open space, saving the marsh, saving the farmland, saves money and is just as Red, White, and Blue as you. Outrage is out, cool economic analysis is in. Arguably, the conservation movement, far from being the embryo for the land ethic, is its destroyer; for it does exactly what Aldo Leopold warned against, it trivializes conservation by reducing its ethical imperatives to mere dollars and cents. "The logic of history hungers for bread," he wrote, "and we hand out a stone."

Ethical behavior of any sort—which is to say choosing between social and antisocial conduct between us as individuals, between individuals and society, and society and the land—is never a matter of dollars and cents except coincidentally. But never mind that. A developer bought some land from a real estate speculator who bought it from the family of a farmer, and the developer got the land rezoned and hired an architect to design a building with pink windows. My example is emblematic, of course, even idiosyncratic. The tastelessness ought to make me laugh, but manages only to put me in a fury. Such excesses infuriate each of us in our own particular way, but I suggest that at some point, our reaction is *not* a matter of individual taste. It is a matter of ethics. And yet only rarely does the concept of the land ethic, with its sense of caution and deferred reward, enter into the process of deciding how we use the land, deciding what kind of buildings we may place upon it. Why is that? I want to know.

G. K. Chesterton, the British writer and social critic, was once asked if he thought that Christianity had failed in England. His answer was that it had never been tried. And so it is with the land ethic in America. The failure, and it is the worst kind of failure of all, is the failure to try.

In our unsuccessful efforts to codify the land ethic in policy—such as for development planning, the stewardship of resource lands, and the protection of critical environmental areas—we have proposed two criteria for establishing the terms of ethical land-use decision-making: *ecology* and *equity*. In the case of the first of these, we can identify (if we choose) an unethical decision through ecological analysis, such as the decision to clear a forest in a way that would destabilize the ecological balances between plants and animals. In the case of the

13

second, equity, we can identify (if we choose) an unethical decision through socioeconomic analysis, such as inappropriately consolidating land for strip mining and consequently depriving individuals of their rights to ownership, safety, and economic use of land.

If we read our Leopold, however, there are *three* criteria, not two. The third criterion is the *aesthetics* of the land. In the case of aesthetics we need not hire an ecologist who, in fact, may be "callous as an undertaker to the mysteries to which he officiates" (said Leopold), nor a social scientist to survey the consequences of diseconomic land use. We need only to open our eyes to the despoliation all around us. The clear-cuts, the strip mines, the outer-city buildings with pink windows require no statistics to produce outrage. They are outrageous at first sight.

There can be no hierarchy among the three criteria of the land ethic—ecology, equity, aesthetics—and I propose none. I do propose that we not ignore aesthetics. Since it is the most universally apprehended of all the criteria and relates most directly to our quotidian surroundings, our *place*, an aesthetic sensibility is the best means by which we can understand and implement the land ethic in a community setting. When our sensibility is offended by buildings filled with pink cold cream, the outrage that follows should not be suppressed. It should be allowed to flourish. It is the most human defense there is against the despoliation of land.

Without outrage, Aldo Leopold will be left without a legacy, for the land ethic will then suffer the worst kind of failure, the failure to try. Instead of cool analysis, then, we should embrace the politics of outrage, and of fury, indignation, wrath, deep umbrage, resentment, exasperation, rancor, and passion that wells up, if we let it, when we see the landscape destroyed. "We are remodeling the Alhambra with a steamshovel," Leopold wrote in the conclusion of *A Sand County Almanac*, "and we are proud of our yardage." When enough of us permit ourselves to feel, as did Aldo Leopold, the anger such an act produces, then perhaps laws protecting the land will follow, and, finally, an American land ethic can begin.

PLACELESSNESS AND PLANNING

Excommunication, exile, displacement: these are among the extreme punishments meted out by society to its miscreants, or are the results of wars or politics. They are extreme because people are banished from their *place*.

Is it not also extreme when place is banished from the people? As I will describe more fully at the conclusion of this book, this kind of reverse banishment is one of my own most vivid childhood memories—and perhaps an informing one for my writing. Those who lived in the Los Angeles of the 1940s could see it coming even then, and I was among them. From a hillside perch I watched as the great conurbated bowl filled up with people and factories and houses and roads and smog, the characteristic haze (which is what Angelenos always called it) that got browner year by year and crept up the side of our mountain.

The rows of valencia and tokay disappeared. The streams, intermittent even in the wettest years, dried up, were forgotten about, got paved over. Puma, coyote, and eagle fled from thirst, fire, and bulldozer. And so did I. Now, under a great multilane expressway interchange lies a schoolyard. Beneath ten times ten thousand tons of concrete and fill is a rotted thong from a David's sling that once sent the smooth stones from the creek beds humming into the brilliant sky. All this was banished from *me*, my "place."

One cannot go home again, in Thomas Wolfe's endlessly quoted and widely misunderstood phrase. Not just because maturity changes perception, but because the home—the "place"—is gone, no longer perceivable at all.

What began during World War II in Los Angeles spread across the country during the postwar years into the potato fields of Long Island, the cow pastures west of Chicago, and everywhere else cheap land could be found on the fringes of cities. As a consequence, by the 1960s placelessness had resolved itself into an issue called "land use." The phrase may even now seem unfamiliar to many, and without affect, but of all the issues of domestic policy, this one has been the most discussed and argued over—whether or not the discussants understand that they are talking policy issues and not just grousing.

When a highway is put through a community, the issue is land use. When a factory spews fouled air or discharges chemical-laden waste into the local creek, the issue is land use. When everybody says that the place we live in is just not the same anymore, the issue is land use. And then everybody agrees that "we've got to have better *planning*." Whereupon our place may be in really deep trouble.

Planning—by which I mean the governmentally sponsored enterprise of drawing maps and making rules to minimize the impact of the eradication of places—is clearly necessary. But as it is practiced in far too many areas of growth and change in the United States, "planning" has become a lulling substitute for resolute political action when our place is threatened with destruction. So we make a plan, and then assume we are safe, as if the plan could transform itself automatically into action to save our place. If planning is, theoretically, precedent to action, in practice it is often a substitute for action, a way to avoid facing the hard political questions of land use.

We should not blame the planners, of course, for they have arrogated no wizardly power to themselves without our encouragement. We are the ones, at least in the years of my own awareness of the issues of "land use," who have ducked the job of dealing with the eradication of place by the ordinary means of political process that are available to us, which is to say that you go down to town hall and yell your damn head off. Instead, we have asked a small group of professionals to turn our human needs for the preservation of place into some kind of technical "process" that would require an alchemy beyond even the power of wizards.

And so, it has been our failure and misfortune to be unable to define the issue of placelessness in concrete political terms. By themselves the words "land use," or "environmental impact," or even "conservation" mean nothing. That is, they mean so much as to mean nothing at all. In political terms, such words and phrases are not only meaningless, they are mischievous, for they divert us from the goal rather than illuminate it. True politics, which in the Greek means "of the citizen" (*politikos*), insists on a language of reality, not jargon that describes a managerial function. In the language of reality, the issue of land use is, after all, experienced as *placelessness*.

In human terms, the opposite of placelessness is *community*. Therefore, if ordinary citizens, having become disenchanted with wizards, wish to figure out what to do about placelessness beyond making a spectacle of themselves at town hall, they must deal with the making of community. Though we often speak of a "community of interest" in a nongeographical sense, the most thoroughgoing kind of community provides a holistic experience that operates within fixed spatial boundaries. Communities can, and often do, embrace large geographical areas in sparsely settled regions, but what it comes down to is that a community is our smallest, truly political (as in *politikos*) unit of society.

The search for community takes many forms in the United States, and community is achieved at varying levels of success. Community strengths can fail to appear in places where they would be thought most likely, or can arise in spite of the odds. In order to find out what determines the difference, I was commissioned, in 1975, by the Conservation and Research Foundation of New London, Connecticut, to investigate various kinds of communities around the country to see how ordinary people, left to their own devices (*politikos*), dealt with the issue of the preservation of place—that old issue the bureaucrats call land use and that I call placelessness. I was, in other words, looking for little nuggets of local good news within the national slag heap of land-use misery. I found three.

The first good news was in the adjoining downstate Illinois cities of Champaign and Urbana, having a combined population of about a hundred thousand, the home of the University of Illinois and far enough from Chicago to escape the kind of hog-butcher development that had been going on in the city of broad shoulders. In fact, just about the first thing the people of Champaign-Urbana told me was that they had a "crisis gap." The gap obtained because the university was no longer growing and, since it was the dominant enterprise locally, the cities themselves were no longer growing.

Although I did not know it at the time, the conditions of economic retraction, as opposed to expansion, would become rife ten years later in Middle Western and Plains states. (There's more on this subject later.) But here, in downstate Illinois, a medium-sized city had achieved what every conservationist inured to the patterns of postwar metropolitan sprawl wished for—no growth. Interestingly, what this condition did for the civic leadership in Champaign-Urbana was to force it to reflect upon affirmative strategies for the improvement of their place as opposed to defensive tactics that are inevitably required when a place is threatened by overdevelopment, as had been the case during the 1960s and 1970s almost everywhere.

For me, the visit to Champaign-Urbana served as a kind of R & R leave for an embattled conservationist suffering from a bad case of futility. The city that I saw was, for the most part, something straight out of an Andy Hardy movie: graceful old homes lining wide, pleasant streets. And even though there was a bit of decrepitude and blight downtown, it was merely shabby, not appalling. Poverty and unemployment were a problem, but seemingly a small one at the time. However, when I voiced these observations to a group of local officials (many of whom operated as civic leaders as well as university faculty), there were cries of outrage. "Have you seen the North End?" demanded Hiram Paley, a professor of mathematics and then mayor of Urbana. When I allowed that I had not, Dr. Paley invited me to a basketball game (Illinois vs. Purdue—the home team lost by an embarrassing twenty points), before which we would take a swing through the infamous North End since it was on the way. After several wrong turns, Dr. Paley found a few ramshackle houses. "Really bad, isn't it?" he inquired hopefully. Though a few houses were abandoned and others listed slightly to port or starboard, the slums of Champaign-Urbana were nowhere to be found. What I saw was a street where Judge Hardy might have lived if he had not been quite so well off.

In the places I was most familiar with—L.A., New York, Washington, D.C.—the inner city festered while metropolitan growth fanned far into the countryside. The fanning-out ruined both the city and the countryside. But this Corn Belt city had a very distinct edge. One could go from a residential street into farmland as cleanly as if a slide had been changed on a projector. There was a reason for this, of course. The topsoil is eight feet deep outside of town, and an acre of agricultural land could sell for a price approaching a city lot. As Lachlan Blair, a professor of planning at the university (now retired), told me, "This land produces three things for our farmers: corn, soybeans, and Miami Beach."

Would that it were ever so. But situations change. Farming was soon to go into decline, and more and more houses in the North End would be abandoned to decay. Still, the Champaign-Urbana of the mid-1970s might well provide some valuable lessons. The question must be posed: Can a sense of community arise, and prevail, in the absence of crisis? Or will civic apathy take over as the local leadership feared it might? The fact is, it didn't. As Robert Pinkerton, a regional planner for Champaign County complained to me, he and his small staff were required to attend over one hundred citizen-group meetings a month.

One of the reasons for meetings was that the state of Illinois had raised the tendency of local governments to spin off services into special districts (in order to bypass debt-limitation constraints) into a high art. According to some estimates given to me, the number of special units of government in Illinois—for lighting, sewers, roads, schools, police, hospitals, parks, and so on—then exceeded ten thousand. In Champaign-Urbana alone there were fifty such districts, which, considering the one or more citizen advisory groups associated with each, indicated that literally thousands of people were directly involved in governance.

Whether this was good or bad was the leitmotif of a freewheeling discussion concerning land and community issues that was held for my benefit. In attendance were Mayor Paley and Professor Blair, along with Susan Stone, a director and founder of the Champaign County Development Council, and Joan Severns, a member of the Champaign City Council.

Said Mrs. Stone, referring to the multiplicity of authorities: "It took us three months just to get a meeting date acceptable to everybody to discuss a municipal swimming pool."

Said Mayor Paley, referring to the vast number of citizen groups: "All we do is hear and hear and hear."

Said Professor Blair, wanting to be fair: "Still, progress has been made."

Said Mrs. Severns, the realist: "But at what cost?"

It seemed clear to me that civic involvement in land-use decision-making served to keep the issues alive even during the crisis gap. At the same time, the legal and practical traditions of Illinois's severely atomized form of local government could serve to cancel out the sense of community hegemony that traditionally provides the motive power for reform. The welter of special districts could make "progress" impossible. Still, in most places that I knew about, "progress" was no solution; it was the problem. As Professor Blair pointed out, "In Mayor

Daley's Chicago, there are seven units of government, rather than fifty." He invited me to draw my own conclusions.

Thus the progress that had been made in Champaign-Urbana was of the most benign sort—the creation of a humane landscape and living environment: a tree-planting program, new and expanded parks, the preservation of the remnant woodlands (so rare in the prairie), the landscaping of unsightly areas, a pedestrian mall downtown, a rigorous ordinance controlling commercial signage. These were just some of the projects that used the high level of citizen involvement in public decision-making to good effect in creating the artifacts of a true community. On balance, it would appear that even a crisis gap was not enough to depress civic energy for good works in Champaign-Urbana. In other places, where such involvement is commonly replaced by the expertise of professional political operatives and consultants, perhaps the outcome is not the same.

"In the beginner's mind there are many possibilities," says the Zen Master, Shunryu Suzuki. "In the expert's, there are few."

Another nugget discovered amid the dross of national land-use failure was Bolinas, California, in western Marin County, north of San Francisco. On the bay side of Marin are the dense suburbs of the city—Sausalito, Mill Valley, San Rafael—which extend northward to Petaluma and Santa Rosa. But the sprawl has not moved westward toward the Pacific. Development has been hindered, thank heavens, by problems of slope and soil stability, lack of highway access, a practically nonexistent water table, extreme fog at times, and a large proportion of the land in public ownership.

Along the narrow, unsuburbanized coastal strip of Marin County, at the foot of the mountains, small agricultural and fishing villages have therefore remained intact, strung out along the two-lane California Route 1, which hugs the cliff edges and is surely the most scenic coastal road in all the United States. One of these communities is the village of Bolinas, located on a peninsula that forms the seaward side of Bolinas Lagoon, a treasured natural area along the coast. Formed by the San Andreas fault, the lagoon is host to a lively heron rookery. Nearby, at Monarch Grove, is the legendary resting place for millions of migrating butterflies.

The community at Bolinas also has some human commuters, though I found them to be in the minority. For the most part, Bolinasites are summer residents, retired people, those who run shops and businesses, and "subsistence residents," which then was about 30 percent of the total population—artists and writers and poets or those who just "do their thing" without visible means of support. In the summer and on holidays the sightseers come, but do not stay long. They are day-trippers, for Bolinas is little more than an hour's car ride from San Francisco. At the time of my visit in 1975, the population of the community was about two thousand, living on some thirty-six hundred acres of the peninsula, which had not much room for expansion.

Marin County is one of those suburban jurisdictions priding itself on the sophistication of its planning. So it was fair for me to ask of the natives I encountered in Bolinas whether or not a bureaucratic, suburban-oriented planning apparatus could do much good for as rural, peculiar, and isolated a place as theirs. The people of the village thought not, for they had already successfully defended the fragile lagoon from any number of destructive incursions without much if any "planning" help from San Rafael, where county planners labored over their maps in a sprawling government complex. The Bolinasites had beaten back a scheme to dredge the lagoon for a giant marina, had sent any number of second-home developers packing, and had turned out in force to clean up after an oil spill that otherwise might well have destroyed many shorebird nesting colonies.

In recognition of this civic energy, in Bolinas and some other remote communities, a new government in Marin County inaugurated an optional "local-input planning policy," based on the notion that the responsibility for planning could be placed on residents themselves in less intensively developed areas. In the case of Bolinas, the residents did not simply provide "input," they essentially took over the process, producing a plan that appeared to their visitor (me) as being utterly unique if not visionary.

I have seen thousands of local master plans of the kind routinely produced by professional consultants. They are as predictable and boring as the tract-house subdivisions they are intended to control. But Bolinas's effort was categorically different. According to Rex Rathbun, who was one of the "Planning Group Coordinators" called for under the Marin system, the community set out not just to prepare a land-use plan, but to devise a kind of community *constitution.* More than one hundred participants, representing about one-sixth of the households, produced the document. As the introduction (preamble) to the plan put it, "The concept of community, including all living organisms and land forms, exists in rare form in Bolinas. The planning process shall attempt to understand, protect, and engender the elements of COMMUNITY [their caps] as they apply to Bolinas."

There was more. An epigraph stated: "Mine is a proud village, such as it is./ We are at our best when dancing. . . ." In the bibliography of the plan, alongside entries describing arcane technical reports, were such reference works as "A Gentle Person's Guide to Crochet and Picture Coloring," and "Postcard from My Mother in Mexico City Complaining of the Smog." The last page of the document was a drawing of Mickey Mouse riding a motorcycle doing wheelies. They don't teach *that* at planning school!

Was this a serious piece of work? You bet it was. The plan called for a growth rate of six new houses a year based on a lottery system; it called for a new mass transit system consisting of a community-owned fleet of jitneys to eliminate traffic problems at tourist-time; it proposed to unstraighten the grid-system roads put in by early real estate speculators; it would protect existing agricultural land and encourage part-time farming by eliminating restrictions on farm animals on small lots; it would ban resort development of any kind in favor of bed-and-breakfast accommodations and youth hostels; it would encourage owner-built "low-tech" design and relax unrealistic building codes; it would prohibit any building within one hundred feet of the lagoon or any watercourse; it would create a public utility district for water and sewage. To implement these ideas, the plan flirted with incorporating the village, but finally concluded that this was the least desirable course: the constitution was constitutionally distrustful of any kind of governmental organization, including their own.

Was the plan "adopted" by the politicians and planners in San Rafael? Well, yes and no. The village of Bolinas has changed little, as residents had hoped, but it is protected less by ordinance than by a combination of community grit (they keep tearing down the Route 1 road signs that would direct idle tourists) and an intractable water and sewer problem that will, perhaps forever, limit development. The most important group that the plan had to persuade was, of course, the community itself. And there it succeeded, wholly transcending the idea of "local input," a supercilious and execrable term if there ever was one.

Indeed, what was going on in Bolinas, as it was in Champaign-Urbana (though for entirely different reasons), was not so much "input" to a professional planning process, but citizen-led, nonhierarchical "vernacular planning" (my term). Vernacular planning, like vernacular architecture, is an organic process, something true communities can do for themselves rather than acquiescing to a remote government that promises—presumably in the community's interest—to organize the oncoming draglines and bulldozers so that they will do the least damage. The Bolinasites would maintain that in any true community, planning for land use *must* be vernacular. Who better than they would understand what it is like to be paved over?

My third discovery was in the neighborhoods of a big city. The very word "neighborhood" conveys warmth and friendliness and is another form of community, one that operates within units of settlement much larger than a tiny village such as Bolinas, but can have more similarities than differences. The question is, can big-city planning work in behalf of protecting community values in a big-city neighborhood? The answer to this question, if asked in Atlanta, Georgia, is yes. In that city, a neighborhood planning program has successfully been in place for over fifteen years.

The program arose when a new city charter called for a city council to replace the old Board of Aldermen and divided the city into twelve council districts. In addition, the charter called for the Bureau of Finance and the Bureau of Planning to be joined at the top under a single commissioner. The head man then (1975) and now (1991) was Leon Eplan, a city planner with a substantial national reputation. (He did not, however, hold this job for all the intervening years, having only recently returned to it from private planning practice.) The significance of tying the city budget to the city plan was not lost on Eplan, nor would it be on any planner. The sheer futility of producing good ideas and handsome reports without the money needed for their implementation is the chief occupational hazard of a profession whose plans traditionally (as they say) "simply gather dust on the shelf." Accordingly, for Leon Eplan, the linking of planning with budgeting was like the tooth fairy come true.

The provisions of the new charter were augmented by a "Neighborhood Planning Ordinance," arising quite naturally from the establishment of the council districts. "In order to be truly comprehensive," the preamble to the ordinance stated, "city plans must be responsive to the needs and concerns of citizens." Such high-falutin' language is routinely ignored in most cities, but in Atlanta it was to become the basis for a big-city version of "vernacular planning" wherein "neighborhood planning units" would be the primary source of planning ideas and principles as well as the object of the enterprise. These neighborhood units were not set up simply to monitor governmental planning, nor to provide "input." Their purpose, with the help of planning advisers from city government who served as resource persons rather than "experts" (even though they were), was to *create*, in a very real sense, the city plan in one-, five-, and fifteen-year versions by means of aggregating the neighborhood plans.

Neighborhood planning did not just emerge accidentally in Atlanta but grew out of manifold social and physical changes that took place during the 1960s, with the combination of economic expansion in a city that was coming to be known as the "capital of the new South" and white flight from in-town neighborhoods to the suburbs after *Brown v. Board of Education* decreed that schools would have to be integrated. During this period, 50 percent of the population changed their address. It was a period, Eplan told me, when "we very nearly lost the city of Atlanta."

In an effort to keep the city from completely coming apart during these worst of times, community groups formed to try to maintain some semblance of neighborhood integrity in the face of urban renewal, highway building, commercial development, and wholesale population shift. During the period, Georgia State University began to monitor the community-group phenomenon and by the early 1970s had accumulated a catalog of such groups that was nearly as thick as the Atlanta telephone directory. According to Joseph E. Parko, Jr., of the School of Urban Life at Georgia State, "The development of a large network of voluntary neighborhood organizations is, I think, the most important factor relating to organized citizen participation in the Atlanta area. The rapid transition of many of these organizations from a crisis orientation to an issue orientation is particularly significant. Neighborhoods which organized initially to combat a zoning change or an expressway [created] mechanisms to involve themselves actively in governmental policy and decision making."

The change from a crisis orientation to an issue orientation was not, however, limited to citizen groups. While new mechanisms were being created in the communities of Atlanta, so were new ones formed in the Bureau of Planning in order to undertake a long-range neighborhood planning program. Starting with the Georgia State catalog, Eplan and a cadre of young city planners interviewed all the community organizations listed to find those that were more or less permanent and at the same time had some interest in planning—however tenuous or unsophisticated that interest might be. As it turned out, 250 neighborhood groups filled the bill, and these were organized into twenty-one neighborhood planning units using the guidelines called for in the ordinance. Thirty-seven of the neighborhood groups, with the help of the young city planners of Atlanta, submitted planning documents. Some of the neighborhoods hired professional consultants whose plans were replete with colored maps and drawings and statistical tables. The poorer neighborhoods sometimes simply submitted lists—"Don't widen the streets," "More playgrounds for young children." But whatever the form, they all had equal weight as the neighborhood unit plans were aggregated and conformed to create the one-, five-, and fifteen-year master plan for the city as a whole in an activity that is repeated every year.

I had the opportunity to interview the first two city planners assigned to carry out the neighborhood planning ordinance. Both were highly trained women with graduate degrees, one a sociologist, one a city planner; one was black, one white; one made the rounds of the neighborhoods in a Volkswagen sedan, the other on a motorcycle; both were twenty-six years old. The sociologist, Shirley Harris, made the initial contact with the neighborhood groups and explained the procedures and the potentials of the program. If she could generate any interest and commitment on the part of the groups to do some actual planning, then Cheryl Pence, the planner, would step in and provide support services to her new "clients."

Both Harris and Pence were overworked but cheerful in spite of taking on a task that was originally thought to require three teams of four people each. (After the initial phase, the staff was, in fact, greatly increased.) I asked them to describe a typical but rewarding community operation. They decided to tell me about the Cabbagetown-Reynoldstown neighborhood plan.

There was a time, they said, when Cabbagetown-Reynoldstown was anything but a community. Cabbagetown was a village of rickety bungalows in an area rezoned for heavy industry that had been built to house the workers of a cotton mill which had long since ceased operation. It was a white, working-class neighborhood. Reynoldstown, which abutted it, was a black working-class community. Said Cheryl Pence, "Five years ago when you asked people in Cabbagetown which way to Reynoldstown, they wouldn't tell you, and vice versa." Added Shirley Harris, "In those days when a black moved to a Cabbagetown street,

25

the boundary between Cabbagetown and Reynoldstown would automatically shift!"

But under the neighborhood planning process, these two places, so suspicious of one another, became a single *community*—and in fact submitted one of the better plans under the program. The coalescing issue was, as was common in those days, an expressway fight, but the coalition remained because it was geographically logical for these neighborhoods to work together as a community, to make the transition from a crisis orientation, as Joseph Parko described, to an issue orientation.

Among the issues was the need for a community park, for a recreation center, for neighborhood renovation, and for changing the zoning from industrial to residential. With the help of Harris and Pence the community established a cooperative grocery store and via a city allocation of $45,000 (one of the virtues of linking planning and finance), began restoring a church to serve as a community center. Best of all, through an all-out community-based fund-raising effort, Cabbagetown-Reynoldstown was able to get enough money together to hire a full-time community coordinator.

While the Cabbagetown-Reynoldstown success story was more dramatic than most, overall response to the program was, and has been, remarkable from the outset. I asked Harris and Pence if they could make any generalizations about their program that might be of help to others. Aesthetics was at the top of the list of community wants and needs, they said—in the form of tree planting, litter clearing, paint-up–fix-up, and open space preservation. They said that people in "the projects," meaning the public housing built in the 1950s and 1960s, were hard to organize, for the residents had had too long a history of displacement and oppression to trust anyone. Many communities, they admitted, failed to achieve consensus because of internal squabbles, one of which had brought Cheryl Pence to tears. Other communities were simply too frightened to submit written plans for fear that they would not be "technical" enough, that they would be laughed at, in spite of assurances from Harris and Pence to the contrary. And, sadly, "Lots of people in our department," they said, "are not into citizen involvement at all—they think citizens bog down the process."

Still, the process was working. "We're really committed to it," said Harris and Pence.

After I had written my paper on placelessness and planning as I had found it in Champaign-Urbana, Bolinas, and Atlanta for the Conservation and Research Foundation (which had commissioned it in 1975), I sent a copy to a friend, Jake Page, who was an editor at *Smithsonian* magazine. He was so entranced by the Atlanta story he asked me to write a fuller version for the bicentennial issue of the magazine he was then putting together. I made several trips back to Atlanta to round out my research, and the article appeared in the July 1976 issue. Since then, in my writings and lectures I have often referred to Atlanta, offering it as an inspirational example of how a big city can actually encourage bottom-up neighborhood planning—much discussed in land-use policy circles but hardly ever put into practice.

So it was with some trepidation that I called up the Atlanta city planning department prior to recasting the story for this book. I just didn't want to hear that the city had abandoned neighborhood planning as unwieldy or unworkable in the fifteen years since I last checked. To my absolute delight and relief I found just the opposite. The program is going strong. Harris and Pence have moved on, but many of the old hands are still working away at it (including Leon Eplan). In fact, when I called, I was transferred to a young woman I remember interviewing, Mary Jane Armstrong ("I'm forty now," she confessed), now the director. Immediately she launched into how the number of participating community groups had increased (to about 350), how they had to add a number of neighborhood planning units (now over fifty), and how effective the program had been.

"Well, that's just great," I said. "Please give my best to everybody down there."

"Sure will," said Mary Jane. "And don't forget to check back after *another* fifteen years!"

———

In our federal system, the states have power over the uses of land. In turn, the states have created local governments to which they have delegated this authority. It should not be construed, however, that "communities" owe their existence or derive any authority from any part of government. They are not creatures of the Constitution or of the states or any state subdivision, but creatures of the people; communities are real places—not a fourth "level" of government, after federal, state, and local, but entities on another plane entirely.

Planning is one of the ways governments can try to help communities, but planning theory, like Keynesian economics, is dominated by big-system thinking. At the beginning of this century, when planning got its start, economic growth needed to be encouraged and large-scale public service systems—roads, education, power and light, water and sewage—provided services as efficiently as possible. Traditional planners still think this way and are puzzled when they find themselves at odds with those whom they would like to serve—the people. The lack of perfect agreement about neighborhood planning at the Bureau of Planning in Atlanta derives from this conflict. Indeed, most professional planners and government officials really do want to practice "top-down" planning—albeit with a modicum of "local input" or citizen participation. That is why the bottom-up communitarian nuggets I found in Illinois, California, and Georgia are so unusual. "Placelessness" in America tends not to be the exception, but the rule.

It has seemed to me, as an advocate of conservation and planning (which must, of course, go hand in hand), that it is a tragedy that our nation has been unable to fashion some sort of national policy to guide our actions. Someday we may try again to enact land-use legislation. And if so, I hope—based on my visits to Champaign-Urbana, Bolinas, and Atlanta—that its central notion will be to encourage and support *vernacular* planning by *citizen* planners to preserve and enhance true community, and therefore a sense of place. Surely it is time for conservationists and their colleagues, who know so much about the community of nature, to learn something about the nature of community.

COPING WITH UNGROWTH

Typically, the economic difficulties that chronically beset agriculture in the United States are described in terms of declining overseas commodity sales volume, or farm bankruptcy, or the need to find new ways to produce more at less cost. Sometimes it seems as though American agriculture were a free-floating enterprise, unattached to the human communities that nourish it every bit as much as do the resources of soil and water. These communities are in trouble, too, and the sense of placelessness among their denizens is as pronounced as that of any exurban village or city neighborhood.

The American country town is in fact a cultural treasure, created by pioneers and homesteaders who, as the editor of the influential British journal *The Economist* put it, "produced just about the most decent, as well as progressive, small-town neighborhood system the world has seen." These communities—the small towns and cities *outside* the orbit of metropolitan growth—are hurting badly.

During the 1970s, many rural towns had stable or even growing populations and were on the increase in wealth, too. In farm counties, real per capita income was, at 91 percent, drawing near to metropolitan levels. Then came the agricultural depression, bringing with it a widening rather than narrowing income gap between the city and country. By 1984 rural incomes had plummeted to 75 percent of metropolitan area levels. The effect has been graphically evident in the rural communities of the 1980s and now the 1990s: boarded-up shop windows, abandoned gas stations with weeds growing through the cracked concrete, and empty schoolhouses with doors standing open and curling linoleum in halls that would never again hear the scramble of children running to class.

There is a poignant irony here. Planning consultants by the thousands are retained to devise strategies to control economic expansion and population increase in the semirural communities on the metropolitan fringe or in popular recreation or retirement areas. But for rural communities in the American heartland, the issue these communities must face is how to control *ungrowth*. There aren't any great programs and planning theories to cover that exigency. If you want to try to cope with it, you're pretty much on your own.

"The problem is," Ben Jones of Burlington, Colorado, told me, "you start living out of each other's pockets after a while." Jones, an optometrist, was voicing a concern that local business and professional people in many other farm communities in America discuss daily.

In small prairie towns such as Burlington especially, the prospect of living out of one another's pockets is not just a matter of business-cycle ups and downs, either. According to a roundup of the economic prospects of rural communities published by the U.S. Department of Agriculture, the rural downturn of the 1980s and 1990s is structural and long-lasting, not cyclical. It's not just a matter of waiting out an economic dry spell until better times come. For the foreseeable future, ungrowth is here to stay. "Most rural communities are ill-situated to benefit from the U.S. economy's shift to service," the USDA economists explain, noting that the kind of businesses showing the greatest vitality are those that serve business itself—data-processing firms, for example, or temporary employment agencies. But while such enterprises do exceedingly well in cities and suburbs, where the clients are, "they are not likely to locate in rural areas, where clients are fewer and much more dispersed."

What to do? In general, there seem to be three responses. Though they are not generally so baldly stated in the literature of rural development, they are as follows. (1) Just let ungrowth roll over you, hoping that neighboring businesses, or neighboring towns, go broke first. (2) Despite the odds against it, send a trade mission to Silicon Valley, armed with tax breaks and other inducements that reach deeply into the municipal treasury of the next century, to see if you can't persuade some manufacturer of microchips to locate a low-slung, superbly landscaped, extremely labor-intensive factory in your town. (3) Pull up your socks and see how you might build back the economy using your own resources.

In the argot of rural development experts, this latter approach is known as a "self-development strategy." According to J. Norman Reid of the USDA's Economic Research Service, it is greatly preferred over any other alternative because it "calls on communities to identify their comparative economic advantages and undervalued local resources and to initiate locally controlled ventures that increase the amount of value added by the local economy." Self-development also, says Reid, includes "motivating community organizations and leadership where they exist or creating them where they do not."

As it happens, Burlington's "Old Town" project fits this definition exactly. Initiated in the late 1970s, the project, which is a re-creation of cow-town life, features, according to Mayor Rol Hudler, an old law office, a general store, "a huge old barn for the production of melodramas," a sod house, printing office, saloon (naturally), and (for balance) an ice cream parlor.

Significantly, the project did not lapse when hard times began to hit Burlington in the early 1980s. Although the town is now making something of a comeback, it lost three hundred people in those years—a small number but at 10 percent a significant fraction of its residents—and several major businesses closed. "We went through this farm economic crisis about two years before anyone around us," Hudler told me. "We were losing businesses and our paper was printing three or four sale bills a week." (Hudler is also editor and publisher of the Burlington *Record.*) But when the going got tough, Burlington didn't forget about Old Town. In fact they kept at it—with financial help from the Colorado Department of Local Affairs, design assistance from the University of Colorado, and coordination by the state's East Central Council of Governments. Though civic pride was a key element that kept everyone going, the primary purpose of the project was to defend the community economy. Said Hudler, "We want to preserve our heritage, that's for sure. But we also want to capture tourist dollars as they come into Colorado." Hudler pointed out that his was the first town you get to in Colorado if you're driving along I-70 as it unrolls out of Kansas. Accordingly, the state government decided to build a welcome center at Burlington, which Hudler thought would stop a fair number of tourists. It just so happens that Old Town is right next to the welcome center.

In economic self-development terms, then, I-70 was the "undervalued local resource," and Old Town one of the "locally controlled ventures" that could "increase the amount of value added by the local economy."

To be sure, not every rural town has a mayor as resourceful as Rol Hudler, nor does it have two exits (as does Burlington) on one of the nation's major east-west interstate auto routes. I asked Maryjo (Jo) Downey about this, in her official capacity as executive director of the East Central Council of Governments (COG). "I've got fifteen towns in the four counties that I work with," she said. "And I already know that only four of those towns are going to be retail trade centers, and that the eleven others are going to have to look to neighboring communities for services."

Chief among the services is, of course, education. In the heartland, a school is more than a brick building; it is a focal point for community pride. According to Jo Downey, when a school closes a kind of panic sets in. The citizens fight to keep the school open, feeling their community might die should it close permanently. In Jo Downey's four counties, three schools had just recently closed, she told me.

Nevertheless, she said, "Once people adjust to the fact that the school is never going to open again, they begin to rally around other projects." And she encourages them, no matter how small or seemingly hopeless an effort it might be. Indeed, I learned that with her energy, enthusiasm, and good contacts with national and state agencies, Downey had become a key figure in holding "The Other Colorado" together. She didn't agree entirely with this assessment. "I work the system," she said. "But if anything is going to happen, only the local people can make it happen." Jobs are, of course, first priority. "First you look at what you've already got," said Downey. "If you can't keep the jobs you've already got, how are you going to go out and find new ones?" All this operates at an exceedingly fine grain, she explained: persuading a McDonald's to take on one or two more employees, for example; or showing a local hardware store how to improve its merchandising program.

A chief tool for Downey's work was a revolving loan fund, operated by the nonprofit "Prairie Development Corporation." The fund is an adjunct to the COG program, and Downey was in charge of that, too. The basic funding comes from the Small Cities Program of the U.S. Department of Housing and Urban Development. Small cities grants are commonly used for public projects—a municipal parking lot, a firehouse, a recreation area—but Downey thought the money would be better spent if it could create permanent local jobs. Among the loan criteria was a proviso that one new full-time job had to be created for every $12,000 loaned by the fund, and at least 60 percent of the new jobs had to be filled by low- to moderate-income persons, which helped insure that they would go to local people.

Though saving jobs, or creating them one by one, seemed to me an arduous and seemingly endless task in this depressed agricultural region of the Great Plains, neither Rol Hudler nor Jo Downey thought of it as a rear-guard action. It was a matter of diversifying local economies based on their local attributes, and slowly bringing employment and population levels into balance with the resource base. Though many experts believe the Plains are in for a long downhill slide, Downey disagreed. "People like it here," she said. "It's small, people look out for each other, you can walk to school, everybody is still full of pride. It's a wonderful place to raise a family." Those little towns, in other words, operate as *communities.*

I asked them about getting some help in mitigating the impacts of ungrowth from professional planners—in the same way that communities beset by just the opposite problem tend to do. But neither Downey nor Hudler were persuaded that "professional" planning would do them much good—although they have themselves demonstrated a quite sophisticated kind of planning that any graduate school would do well to teach. They had become experts in their own right. But what about those towns, whole regions even, that do not have people as skilled as these two or a state government as committed to local economic vitality as is Colorado?

Recently, Jo Downey told me, she was asked how she would recommend bringing about a population decline gracefully in a rural town. How would you even up the number of jobs with the number of people who need them? "You don't," she replied slowly. "I know it sounds awful, but you mainly just have to wait for people to die."

WHAT DO
PEOPLE WANT?

One fine spring in the mid-1970s I was invited to a New England town that was undergoing extreme residential and commercial growth. The purpose was consultative. I had written much about open-space preservation, and so my advice was sought. It happens. Once arrived, I was taken on a tour of the town. I was shown the village green and the Revolutionary houses. I was asked to climb to the top of a drumlin to view a lush valley sprinkled with white farmhouses and laced with stone fences. I was driven to country-road vistas of apple trees in bloom and soft meadowlands. At the end of the day, I sat on my host's deck and admired the view of pasture and woodland and a dramatic ridgeline of greening hills. We had a few beers and I reflected on what a fine place this would be to live in and how lucky he was.

The following morning, I had to get to work to earn my consulting fee. It was meager, but the New England work ethic had somehow been infused in me by the landscape, so the low pay didn't make any difference. It did, however, permit me a measure of independence in my judgment, for if I were not invited back for an encore, it would be all the same to me. And so the conservation commissioners of this town arrived at my host's house overlooking the pasture and wood-land and the dramatic ridge of greening hills. Coffee and sweet rolls were served, and then, at last, a map was unfurled on the dining-room table—a map being the sine qua non of discussions like these. It was an open-space map, said to represent one of the most ambitious pres-ervation plans in the whole state. I took a long look at the many areas colored in various shades of green, but I was unable to make any comment at all. In spite of my lengthy tour the day before, only in one or two instances had I been shown the land that had been pro-posed for preservation.

What this rather startling disjunction suggested to me—and I have encountered it many times since—was that there must have been two sets of values operating with regard to the preservation of place. One was a mapped set of landscape-preservation values capable of being rationalized as public policy; the other, which I had been instructed in the day before and which had moved me greatly, was a set of landscape-preservation values deriving from ordinary personal perception. Only in a very minor way did the two sets overlap. The values of the place and the proposals of the plan were essentially separate.

Why in the world does this happen? We have difficulty, evidently, rationalizing the expenditure of public funds for open-space acquisition merely because it *looks* good or possesses mere cultural values. Instead we have to create constructs to rationalize public expenditures that if not artificial are often wide off the mark in terms of what people really want.

Here is how it works. Land is "saved" (from bulldozers, draglines, and other instruments of destruction) in one of three ways. It is bought or, sometimes, bought back from private interests by the public (which once owned it, of course) to serve a public purpose; or private interests are required by the public not to use the land in certain ways if there would be a dire secondary effect stemming from such a use, such as damming up a stream and depriving others of water; or, finally, private owners are paid not to change the use of the land, a more recent and complicated maneuver. The payment may be made in a variety of ways, although most of it is in the form of negative income: allowing developers to build at higher densities to produce a land surplus that can be preserved, for example, or reducing taxes on farmland.

Since the exercise of any of these public actions tends to reduce land values and thus affect municipal economics, if not require outright expenditure, the public decision to preserve the land one way or another must be convincingly rationalized. And sometimes the rationalizations replace the primary, human impulses of choosing what land to save. This was the case in my New England town, where the rationalizations were set forth as the *primary* values even though they were not. They were simply the arguments for saving open space that were thought to be politically workable. Thus, while the impulse to the preservation of place is derived from a largely nonrational aesthetic sensibility, open-space planning is often based on politically justifiable approaches that can be (and are) rationalized in solely nonaesthetic terms.

This phenonemon is a form of political dishonesty, gladly entered into by land-use planners and their conservationist allies, and it has cost us much. Let us take a look, by way of illustration, at three of these substitute rationales in turn—open space as an economic benefit, ecological determinism in land-use planning, and the social requirements of outdoor recreation.

First, open space. Environmentalists discovered the value of cost-benefit analysis as a device to rationalize public decisions to purchase open space at the municipal level in 1958. That was the year Roland Greeley, a professor of planning at MIT, published a famous letter in the Lexington, Massachusetts, *Minute Man* to the effect that if the town of Lexington, a suburb of Boston and his hometown, would buy up some two thousand acres of open land it would save the taxpayers money. The basis for the claim was that if the land were developed in accordance with the zoning then in force, the new houses would not pay their way. In fact, the annual cost of schools (this was at the peak of the baby boom, remember, and new schools were being built by the tens of thousands in American suburbs), fire and police protection, sewage, drainage, and public welfare would be far greater for the taxpayers of Lexington than the annual cost of retiring a twenty-year open-space acquisition bond, even a multimillion-dollar one.

Greeley's letter was copied onto thousands of stencils, mimeographed, and sent all over the country by open-space preservationists eager to make their case at town hall. By applying their own numbers to Greeley's municipal open-space math, preservationists could show that most suburban open land, typically zoned for half- or full-acre lots, was susceptible to the rationale that preserving public open space costs less than permitting developers to create their subdivisions of split-levels, ranchers, and center-hall colonials. Therefore the land to save was the land that was about to be built on. The race for open space had begun, and *which* open space didn't seem to make any difference.

Developers, the traditional enemy of the landsaver, fought back. The Urban Land Institute, under a grant from the National Association of Home Builders, sought to produce a definitive study that would prove that single-family homes *could* pay their own way if the calculations were made differently. Moreover, developers during this period would often characterize themselves as social reformers, asking where all the ordinary people would live if the suburbs were to become one gigantic nature preserve.

In a valiant effort at compromise, and to bring some sense of order

into the open-space preservation movement, author William H. Whyte
(*The Organization Man, The Last Landscape*) published an influential
report entitled *Cluster Development* (American Conservation Association, 1964). The idea was that low-density zoning be maintained in
the suburbs, but that the allowable number of houses be put on small
lots—that is, "clustered"—so as to produce a large amount of leftover
land that could be aggregated into a large open-space holding for
community or municipal use. Although cluster development is today
permitted in many localities, the idea did not really succeed during the
1960s and 1970s. The land savers were less than persuaded since they
weren't interested in houses of *any* kind. And municipal officials
couldn't see how clustering would solve the baby-boom school-and-
service cost problems. As for the developers (at least the big, well-
capitalized firms), well, they smelled a larger opportunity.

If, the developers reasoned, the primary issue making their lives
difficult was the Greeleyite argument against development because of
the municipal tax-cost liability of single-family houses on large lots,
they could fashion an effective petard for the land savers. This they
did, and called it "planned unit development." By agreeing that development should pay its own way, even agreeing that a modicum of
open space should be preserved, they backed their way into builders'
heaven. They proposed high-density, low-children residential units
including garden apartments, some highrises, and townhouses, along
with a smattering of single-family homes, their old standby in the '50s
and '60s. Some of these developments were described as "new towns,"
although for the most part they were simply new suburbs at the far
edges of large metropolitan regions. In any case, they could pump
fresh blood into the tax base since not all tenants or owners would be
of that uniform species that then produced 2.4 school-age children per
breeding pair. Moreover, through economies of scale, a planned unit
development could provide many of its own municipal services. Some
could even offer their residents a large amount of open space—up to
25 percent of a site in some instances. But in terms of the larger issues
of land conservation, they were, and have been, a disaster. On a site-
planning basis, the PUDs (as planned unit developments were called)
and the new towns might be wonderful, but they attracted less well-
planned development around them, creating in time high-density "outer
cities" that grossly distorted regional development patterns.

Thus, the countryside accessible to metropolitan centers turned out
not to be the countryside that the land savers had in mind at all, in

spite of the fact that the cows sometimes cohabit with the condominiums. So much for the new municipal math. By capitulation to cost-benefit analysis, landscape preservationists not only failed to make a convincing case, they may well have abetted a land-development pattern wholly inconsistent with even the most rudimentary landscape aesthetic—of apple trees, authentic villages, and the distant green ridges.

———

The difficulties with ecological determinism and the social benefits of recreation, two other substitute rationales for the preservation of place, may not be so destructive, but they can also significantly distort public policy. With regard to "the ecology" (as television newscasters are wont to say), the postulates are attractive to conservationists. Sir Frank Fraser Darling, the British ecologist, has maintained that landscapes in ecological balance are also beautiful to behold. This may be true, at least in some cases. But the reverse is false, and the extent to which ecological determinism implies that nonecologically balanced landscapes are valueless is the extent to which the rationale is mischievous. The apple orchard is manipulated agronomically to produce a crop but may still be beautiful and worthy of preservation.

Certainly there is nothing wrong with ecology as a way to understand how the landscape functions. Moreover, ecological analysis is potentially helpful in justifying the preservation of wetlands, alpine environments, deserts, and other habitats that contain a delicate interlocking of creatures, plants, climate, and topography. But such insights are not endlessly projectable to every copse and lea. If ecology as a discipline is neutral—that is, value free—this is not the case for ecological *determinism* as a means for a government to decide which lands shall be preserved and which built upon. Ecological determinism—the invention, pretty much, of the brilliant landscape architect Ian McHarg (see *Design with Nature*, 1969)—tends to insist that all land-use policy questions can be answered by understanding the biological linkages, especially those related to hydrology. In the hands of the unimaginative, however, the result is that water-related landscapes are preserved but little else. Such an outcome takes no account of aesthetics or the so-called cultural values, except by happenstance.

Like the land saver's cost-benefit analysis, ecology too has been eagerly embraced by the developers. In the old days, when all a builder would do for "the ecology" was to leave a couple of trees standing, citizen outrage could often bring a project to a standstill. But after the developers learned about ecology, they were quick to prepare computer-generated maps showing unbuildable gorges, swamps, and outcrops splashed with green ink and labeled "conservation area." Nothing wrong with this, of course, except that it would often delude the land savers into giving up a fine visual landscape, such as a meadow or even an old apple orchard. Because no value under a system of ecological determinism could be established for them, the merely aesthetic or historical areas were often sacrificed in exchange for not building on land that the developer couldn't build on anyway.

———

The third justification for land preservation that is often mistaken for a primary "value" is the need for sites for outdoor recreation. I have always sensed something imperious in much of recreational planning, as if outdoor recreation were defined as a set of leisure-time activities necessary to the underclasses but categorically different from the interests of those who plan the recreational facilities for them. Accordingly, where the intelligentsia of the out-of-doors (that is, you and I) treasure the slap and gurge of a canoe moving across a wilderness lake, the masses (that is, Joe Sixpack) are required to toss beer cans out of a hired aluminum outboard roaring across a reservoir. If the wilderness lake is too crowded, it is judged a failure. If the reservoir is not crowded enough, it is judged a failure. Surely we all, regardless of socioeconomic status, respond in pretty much the same way to a beautiful landscape. Why is it then automatically assumed that it is appropriate to destroy landscapes and the natural ambiance to provide for "public recreation"?

On the shore of the Hudson River near where I lived for a spell, conservationists (and I was among them) had argued for years that a certain point of land jutting into Haverstraw Bay, favored by many for bird-watching, rock sitting, and similar activities, should be preserved. At length we were successful, and with the help of a federal grant the county (Westchester) stepped in and bought the land, whereupon they bulldozed it clear, covered a meadow with a parking lot, blasted aside our sitting-rocks for a boat-launching ramp, installed swings, picnic tables, charcoal grills, grass, signs that said "No"—and immediately complained that there wasn't enough money for maintenance. A lot of people, from all walks of life, had *liked* that point of land, for what it was. Now it is a mere "facility."

The same thing has happened to many of the national parks. The reader is directed to Edward Abbey's *Desert Solitaire* (1970) and Joseph Sax's *Mountains without Handrails* (1980). The question is not *whether* the popular national parks are surrounded by tawdry gateway communities, choked with automobiles, and insensitively operated by the National Park Service. Rather, the question is *why*.

The reason is that a policy justification of national parks (and of other government recreation lands) has been substituted for the primary values that led to their preservation in the first place. The justification is "outdoor recreation"—one of the least expensive ways, presumably, that a society based on the exploitation of resources and labor can pretend that it believes in the sanctity of nature and in individual dignity. Is the only value of two weeks among the tall trees to create a profit for the "leisure-time" industry? Is it unpatriotic to presume that our recreational needs are a bit subtler than the planners suppose, that they are related also to untrammeled nature that doesn't produce a profit that can be talked about in town hall or in the halls of Congress?

I would suggest that the selling of outdoor recreation as a justification for landscape preservation has led to the destruction of landscapes, not their salvation. This is what I learned from my suburban Hudson River debacle, and what is clear to me every time I visit the most popular of the national parks.

When one loses faith in the leadership, one must resort to the wisdom of the people. During the early years of my career, which was in the advertising business in New York City, I learned that knowing "what people really want" is the difference between success and failure. To find out what people *think* they want is easy, but to find out what they *really* want takes genius. Quite often, creative intuition is a better guide than the most elaborate statistics derived from market research. It was creative intuition that led one of my co-workers, a copywriter named Shirley Polykoff, to create a brilliant campaign for a small-bore client called the Clairol Company, with the headline, "Does She or Doesn't She? (Only Her Hairdresser Knows for Sure.)" With this notion, which every woman immediately understood, she not only put the makers of that product into the corporate big leagues but created a huge new market that today everyone takes for granted.

Great copywriters such as Shirley Polykoff don't believe their intuition can operate without nourishment, however. Like a good politician, they get out there with the people. Shirley liked to cruise around department stores, listening. A more organized way of listening favored by advertising agencies then (and now) was something called the "focus group interview." To an outsider, an ad agency focus group might sound like the most inane enterprise imaginable—a group of housewives comparing the merits of laundry soaps, for example, as if they were discussing, say, energy policy, or athletes talking about jock itch so seriously that it sounds like the greatest health problem since yellow fever. But sometimes the writers and advertising strategists (such as I), looking through a one-way mirror at a group in session around a conference table, would be hit in the head by a little something that one of the participants said—and there would be the seed of a great campaign. "Get them to talk more about so-and-so," would come an urgent plea from an excited writer through the interviewer's earphone.

By the time I was fighting the land-use policy wars in Washington, D.C., Madison Avenue was several years behind me. But I remembered those focus group interviews. Since the conservationists were getting pasted at every turn by the opponents of the land-use bills, it seemed to me that maybe we could concoct a better strategy by using Shirley Polykoff's trick: *listening*. So I cooked up a pilot project called "Expectations of the American Land" (after Thoreau's line, "Who would not rise to the expectations of the land?") that was a pure steal from the Madison Avenue focus group interview.

I chose the Minneapolis–St. Paul metropolitan area as the venue for my experimental focus groups. Three "landscape value sessions" were held—in an inner-city area, a suburban area, and a rural area. In all, about thirty-six people participated in the project, which I described (here somewhat edited) as follows. The year was 1974.

"Expectations of the American Land" is a series of citizen forums in cities, suburbs, and rural areas throughout the United States. The object of these meetings is to get behind the rhetoric of land-use planning to a basic understanding of how Americans really *feel* about their land and landscape. We believe that the insights so gathered can have a sigificant impact on national, state, and local land-use policy.

The forums, made up of twelve participants each, will engage in an informal and candid discussion about personal values as they are associated with an emerging public consciousness that the American land ethic has a "cultural" meaning as well as an economic one. The discussion should focus on personal experiences and beliefs about land use and landscape and the basic impulses, as well as they can be expressed, that have led to the growing demand that land-use policies be developed that will make our communities worth looking at and living in. What is sought in each forum is passionate statement rather than a critical analysis of planning technique. Moreover, a spontaneous interaction between forum members is of greater value than are considered responses to questions posed by the moderator.

As it worked out, I did not have to pose many questions. The discussions took off spontaneously and ran on their own fuel. All I could do was give them a bit of a nudge from time to time to keep on the topic or develop a promising line of inquiry. The responses were varied and hard to analyze in a systematic way. This much can be ventured, however. The discussions had nothing to do with cost-benefit analysis, ecological determinism, or the statistics of recreational demand. Instead, they indicated civic confusion and extreme political frustration on the part of virtually all the participants.

So much confusion surfaced, in fact, that "values" of the kind a consultant to land-use policymakers would dearly love to record, ascribe numbers to, and see decisions made by seemed almost moot. As one annoyed participant observed to me at the end of one of the sessions, "What's the point of talking about 'values' when the processes of the political and economic systems are immune to such values?" This was the very point of the exercise, I told him: to change the system. But he just shook his head and clamped his mouth shut as if to show the futility of speaking about it at all.

This view was unique only in its bluntness. The very first topic taken up in a meeting of farmers in a rural county on the far edge of the metropolitan area was a story that had the sense of legend about it. It was a circumstance that had taken place many years before but was felt to have a contemporary applicability, given the intense development pressures the outlying areas were feeling.

"Albert," began one of the farmers in the group, "you might want to tell about what happened when the federal government took over . . ."

"Well, I'll tell you," said Albert, glad to be asked. "We seen men walking across our lands, and they must have been taking soil samples, that's all I can figure. We were wondering what they were doing. And then, all at once, the last week in March it was, there comes a federal officer—big cap and all—and gives us a warrant to move in thirty days. How in the world can you move thirty-five sows and twenty-five cows and three hundred chickens in thirty days? That's the kind of orders they gave us."

"When was this?" I asked.

"Oh, this was the tail end of World War II," said Albert.

"Why was the land taken?"

"Oh," said Albert, "they just condemned it to put some kind of factory on it. I don't remember quite right."

As it turned out, the mythic force of the legend dominated the session. Stories were told about builders who threatened to take this rural community to court unless they upzoned land so that it could be more densely developed. There were stories about farmers who thought they *had* to sell out. That was the impression they got, just like Albert did from the fellow in the big cap. One man recollected about an uncle who had done this. "He turned around and sold for about $1,200 an acre and bought other land for $450, so he has a cash reserve in the bank for his old age and still has 160 acres. But it wasn't quite what he wanted. No, it never is."

"When we moved out of that area," said Albert, back at the myth again, "we were just like orphans. We couldn't adjust to no different area. It takes a while, because every square foot of the land you've got to know if you're a farmer."

"I can't move out," put in another. "I'll stay here. I'll fight. I'm going to stay on my land until . . . as long as I can."

"I'm going to live and die on my farm," said a third. "I'm attached to the community, churches, friends, neighbors—all that is worth something to me. You can't buy that with money. Isn't that right?"

"Right. That's right."

"Yes," said Albert, his eyes closed, thinking back.

Later, of course, they all agreed you'd be a fool not to sell out for the really big money they'd heard that some of those developer fellows were offering.

In the suburban session, the focus group members spoke for a while about tearing up Montana to coal-stoke the industry around Minneapolis.

"I think it's immoral to go out there and do to Montana what they did in northern Minnesota to get the iron ore out," said a women who wrote a column for a suburban newspaper.

"That's hardly a scratch on the surface compared to what strip mining's done to the South," observed an architect.

"I've been to Kentucky, I've been in Appalachia," said a school-teacher, shaking his head.

Then someone asked, "Okay, so that's the position you take. All right. Let's say we're *not* going to take the coal out of Montana then, so the industrial plant in this city is not going to keep growing any more. Tell me, what's going to happen to this metropolitan area if you don't take the coal out of Montana?"

The wife of a physician complained that such a discussion was irrelevant to her. "A lot of us are involved with issues that are much smaller than that, with problems that are a lot easier to cope with and don't cause a situation where push comes to shove, when you have major forces clashing."

"Most of us here," she went on, "are involved in issues that have to do with relatively small areas of land—a matter of twenty feet on one side or another of a stream, whether to build on these five acres here or whether to move over a few hundred yards. And we can't get anywhere even with *those* kinds of land-use problems."

Later they talked about an ecologist who had been appointed to a governmental commission.

"He was on our team when we were trying to clean up the creek and save it," one woman said. "Now he's on the commission and I don't even go to their meetings anymore because I have never heard them turn down any developer when he asked for anything."

"But in that position he can't be arbitrary or capricious to anybody," put in a man who wanted to be fair.

"Oh, bullshit," said the woman who wrote the newspaper column.

At the inner-city session, a professor at the University of Minnesota said, "I get so damned depressed, you know. I've become a radical sort of environmentalist, mau-mauing state agency meetings and things like that. I am distrustful of planners. I am distrustful of people who come to me and say they are going to help me improve our urban landscape, particularly if they are officials, because I think that the urban landscape is up for sale to the highest bidder."

Tales of civic outrage ran around the table, of freeways and highrises that were constructed despite efforts to prevent them.

"You know," said one woman, "I'm sick of going over to the legislature and lobbying and looking eye to eye with guys who get huge salaries to do what I do on behalf of the environment for nothing."

"All we're doing," I said, "is talking about governmental processes, not perceptions of a more humane landscape."

"I'm sorry," said the woman.

"I'm not sorry," said the professor. "No, I wouldn't be sorry because I happen to feel very strongly that the process is impeding the vision, not the lack of vision impeding the process."

And so it went. But in spite of their confusion, their despair that anything could be done, and their panic over the loss of *place*, visions of landscape quality crept in.

"I need trees," said an employee of the 3M Company. "Trees are now used as an economic thing—all the same type, all the same heights, all harvested when they're twenty-five years old for economic purposes. They're not grown for my needs. My needs are for a huge tree that's tangled, jumbled, not economically worthwhile at all."

"You know," said a woman, "I heard something that was *very* interesting. St. Catherine's College is right in the city, but close to the river. And they have a little woods in back, but it's *very* little. And they saw a *deer* in there. A deer!"

"No kidding."

"I mean, that's amazing when you consider that the deer must have come through backyards . . ."

"That's really an exciting thought—that a deer can actually get into the city. You know, if the city could re-create itself so that this kind of thing could normally occur . . ."

Diversity was what the city residents recommended. "As soon as you simplify the environment, you lose the safety," one said. And they were concerned with small spaces, not large parks, which they thought could just as well be natural areas, not developed for recreation. They disliked both suburbs and automobiles. Suburbs because they destroyed the countryside, which they did not want to have destroyed; cars because they destroyed the city. They discussed gardens—for flowers and vegetables in small spaces. And they thought that the bulk of the streets could be done away with, used instead for gardens and trees.

They spoke of funny, surprising little places in the city and decided that you don't get that kind of thing with planning. In fact, the point was made that planning is probably antithetical to true urban diversity, the jumble city that is productive of a good urban life-style.

Safety, surprise, and (that recurring theme) the need for trees came together in the remarks of a young woman who was a Vista Volunteer. "There's value in ugliness. I live above a warehouse, and I can leave my door unlocked. My windows are open. Sometimes when I do lock the door, I leave my key inside, and lock myself out. But I can crawl up into an open window in a matter of seconds. And because where I live appears to be ugly, it is very safe. Nobody suspects that anybody would want to live there."

And then she revealed the true secret of her place. "In the back I've got my roof garden and I look out my window and there's an old box-elder tree which fills up my window. So what if a box elder is a weedy tree. It's nice and green. I lie in bed and see it against the sky."

If in the city the perceptions were related mainly to life-style, in the suburbs there was a more abstracted notion of natural beauty. "I have a real love for idle land," said a high school science teacher, "land that people will just keep their cotton picking fingers off of and let it go its own way."

Their talk was of childhood summers in the out-of-doors and of their effort to re-create that spacious sense for their own children in a metropolitan milieu.

One exchange seemed to express not only the suburban view of the landscape but also the most profound kind of "value" in terms of the preservation of place. One participant put this question to an avid open-space preservation advocate: "But why," he asked. "Why do you care so much about open space?"

The woman answered, "It's sort of like a sense of security. We look at the natural order of things as ongoing. To see a river continue on is life."

And a man added, "A person's sanity depends on associating with and being able to know that the river is there, and that it's going to be there. Whereas everything else we're associated with is going to be here today but gone tomorrow. Yet, you know, that river . . ."

In reflecting on this exchange, it occurred to me that the suburbs were just as dangerous as the city but in a different way. People are undependable in the city, and that is dangerous. But in the suburbs, nature itself seems undependable, since the landscapes are so massively transformed by new development. Walking in the woods may involve something other than recreation. Perhaps it is a compulsive effort to reestablish the permanence of the natural order, an escape from the placeless suburbs to natural dependability.

The farmers seemed to understand this notion intuitively. One of them, a bit of a poet, put it this way. "Most of those new people," he said, referring to a newly built subdivision adjoining his land, "they like to have a farmer living near them, so they can sit and look out the window and watch everything he does. And they do. The older people and the kids especially. A lot of people say, 'Oh, we watch you all the time. We listen to you sing.'"

What are we to make of this? Listening to a farmer sing as he walks among the beans in summer. Lying on one's bed in just such a way so that the view of a box elder will fill up a window. Knowing that to see a river continue on is life. These expressions of place are affecting and yet poignant, for the dominant theme of all the focus group interviews was of the *loss* of place, of personal locatability. The land-use changes were too many, too big, too fast even for the most exuberant and adaptable of citizens. People sensed their lives in disarray. They believed that they were being manipulated by government and business, and yet they still seemed reluctant to admit that a humane landscape and living environment was wholly out of reach, if only they could really *organize*. But then, when that thought was uttered, the hopelessness seemed to return, sometimes with a shrug and silence, sometimes with a kind of protorevolutionary stridency.

At the forums there was compulsive talking and unburdening, a reluctance to end the sessions. One of them went on for four hours and then continued past midnight in a parking lot.

Did my experiment prove anything? Possibly this: there would appear to be a difference between authentic landscape values deriving from the need for a dependable *place* and the dry intellectual constructs that planners and the professional analysts employed by big conservation organizations have developed to justify their arguments. I believe that if we continue to mistake the justifications for the reality, we will continue to be frustrated in our attempt to create, or re-create, humane and workable landscapes for living. We will lose both land *and* community. We shall fail not just because we are wrong in some narrow intellectual sense, but because we shall move no one to action.

If we want to move people, we will have to ignore the academics and the bureaucrats at least for a moment and adopt Shirley Polykoff's creative approach. We simply have to get out there and *listen*—listen to the pleas of farmers singing in the fields, of inner-city dwellers grateful for trees, of suburbanites hoping that their rivers will continue on.

II

DOWN A COUNTRY ROAD

In towns and cities, and in suburbs and exurbs, land is commonly thought of as space. In truly rural settings, however, where commercial agriculture takes place, land is a resource. For the most part, conservationists—with the exception of those concerned with soil erosion—have traditionally paid scant attention to rural land. They were concerned, mainly, with metropolitan areas on the one hand and the untrammeled wilderness on the other. The "land between"—which is slightly more than half the total acreage in the coterminous United States—was terra incognita.

Then, in the late 1970s, the U.S. Department of Agriculture published a study showing that between 1967 and 1977 some twenty-nine million acres of rural land had been urbanized—a rate of loss, in effect, of some three million acres a year. This statistic was later confirmed by a federal interagency project, the National Agricultural Lands Study, set up for the sole purpose of validating the earlier research. Given the findings, it didn't take long before conservationists concerned with land and landscape realized that at three million acres a year the greatest patch of prime farmland on the face of the earth could soon be decimated.

This loss of farmland, of the small and medium-sized farms with it, and of that most important collateral resource—water—remain issues that must command the attention of all of us.

LOOKING FOR
DEANE HOISINGTON

It does not seem so many years ago that I came east to attend college. To be sure, I was suitably impressed by New York City, visited en route and shown off to me by a beloved uncle who took me riding on the IRT, to the top of the Empire State Building, and across the harbor on the five-cent ferry to Staten Island. But my destination was New England, in whose timeless rocky hills our forebears had settled centuries ago. Here was the greatest contrast—cool, green—with my dusty California valley hometown that even then was filling up with tract housing and other whatnots of metropolitan expansion across the great megawatt bowl called Los Angeles.

By good fortune I signed up for Geology I in the first semester of my freshman year, a science course favored by the nonscientific because it specialized in field trips, weather permitting, under the enthusiastic direction of Professor Joe Peoples. Professor Joe showed us the dinosaur tracks, the trilobites, the schist and gneiss, and granites as old as God. But, just as vividly, there was recorded on my brain, or perhaps somewhat deeper, the rural landscape seen through bus windows, or at a distance from the geological sites under study—the beautiful hill farms of New England. For a westerner used to the dry talus slopes of the Coast Range, this was a revelation, a landscape that I had thought could only be dreamed of: fieldstone fences, arching elms shading a pasture, lowing cattle at streamside, white farmhouses tucked crisply beneath the brows of hills, red barns. And as the semester passed, autumn's golds and reds gave way to winter's miracle of white—a miracle at least to one who had never before seen an eastern woods fill up with snow.

The following spring, eager to get out into the landscape again,

I decided to see more of New England by hitchhiking up to Williamstown, Massachusetts, to visit a friend, for my geological explorations had been confined, mainly, to a smallish patch of central Connecticut favored by Professor Joe. The Berkshires seemed like a perfect destination.

An interminable number of short hitches got me through Hartford, then a good long one to Windsor Locks, then another on to Northampton, where I spent the night in a guest house of the kind that still hangs on in New England. Next morning, the sky was brilliant, the sun warming, and I got on the road early. Soon enough, an old pickup truck with Vermont plates stopped. I climbed aboard and settled in for the ride northward along U.S. Route 5. Evidently I slept, for when I next looked out of the window we were in the deep countryside. "Where are we?" I asked the driver, a long-faced, quiet man. "Why, Vermont," he replied levelly, just a hint of reproach in his voice. "You were sleeping." I had overshot the Massachusetts cross-state highway that would take me to Williamstown. The only thing to do was get out of the truck and hitchhike back.

But it was Vermont! As soon as the pickup rattled out of sight, the very idea of just *being* in Vermont filled me with wonder. What had brought me to this exotic place, so antithetical to the megalopolitan semidesert of my growing up? Not just a pickup truck certainly. This was *deep* New England, unfactoried, totally rural. Here, the Connecticut River was innocent of mills or the great wharves for the seagoing sailing ships that one of my ancestors had brought to berth two hundred miles downstream 150 years before. So instead of seeking a ride back down to Massachusetts, I walked along the highway till I came to a rutted dirt side road, cutting between two pastures. I scrambled over a stone fence bordering one of them, found the center of the field, and sat down amid the cow pies and early wildflowers of Vermont. It was many hours before I moved from that spot, for it was there that I felt as much at home as in any place I had ever been before.

This happened in the spring of 1950. I was not to return to Vermont for another thirty years.

———

Deane Hoisington brought me back to the Green Mountain State. He was a famous man, at least to me, and I wanted to know what became of him. For most, that kind of mystery ("what ever became of . . . ") attaches to movie stars like Ann Sheridan or deposed Third World colonialists like Ian Smith. But my curiosity pertained to the fate of a Vermont farmer, for that is who Deane Hoisington is, or was. My connection to him was through an article in *Fortune* magazine, issue of February 1939.

I had first come across the article while poking around some dusty piles of books, reports, and magazines at the Library of Congress. For the most part I was looking for government and academic research reports on the loss of farms and farmland in the U.S. The trouble was, these sources were dry, numbers-oriented analyses that smelled of must and mildew rather than a freshly cut field or even a barnyard. But there, in *Fortune*, was the real thing—watercolor illustrations by Paul Sample, and an appealing article to accompany them. It was all about a farm such as the one in whose pasture I sat, at age eighteen, one unforgettable spring day nearly three decades before. "A Vermont Farm," was the title, and the subtitle, "to which Deane Hoisington, the owner, gives sixteen hours labor every day and from which he takes independence and a good living." I read that Deane Hoisington, the third Hoisington to farm the place, was in his early forties at the time the article was written, which would put him in his early eighties now. Not impossible, I thought. Anyway, there was his son Conrad, who I read was six or seven, which would make him roughly my own age; and if he did as the article said his father wanted him to do, he could be the proprietor of the Hoisington Farm now, taking for himself and his own family independence and a good living. Unless, of course—and I didn't much want to think about this possibility—the place had been sold off.

The farm, located in Hartland, a Connecticut River town, had been purchased by one Cyrus Houghton Hoisington, of Windsor, Vermont (the next town down the river), in 1864. Paul Sample's illustrations show that probably not much had changed between 1864 and 1939. The barns are painted as an attractive jumble of structures, which Sample has backed up with the mounded green of sugar maples. In the foreground, a pasture, Holsteins are peaceably a-grazing on a summer's day. No sentimentalist, though, the artist has placed a couple of telephone poles in the foreground, to show that this is, after all, a modern, working farm. That much, in any case, was a change from Cyrus's time, as were, no doubt, the blotch-coated Holsteins. More likely Cyrus had had Jerseys, smaller, with an all-over brown color.

Elsewhere in his portfolio, Sample depicts the place in snow time, in one painting with Deane Hoisington hauling milk cans on a horse-drawn sled, and in another sledding logs to a sawmill. And then there is the painting of Deane himself. It shows the face of a man who works hard, all day, out of doors. A resolute expression; but the eyes are calm, benevolent, looking into a middle distance. It is a true farmer's face. The children, nine-year-old Joyce, shown seated atop a white horse, and little Conrad, are looking on. All about them stand the hills of Vermont, always seeming to be serene and permanent.

The Hoisington place is a hill farm and Hartland is about halfway between the Massachusetts border to the south and the Canadian border to the north. In 1939, according to *Fortune*, the farm was worth $4,500 and the Hoisingtons grossed about $3,000 a year, which was not bad for those Depression times. The farm was 250 acres in all: 65 tillable acres, 35 acres in woodlot, and 150 acres in pasture for twenty-four milk cows, eleven calves, one bull. There was also a summer garden, two hogs, chickens, and fish in the brook. So the farm provided not only cash, but sufficiency and a good life. "A living," said *Fortune*. "And that means good food, good clothing, a good house for his wife and two small children. It means freedom from debt, independence, self-respect." My research had told me what was most likely to happen to farms that provided, once, a whole living, and I knew too that a New England hill farm in particular was a vanishing species; yet I wanted very much for the farm to be there still.

I did not set out for Vermont immediately after finding the article about Deane Hoisington in the dusty stacks of the Library of Congress. I procrastinated for several years, in fact. But then, one spring day, I resolutely loaded up the station wagon with camera and clothes and a tape recorder and a notebook, and took off. North. From Maryland through Delaware, New Jersey, New York, and into New England. Still, not wishing to get the bad news I feared all at once, I didn't go straight to Hartland, or Hartland Four Corners, or North Hartland— wherever the interstate paralleling the old Route 5 would dump me out into the Vermont countryside—but instead decided to check some facts indirectly by seeing my friend George Dunsmore in Montpelier.

George looks like a dairy farmer, perhaps because he is. There is a healthy, creamy-richness about him, rounded and sturdy, like a milk can. He has a "pretty big" dairy operation in St. Albans, Vermont, at the top left-hand corner of the state, where New York, Canada, and Vermont separate to create the blue vastness of Lake Champlain. George Dunsmore was also commissioner of agriculture for his state, with an office two flights up in a no-nonsense, slightly down-at-the-heels government building in Montpelier. He was genuinely glad to see me, but worried that I was huffing and puffing up the stairs. He put me into a slatted wooden armchair of the kind that all sensible government office buildings have been equipped with for the last one hundred years.

"Well," George said. He likes to get right to the point.

"Ever heard of Hoisington Farm?" I asked.

"Nope."

"It was—is—a hill farm. In Windsor County," I added.

"Still nope."

"Are there any hill farms left?"

"A few," George said.

Like anybody else who is a commissioner of something, George had buttons on his phone, but in Vermont it may be better not to use the buttons if you don't have to. He yelled, to no one in particular, to "send in Bob and Steve." I guessed I was about to learn something of hill farms, Vermont, and their future. And perhaps the future of rural land everywhere, save those places that exist only in the memory.

Bob and Steve did in fact come in, plunking themselves down easily onto two other slatted wooden chairs, like detectives in a TV series. Robert Wagner was a land-use planner and Stephen Kerr was in charge of agricultural development. They were young, bearded, modern, tough-minded. Windsor County, Steve told me straightaway, was in a part of the state where dairy farms were quite numerous in the 1930s, and fairly evenly distributed throughout the hills and dales. "But," he said, "thousands of hill farms have just disappeared."

"We lost a lot of farms," George added, "with the bulk-tank law, which went into effect around 1960 and outlawed the forty-four-gallon can." I remembered the Paul Sample painting in *Fortune* of Deane Hoisington hauling just that kind of can on his sleigh through the snow.

They told me that many of the hill farms were now owned by speculators. "They're growing up to brush as people sit on them," Bob Wagner said. To a Vermonter, sloth includes sitting on land just as much as sitting on one's backside. Then George told me what I had observed while I was winding around the hills and dales of Vermont, avoiding Hartland. "The forest cover in Vermont has gone from twenty-eighty," said George, "to eighty-twenty." By this he meant that those earliest settlers who came up the Connecticut River Valley had managed, within a century or less, to clear four-fifths of the land of trees and rocks so they could grow crops and pasture animals. Early on, Vermont was the chief producer of wheat—in colonial times it was the breadbasket of the colonies (though Vermont was not one of them). Later on, they specialized in sheep, a natural for the steep, wet pastureland. But they lost that business too. The Erie Canal, and later the railroads, opened up the western lands, and so Vermont went in for cows. At first, they had a corner on cheese, but stiff competition came from Wisconsin and elsewhere, so that now they specialize in milk which, because it is perishable, cannot be overrun by producers in the Middle West.

Actually, the hill farms started going under in Vermont with the mass migration after the Civil War to the flat land that was discovered in Illinois and Iowa, Wagner said. And then the forest cover came back, so that now it once again blankets the landscape, or at least 80 percent of it, and the old houses and barns are rotten, with only the cellar holes remaining, and the stone fences that once wound through the pastures are concealed by the spindly second growth of brush and hardwood saplings.

Hill farms. The abandoned hill farms of Vermont. "One of the saddest and most beautiful trips you can take around here," said Stephen Kerr, "is to drive up Route 125 to the top of the Green Mountains at Ripton, and just look at the remains of the farm fields that were up there. You get out on the escarpment and look across the valley and you can almost picture what it was once like. What you had was hundreds of farms on that shallow but very loose and tillable soil. Those places were farmed for about fifty years, until they literally exhausted the land. Back then we didn't have lime, we didn't have chemical fertilizers. And a lot of people actually starved to death. Look at the gravestones. Farmers died at the age of thirty, kids at six months."

George said, "Once John Deere came along, all the farmers went down into the Champlain Valley." There is a theory one hears in discussions of agricultural history that John Deere, a Vermonter from Rutland, was personally responsible for changing Vermont—and all of New England for that matter—and for opening the West, permanently modifying the course of history in a young nation by figuring out how to mass-produce a steel moldboard plow. Born in 1804, Deere apprenticed as a blacksmith at the age of seventeen and set up his own smithy in Vermont. But in 1837 he too moved west with those farmers whose land had run out in the hillsides around Rutland. It was in Illinois that he first produced the famous steel plowshare that with a stout team could cut deep into the bottomland loams and zip open the tough prairie sod, turning long black furrows on land that had formerly been unplowable. And so Vermont kept shifting its agricultural gears: from wheat to sheep to butter and cheese, and now, principally, to milk.

But even dairy farmers were getting scarce. "There are only about three thousand dairy farms left," George said. His figures showed that Vermont was losing about a thousand farms a year. He handed me a state report. In Deane Hoisington's day, there were five times that many dairy farms in Vermont. I peeked at some more figures. Only thirteen dairy farms were left in the town of Hartland. Thirteen. The chances of Hoisington being among them was beginning to look pretty remote. Up until 1963 the cows outnumbered the people in Vermont; now it was decisively the other way around.

George Dunsmore gave me a quart of his own fancy grade Vermont maple syrup. "SUNSET VIEW FARM," the golden label said. Consolation prize.

———

After leaving George's office, I should have zipped right down I-89 from Montpelier to White River Junction. But even though I had resolved, at last, to relieve the suspense of whether Deane Hoisington was alive or dead and find out what happened to his farm, I still wanted to creep up on it slowly and deliberately—in a Vermontish way, I suppose.

So I took U.S. Highway 302 southwestward to beyond Barre, then swung south down state highway 110, which is surely one of the most beautiful country roads in America. (Asked about it later, a Vermonter said, "Yes, well, it's not too bad.") Roads such as 110 in Vermont wind through the narrow valleys of the Green Mountains, once a vacant area between the colonies of New Hampshire and New York, each of which claimed this "land in between," as they prophetically called it. But Ethan Allen cleverly played off the Yorkers against the Hampshiremen, and the Continental Congress against the Canadians and the British. In 1775, Allen and his Green Mountain Boys seized Fort Ticonderoga, not to produce a victory for the colonies against the British, but to give himself a good bargaining position with the Continental Congress so that the independence of the land in between, then called the "Hampshire Grants," could be secured. The Congress was waffling on statehood, so Allen and his colleagues called a convention of patriots from the Hampshire Grants to form "a separate district." In their declaration, the district was called "New Connecticut," but they found the name had already been taken by some Connecticut settlers in Pennsylvania. Later, at a convention to adopt a constitution for the new republic, in 1777, a name was decided on, suggested by Thomas Young, who constructed "Vermont" out of the Latin roots for Green Mountains.

One of the signers of the new constitution was Ebenezer Hoisington, the grandfather of Deane's grandfather, who had in 1864 established Hoisington Farm in Hartland, where I was now headed.

As I traveled down 110, the bottomland farms seemed honestly poor but neatly groomed. The houses and barns were clustered into farmsteads that surely have looked much the same for a hundred years. And up the hillsides were the high meadows, many of them overgrown now, but enough still open for the New England countryside aesthetic to be in evidence—in fact, prevail—where in other places, such as New Hampshire, the vistas are closed up, closed *off* by the second growth that covers the pastures and makes the stone fences irrelevant. This is the sign of categorical change in a landscape, a change that had not yet, or at least not entirely, taken place in the Republic of Vermont. It was a friendly landscape that I traveled through. A farmer, trimming up a hedgerow near the road, waved as I went by. So did the driver of a Farmall—the kind of tractor that the big producers in the Middle West haven't seen for a generation. On an impulse, I drove up a dirt road that didn't seem private, to gain a wider view of the ranks of hills and valleys: woodlot, open meadow, hamlets, the spire of a Congregational church in the distance, rising up behind a low hill. For the purist nature lover, this is perhaps too much a man-made landscape, but I say the hand of man has been a good influence here, aesthetically, even if motivated by ordinary economic concerns, because the scale is right in Vermont. It is human. It is not the scale of big banks, big capital, big business, big government, or big farms.

And yet, as I took photographs from a dirt road on the flank of a green mountain of the ranks of mountains and valleys beyond, disappearing to a blue-green haze in a mystical distance, I could see the brush. Brush, that harbinger of change, of closing up, of a rural economy closing down. I was reminded of Richard Brautigan's nightmare story, "Trout Streams in America," where the streams were rolled up, carried away, had to be bought by the linear foot at the hardware store. Would the Vermont landscape too be rolled up and carried away? Or shredded, or sliced into turves and stored behind the garage? It hadn't happened yet, I thought, and maybe in a place such as this, with the help of people like George Dunsmore and the many others who try to save the landscape, it may not. But I captured the scene on my roll of Kodachrome anyway, and hoped these slides would never have to be put into the file I keep of places that used to be.

Down the hill. Onward. I see a cloud of dust being raised by a car coming up toward me. I pull off to the side, as does he. It is the postman. He waves.

What I have to do, I thought, is to get a place to stay the night, so that I can look for Deane Hoisington while fresh, in the morning. I stopped the side trips, the pauses, the photographic forays, and went straight for that stage set of a Vermont village, Woodstock, where the first rope tow for skiers was established in 1935, and where Rockresorts built a new hotel, the Woodstock Inn, to look like something pre-Revolutionary.

Rockresorts being considerably out of my price range, I chose a distinctly post-Revolutionary nonchain motel in South Woodstock, a little hamlet down the road. I did pause long enough in downtown Woodstock proper, however, to locate a place that sold U.S. Geological Survey topographical maps. I purchased the Hartland Quadrangle in order to see whether I could figure out, from the 1939 *Fortune* article, if Deane Hoisington's place had become an interchange on I-91, or Hill Farm Condos, or a whacked-up landscape of uninspired vacation homes. The imagination ran riot in the motel that evening, unstilled by a couple of scotches and a long walk around South Woodstock to clear the mind. A farmer was cutting weeds along a fence line with a sickle bar on a Farmall. He waved. It was dusk, and cooling down from the summer's day. He raised the cutting bar, and tooled the little tractor briskly down the highway while I trudged back to the motel.

I consulted the *Fortune* article again. "Deane Hoisington's farm," it said, "is usually called the Andrew Hoisington farm, after Deane's father, who died six years ago [that is, in 1932, assuming the article was written during 1938], and before that it was called the Cyrus Hoisington farm after Deane's grandfather, who bought it in 1864. It is a mile and a half above Hartland village, a thousand feet up, lying on both sides of the rutty steep road. . . . The fields slope up northward back of the house to the wood lot, and the pastures fall away steeply southward below the barns. From the house, and only partially cut off by the barns, is a long view down the Connecticut Valley. The road through the farm goes on up over Miller's hill, famous in the neighborhood for its widespread view of the White Mountains to the north, the Green Mountains to the west, the lonely shouldering outline of Mount Ascutney to the south."

Good old *Fortune*, accurate as Babbitt could wish. I ought to be able to figure out the exact location of Hoisington farm by applying that description to the map. But there was no "Miller's" hill on the quadrangle. There was Mace, Tinkham, Cobb, and Rabbit, but no Miller's. Moreover, most farms (tiny solid black squares for houses, open squares for barns and outbuildings) did lie on either side of dirt roads (solid or dotted lines), and most of the places were at or near the one-thousand-foot contour line. Damn. I slept fitfully in my post-Revolutionary motel room, the window flung open to the pasture behind. I heard shufflings, snorts, and occasional hoots and barks all night long.

I needn't have fretted, I guess. It *was* there after all—the house, some of the old barns, and a new barn, all marked by a handsome sign, saying HOISINGTON FARM, and below it, "Reg. Hampshires." The pastures were still open, the view down the Connecticut River Valley just as vivid, the White Mountains to the east, the Green Mountains to the west, and the "lonely shouldering outline" of Mount Ascutney to the south. I will have to tell you that my eyes filled at seeing this place, for reasons too complex to understand fully but going back to my sojourn in the middle of a Vermont meadow in 1950. To find the farm still here! It was not exactly as Paul Sample painted it, but he had got the feel of it, and some of what he captured remained: to look down the sloping pasture to the village of Hartland Four Corners, bordering Lulls Brook, unrolled up, with the trout surely dancing on their tails as the mayflies lit on summer evenings, where Deane took Conrad a-fishing after chores. And they would trudge up the hill to the big warm kitchen where the yeasty smell told that this was Mrs. Hoisington's bread-making day. And then Deane and Roy Patterson, the hired man who lived in a house a ways up the hill, would go into the milking barn and hook up the de Laval milking machine. And . . . and . . . and. My mind was racing with the magic of where I was, and how I had come to be there.

Mary Davis, the Hartland town clerk with offices in Damon Hall, where Deane had come for Town Meeting and where I had gone first to inquire, had known the place. "Hoisington farm? Oh, sure," she had said the minute I asked, "just take the second road. A nice young family lives there now."

And they *were* nice. Nancy Dillon and two young children came out of the farmhouse as I nosed the car into the drive. They were glad to show me around.

Nancy Dillon and her husband Dennis Dillon were both born and brought up in Windsor, the small city a few miles down the river where the Vermont constitution was signed by Ebenezer Hoisington. The Dillons had been trying their hands at sheep raising, which accounted for the words "Reg. Hampshires" on the sign out front.

"We tried to make a living," Nancy Dillon told me in the big old kitchen where Maude Hoisington used to bake her bread three times a week. "We tried for five years. But we're just too far away from the top breeding areas here. So Dennis has to work as a fuel oil salesman."

"What about the Hoisingtons?" I asked.

"Well, they sold the place in 1963," Nancy said. "Mr. Hoisington died a few years ago. Mrs. Hoisington lives with her sister down in Windsor. She comes up here sometimes."

And Conrad and Joyce?

"I think Joyce lives down in Massachusetts. The son is in Iowa. Neither of them wanted to keep the farm."

Nancy Dillon looked at me. "We're just renting the place, you know. Matter of fact, I don't know how long we'll be able to stay here."

Oh.

I walked the fields after our interview. The back pasture was being hayed by a neighboring farmer. But the main pasture, on the side of the road where the milking barns had been, was growing up to brush. Hoisington's sawmill, where he had cut lumber for mending the barns, and cut logs for heating and cooking (sixteen cords a year), had been converted into a summer cottage. I waded through the tall grass of the front pasture, the bindweed grasping at my ankles, to the place where Paul Sample had stood to sketch his most appealing watercolor of the farm. I looked up the slope, at where the barns had been. It was true the land was still there, still open, and the house, now well over one hundred years old, was in fine shape. And the woodlot up the hillside beyond framed the scene, just as it had for generations. But this was not a working farm, not an *operation* anymore. If only the Dillons could make it in the sheep business. I had been reading that sheep were coming back in Vermont. In fact, in the past ten years the number of sheep had increased fivefold—the fastest-growing sheep population of any state in the Union, according to my source. The best thing about sheep was that they keep the brush from coming back into the old cow pastures.

If the Dillons could just produce enough wool, lamb chops, and fleece to keep the wolf from the door and the pastures open, I was thinking, then the absence of the Hoisingtons from Hoisington Farm would not be such a cause for sadness. But as it was the Dillons—and the farm—were bucking what I have come to call "Coughlin's Law," so named for Robert Coughlin, a well-known regional planner based at the University of Pennsylvania, who has specialized in the study of the conversion of farmland to nonfarm uses. Coughlin's Law states that the pivotal moment in the process of change in land use from rural to urban in a given area is when farmers begin to sell their land to nonfarmers. There is worse news: Coughlin's Corollary, which states that once an *investor* takes title to a tract, it is a near certainty that it will never be acquired again by a farmer or other rural owner-user. There are exceptions to Coughlin's Corollary, but few. Most of the time, it decrees that when ownership of farmland passes out of the hands of the primary user—the on-the-land farmer like Deane Hoisington—it begins a journey of new ownerships that takes it farther and farther away from its primary land-resource value and closer and closer to mere real estate, the surface upon which to build second homes or condos.

The inevitability of the one-way pattern of land transfer reminded me, when Coughlin had first sent me the study in which he formulated these laws, of how in the good old days in my neighborhood we would take a piece of the squarish wild wheat found in old fields and put the stem end of the spike just under our shirt cuffs. By lightly rubbing on the outside of the cuff, just so, we could make the wheat disappear, right up under the sleeve. This happened because when we would apply a bit of motion and a bit of pressure to the wheat spike, its configuration of tiny, invisible barbs, which all lay in the same direction, decreed that the spike would not just move back and forth, but would disappear—every time. We were amazed of course. Just as we are amazed when, suddenly, the farms disappear. A little pressure, a little motion, and what you have is Coughlin's Law and its inexorable Corollary.

And the Hoisington place had begun that journey. Except for a house lot on the back pasture, fronting on another road, the land was owned, Nancy Dillon told me, by two people. One of them a summer resident from Boston, the other a real estate woman from town.

I found Maude Hoisington, then eighty-one years old, in a back-alley apartment in Windsor. The historic town is now an industrial center on the Connecticut River. Nancy Dillon told me Mrs. Hoisington lived there with her sister, for the convenience. It was a ground-floor flat, in an old frame house that had been built in the alleyway, its entry shaded by steps going to apartments above. As I approached, Mrs. Hoisington peered through the screen door suspiciously, and then, when I identified myself as the fellow who had called ahead, she let me in. We sat in a tiny parlor, scarcely ten by ten, with a rag rug on the linoleum floor. She took the rocker, and I the couch. The room was filled with photographs and plants, possibly a hundred of the former, and half that many of the latter. Mrs. Hoisington was small, compact, energetic, bright-eyed and talkative, like a character from *Mary Poppins* or *Rutabaga Stories*. Her speech was Vermontish—at least Vermontish in the Connecticut River Valley way, which is what stage New Englanders like to imitate. Maude Hoisington wanted to talk about Deane mostly, but about Conrad and Joyce too.

"Deane went in '78," she said. "'Twas a blood clot in leg." She sometimes dropped the definite articles as many still do in rural England. "He was in terrific pain." And the pain went across her own open face. But quickly as it came, she shook it off. "We built a nice house in the back pasture after we sold the farm. Well! Didn't Deane have a fine time fixing up that house? He had always wanted a woodworking shop."

They had kept a house lot on the back pasture, which fronted on another of the town's graded dirt roads, and, it appeared, a family trust still owned the place. Joyce, the daughter who now lived down in Massachusetts, and grandchildren, and possibly great-grandchildren (it was impossible to follow Mrs. Hoisington's rapid-fire explanation of the pictures she kept pointing to around the room), would be coming up to stay there for the Hartland "Old Home Days," the

Fourth of July celebration. Joyce, Mrs. Hoisington told me, had been valedictorian of her class and was musically inclined.

Maude Hoisington, nee Jackson, had first come to Hartland in 1922 at the age of twenty-one to visit an uncle. She came from Ludlow, a farming community some thirty miles to the southwest, and grew up on a hill farm. She said then that she'd never marry a man who lived on a hill. But she met Deane—tall, quiet, and good-looking—at a Grange dance. Two years later they were married. I tried to imagine Mrs. Hoisington at a Grange Hall dance in a pretty frock. Maude Hoisington was one of those women who carried all the ages of her life in her face, and as she spoke about the old days, her face would brighten with youth, or cloud, depending on whether she was describing good times or bad. "I can't just remember when we sold the farm," she was saying, "and moved to the new house. It was the fall of '62. I wish I could ask Deane. He couldn't go on with the farm any longer." And her face looked all of its eighty-one years.

As it turned out, Conrad didn't want to take over the farm. He had gone to Iowa. "He's worked there since Khrushchev came to visit," said Mrs. Hoisington. He had gone to work for Garst Farm, the seed farm that the Russian premier had made famous. "He doesn't farm for himself," Mrs. Hoisington explained. "Well! You can't own your own land out *there*. Costs like the dickens, it does. It's only people who inherited the land back when their ancestors bought it up before railroad went through."

"Now Conrad," said Mrs. Hoisington, warming to a favorite subject, "he came back from the Army. The young heifers were freshening, and Conrad took care of it all. Chickens, too. But what drew him out to Iowa was, he didn't like cows. He loved land-farming and the big machinery. Well! Didn't he like driving the tractor here, even at night with the lights on!"

Deane had not been well while Conrad had been in the army. Like me, Conrad had served during the Korean War. And there was the unspoken thought that, as his father before him and his grandfather before that, Conrad would take over the farm. Said Mrs. Hoisington, "I told Conrad, 'When Dad's well, if you don't want to stay here and farm, you've got to tell your father. He wouldn't want you to do it if it isn't what you wanted.' And Conrad never made me an answer at all. And then the next spring, he told Deane he just wanted to go."

Pausing, she smoothed her dress, looked around the room at all the photographs and plants. "Well! This is near to Conrad's birthday. Conrad, he chose a summer Friday to be born—a beautiful hay day." Whereupon Mrs. Hoisington took me for another tour of the photographs, and urged me to go see the new house that they had built on the back pasture when Deane had to retire and sell the farm. "I never could see why city people wanted to buy that farm," she said.

And that, in a nutshell, is the modest story of how a single farm became real estate rather than continuing as a viable operation. Writ large, however, the story is part of the changing pattern of the "structure of agriculture," and is repeated tens of thousands of times in Vermont and elsewhere. Good farms, like the Hoisington place over three generations and one hundred years, did not provide a "cash profit" as *Fortune* put it, but only a living. And, like the wheat spike, it disappeared when just the right pressure and movement was applied, for the process of the loss of farms and farmland never seems to go backwards: the farms move inexorably from active use to inactive ownership by estate owners or investors, and when the opportunity is right, are sold by the investor-owners to those who will "improve" the land and in turn sell it to an end-user. It is, as always, the "middle man" who makes out best in this process. Not the original owner-user: the farmer or the farmer's heirs sell the land to summer people or other investors at or near the value of land for agriculture, not for a more intensive and economically rewarding use. And there are few bargains for the end-user—the suburban house or recreational condo buyer—when the chain of transactions is finally completed. This is the invisible dynamic that has started on Hoisington Farm, where one can still stand, as if nothing at all had happened, and look across the pasture to the bright track of the Connecticut River winding through the placid New England hills.

———

Is there anything to be done, save to wallow in nostalgia and hope that Dr. Coughlin's relentless diagnosis will, this time and for this place, somehow not turn out to be the case?

The most thoughtful general answer to that question was provided in the late 1970s by Bob Bergland, former congressman, Minnesota farmer, and perhaps the most interesting secretary of agriculture since Henry Wallace. Bergland set up what became known as "the structure study." Its report, issued in 1981 and entitled *A Time to Choose: Summary Report on the Structure of Agriculture*, made a strong plea for protecting the kind of farm Deane Hoisington's once was. The study group believed that present tax policies are biased toward the larger farmers and wealthy investors who unfairly exploit smaller farmers and their heirs. They believed that modern agricultural technology may not altogether be a good thing for keeping small-farming alive—the kind of technology that is represented by those big, $100,000 four-wheel-drive tractors the farmers love in Iowa, with the hi-fi and air conditioning and the three-hundred-horsepower, turbocharged diesel engines whose two-hundred-gallon tanks can keep a tractor going all day or night, turning over a fifteen-foot-wide strip of black dirt at a speed faster than most people can walk. The study group also believed that marketing techniques have unfairly benefited the large operators rather than small- and medium-sized farms. The bulk milk marketing law may be a good example of how this works. As George Dunsmore pointed out back in Montpelier, it was that law alone which wiped out a great number of low-cash, low-profit operations such as Deane Hoisington's. They further believed that farm commodity and credit policies have been of greater benefit to larger producers, and, finally, that in rural areas, as local economies change from purely farm-based to something more "suburban," the impact on farm structure will be significant, for in such places, what is a farm except a subdivision waiting to happen? *A Time to Choose* listed page after page of practical remedies, ranging from research and marketing initiatives to changes in the tax structure.

But apparently, we have chosen. Few people ever heard of the report. And despite subsequent papers and books on the subject, spawned by Bergland's vision, his effort has had no discernible impact. In fact, it is not even possible to get a copy of his report from today's Department of Agriculture. Just to check, I called the department's general number, was passed through to the "Subject Matter Section." The woman answering said, "Oh, *that* report. That was done by a previous administration. We wouldn't have any copies of *that.*"

One hundred and fifty years ago, the son of a small farmer in Ecclefechan, Scotland, a man who was later to fight the British Corn Laws which enriched the large landowners, coined the term "cash nexus." At the time, the Industrial Revolution had brought a great army of peasants dispossessed by the enclosure of the open fields and commons into the dark satanic mills that made England the "work-shop to the world." Thomas Carlyle, essayist, philosopher, and social reformer, keenly felt the shallowness and emptiness of lives bereft of all meaning save "Cash Payment as the sole nexus . . . between man and man."

Such feelings were mine too when I left Maude Hoisington, not to visit (as she requested) the new house she and Deane had built on the back pasture in 1963, but to take one last look at the old farm, such as it was. And standing under the line of sugar maples along the dirt road that once joined the barns and pastures but now divided them into separate "ownerships," I looked again down the slanting fields, soon to grow up to brush, to the vale of Lulls Brook as it wended its way to the bright Connecticut River beyond. The *Fortune* article, with a Carlylian fervor one would not have expected in a magazine directed to the chieftains of American industry, had drawn the distinction several times between the large, commodity-crop farm owner of the plains and the small-scale farmer like Hoisington, as the difference between "profit" and "a living." A profit was cash, of course. But a living was a life.

"In terms of a living," said *Fortune*, "the farm means a lot. A comfortable house, warm clothes, plenty of good food. It means, too, self-respect and the respect of the community. It means long hours of hard but satisfying work. It means an occasional Sunday drive and picnic or a visit to a neighbor's, and once in a while the movies or a Grange supper or a show at the town hall. It means doctor's care. It means schooling for the children, and a hired girl in the house for busy times. It means cold, dark winter mornings, and hot summer mornings with mist lying low in the valley. It means friendliness and hospitality to neighbors, and warm family affection. And the Hoisingtons hope that nothing will happen to keep it from meaning continued independence and security, a home and a job for them and, after them, for Joyce and Conrad."

There was no reason for me to stay. I had come looking for Deane Hoisington, both literally and symbolically. Like his wife Maude, I wished he were here, but he wasn't. The "cash nexus" had got us—the only connection not just between man and man but between man and land. I backed the car up into the Hoisington driveway, turned, and headed down the dirt road toward the interstate that paralleled Route 5. Just then, a dusty old pickup passed me going in the opposite direction, and its driver, a long-faced man who seemed familiar some-how, waved at me. I waved back, watching the truck through the rear-view mirror, and, with my memory jogged, images from thirty years before began crowding vividly into my mind. And as in a dream, I saw myself stopping the car, getting out, and yelling, "Wait! Wait!" at the truck rattling out of sight up Miller's hill and into a dream of rural Vermont as if time past and present and future had joined into some insistent, convoluted topological knot.

But of course I kept on, passing through the village center and then swinging onto the I-91 access ramp. I sped up to merge with the onrushing traffic south. Goodbye, Deane Hoisington, I thought to myself, forcing time and reality to snap back into place again. Goodbye.

A PORTION OF LAND

Calvin King is a young black farmer in the Delta Region of Arkansas—those flat cotton-and-rice counties that comprise the eastern part of the state, flanking the Mississippi River. King, one of ten children, is a part-time farmer. When he isn't farming, he serves as director of the Arkansas Land and Farm Development Corporation, a civic organization that deals with an issue that has come to be called black land loss. King is bright, with an open, unguarded, casual manner. He is educated, articulate, but his eyes often show hurt: not for himself, but for all those black farmers in the Delta whose land he is trying to save.

I went to see King because I had been reading my Thomas Jefferson, and I feared we had not been living up to what the Sage of Monticello expected of us in the way we deal with land ownership in the United States. Jefferson said that the land of America is given as "common stock for man to labor and live on." The small landowners, he said, are "the most precious part of the state."

These views are contained in a 1785 letter he wrote to Bishop Madison, president of William and Mary College and a cousin of President James Madison. At the time, Jefferson was on a trade mission to France and had been invited to Fontainebleau, the ancient and opulent royal hunting "lodge" located some forty miles from Paris. Characteristically, he took off for the hinterlands once he had arrived at the village (actually a sizeable town of fifteen thousand). On a hillside path, he encountered a "poor woman" walking in the same direction, and he asked her about her life on the king's estate. "She told me," Jefferson wrote to Madison, "she was a day laborer at 8 sous or 4d. sterling a day: that she had two children to maintain, and to pay a rent of two livres for her house (which would consume the hire of 75 days), that often she could get no employment and of course was without bread." After parting, Jefferson gave the woman twenty-four sous, whereupon she burst into tears.

This little drama on the hillside above Fontainebleau led Jefferson to some of his most important speculations on what we now call civil rights, especially as they pertain to "that unequal division of property which occasions the numberless incidences of wretchedness" he had seen throughout monarchical Europe where there was no common right to own and use land for one's subsistence. Despite owning slaves himself, which to his sorrow the economics and traditions of Virginia plantation agriculture demanded, Jefferson looked forward to a better day for everyone. "I am conscious," he wrote of his own country, the nation he had helped to create, "that an equal division of property is impracticable, . . . but it is not too soon to provide by every possible means that as few as possible shall be without a little portion of land."

And so, with Jefferson firmly in mind and heart, I set out for Arkansas to see how the battle for a portion of the land was going down in the Delta.

Not well, it turned out. In fact, the very day I met Calvin King he had not succeeded in persuading a government official presiding over a farm foreclosure to hold a private, as opposed to a public, auction of farm equipment and household goods, dashing the dreams of a family that had taken a chance, tried hard, and yet failed. The difference between a private and public auction has to do with the amount of money one would receive from these sad proceedings—the private auction producing a great deal more, perhaps a whole order of magnitude greater. But the private sale would be complicated and difficult for the busy government executive to manage conveniently.

Calvin King had a loan of his own, in fact. He told me that he had tried recently to get an extension on the loan from the Farmers Home Administration—which is supposed to be the lender of last resort, under the law. But the FmHA declined, because the area was "not feasible for farming." How it changed from being feasible in the first instance to unfeasible later was a mystery to Calvin King. He explained that it was virtually impossible for most farmers to operate without the ability to borrow against next year's crop in hard times. "All the big landowners are in debt over their head," he said. "So in effect, then, you only have a right to be a farmer if you are a big farmer."

Foreclosure of loans, and plain lack of credit, is only one way that black landowners are losing their patrimony. Another is the shameful practice of the "partition sale." One case King told me about, which

70

was written up in the Little Rock *Gazette,* concerned the farm of John Dallas Griggs, a former slave who had bought 380 acres of land one hundred years ago in the Delta, near Forrest City, a sizeable town halfway between Little Rock and Memphis. One day, according to Griggs's great-grandson, Troy Glasper, a woman showed up on the place saying she was the illegitimate daughter of old John Griggs and wanted her share of the land. The law on such matters, in Arkansas and in some other states, requires that if such claims cannot be amicably satisfied the court decides whether the land can be physically partitioned in an equitable way, assuming the claims are valid. But if the land cannot be partitioned equitably—and this is the ruling more often than not—then the land must be sold at auction, and the *proceeds* of the heirs' property divided, rather than the land itself.

And that was how the old Griggs farm was lost, after the family had hung on to it through thick and thin for all those years. When the woman sought to sell what she claimed was her undivided interest in the land, a white buyer acquired her interest in the land and told the family he wanted to buy the whole property to settle the matter. The family refused, and so, as allowed by law, the buyer brought the issue to court to force a partition sale. The moves were familiar to all. The judge said, as could be expected, that the land could not be divided and had to be sold at auction. The bid price was $180,000, a small fraction of its real value, Calvin King told me. The Griggs family, as the bidder well knew, was land-poor like all small farmers, and obviously could not meet this price itself. And so the land was lost.

The family had hired a lawyer, of course, to prove that the woman who claimed a share of the property was not, after all, a legitimate heir. It surprised them that the lawyer had failed. It was only later that Glasper found that the lawyer had an interest in the company that subsequently acquired the land, although he was not absolutely certain that the lawyer's interest preceded the court case, according to a careful statement he made to the *Gazette.* Sometimes, Calvin said, those coveting a piece of land will themselves seek out a distant relative, often going to New York or Detroit for the purpose, and purchase the heir's undivided interest for a few hundred dollars if the heir is down on his or her luck—as many in northern ghettos are. As the owner, then, of an undivided interest, the white buyer or real estate speculator can force a partition sale to acquire land for as little as a tenth of its actual value.

If partition sales such as these don't get black landowners, then they had better watch out for tax sales and something called "adverse possession"—although the latter technique is not so blatantly practiced any longer, according to King. Adverse possession is a way to acquire land at no cost, simply by moving onto it or fencing it off, paying taxes, and then claiming ownership after a period of years, usually ten. Often, the land so acquired was originally owned by blacks and adjoined a white farm.

Tax sales come about, as do many of the other difficulties encountered by black landowners, because the owners are sometimes simply not notified of what they owe, or, if they are notified, are not told of the consequences of failing to pay back-taxes. Any legal document, King told me, is likely to be unintelligible to many black people in the South, particularly those who are elderly, as most of the landowners are. "The out-migration pattern in Arkansas," King said, "has meant that a whole generation of blacks left to seek better employment and a better way of life in urban areas. In most cases, they leave behind those who are less well educated—the older ones in the family, their parents—and no one is around to really look out for the property from a management perspective. In my family, for example, everyone with a college degree, except for me, has gone on to some other area to live. That happens all the time, and the older blacks are not inclined to make out wills or deal with any legal document."

This is why King tours the state putting on workshops to help black landowners understand that, unless they are alert to chicanery as well as the ordinary responsibilities of land ownership, they can lose their farms. Although there have been changes in the official definition of what constitutes a bona fide farm as opposed to a "rural residence" (an issue in itself because the current definition tends to undercount black-owned farms and thus eliminate them from government assistance programs), there were two thousand black-owned farms in the twelve-county Delta region in 1970. At the time of my visit only a quarter of that number remained. Blacks had lost some twelve thousand acres of land, even though seventy thousand acres of new cropland was brought into production in the region.

"By the year 2000," Calvin said, "American blacks may become a landless people." Clarence Wright, known as Butch, a colleague of King's and a regional director of the Save the Children Foundation, told me there was a larger social issue beyond the mechanics of ownership and credit and the shifty dealings of white banks, white lawyers and judges, white real estate agents, white government officials. "Black people don't come back to the land," he told me, "not only because there are policies and practices that discourage it, but because a whole generation moved away from the South. We've lost the bridge."

There is a finality in that metaphor—losing the bridge, the bridge back to both a heritage and to social and economic security. As I talked with these earnest men, in their overheated office with creaky floors on the second story of a building whose access was an iron stairway from an alleyway in Forrest City, Arkansas, Calvin King and Butch Wright seemed like soft-spoken yet passionate Zionists, worrying about the diaspora.

It is, I suppose, amazing that blacks have any land at all. After the Civil War, according to a 1982 report by the U.S. Civil Rights Commission on black land loss (with the incoming Reagan Administration, the composition of the commission was changed and it did not pursue the issue), a Reconstruction program to distribute land to freed slaves was quickly abandoned by the new president, Andrew Johnson. A couple of years later, a bill introduced by Representative Thaddeus Stevens to grant forty acres and fifty dollars to former slaves who were the heads of households was defeated by Congress. And so it was that sharecropping replaced slavery in the South, with scarcely any change in the status of black laborers. Their lot was constant indebtedness in a system in which half a crop was owed to the white landowner, who kept all the financial records and handled sales. Thus did landowners manage to keep the "croppers" in a state of permanent indebtedness— by underpaying for the crop and overcharging for credit for household needs and supplies at usurious rates of up to 100 percent. In many states, there was no escape from this peonage. In South Carolina, for example, it was illegal for a landowner to recruit sharecroppers from another landowner. The difference from actual slavery was slight.

For a whole generation after Reconstruction, blacks were unable effectively to become landowning farmers themselves. During the "golden age of agriculture," around the turn of the century, small, black-owned banks and other lending institutions began to appear in the South. Good climate, good prices, and access to credit meant that industrious blacks could, finally, begin to own the land they farmed. By 1910, in North Carolina, South Carolina, Mississippi, Alabama, and Georgia, there were some 240,000 black-owned farms, accounting for 16.5 percent of all Southern landowners, according to the Civil Rights Commission report. Another 670,000 blacks became tenant farmers, constituting 43.6 percent of all Southern tenant farmers—a category which, unlike sharecropping, could lead, for some, to full ownership.

This was not easily achieved, however, since blacks had to fight whites at every turn to get their stake in the land. Effectively, only those blacks "approved" by whites were permitted to become tenured farmers. This meant they had to be judged "safe" and to "know their place." If blacks wished to operate outside this system of not-so-benevolent patronage, they had better have all cash to make the purchase of land. Indeed, they often had to offer twice the amount the land was worth to acquire it. And even then, they were not allowed on the best land, but only the least fertile, the farthest from transportation routes, and at a safe remove from white schools and churches. All in all, the amount of land blacks were able to acquire signified an incredible achievement, given the adversities.

Then came World War I, and the cotton market crash—an event particularly hurtful to black farmers, since they could get loans for little else than cotton: bankers claimed they could trust them with no other crop. And so began the long slide of reduced landownership among blacks in the South. Even during the Depression, when an effort was made to have equitable federal agricultural programs, landownership by blacks declined by 8 percent in the South (between 1930 and 1935), while ownership increased among whites by 11 percent. After World War II came the mechanization of Southern farms, and the tidal wave of displaced rural blacks inundated Northern cities—Chicago, Detroit, New York—changing both the North *and* the South dramatically. Between 1945 and 1959, black tenant farmers, hardest hit by mechanization, declined by 70 percent. The overall decline in black landownership during the period was 33 percent.

But that was only the beginning. "A dramatic shift in black agriculture occurred during the decade between 1959 and 1969," according to the Civil Rights Commission report. "In this short time span the number of black commercial farm operators in the South declined by 84.1 percent. In contrast, white-operated commercial farms declined by 26.3 percent during the same period."

As for numbers of black-owned farms, these statistics too are alarming. Here are the numbers from the commission's 1982 report, the latest available:

1900	746,717
1910	893,377
1920	925,710
1930	882,852
1940	681,970
1950	559,980
1959	272,541
1969	133,973
1978	57,271

Quite obviously, if this trend continues, and it has, Calvin King's concern that his people would be landless in a matter of a few years was no hyperbole.

To give me an idea of Delta farmland and its ownership, King took me for a ride around St. Francis County, of which Forrest City (where his office is located) is the county seat, with side trips into adjoining Cross and Monroe counties. These are counties with good place names: Pine Tree, Palestine, Greasy Corner, Ragtown, Birdeye, Twist, Madison. I add Madison because it recalls the letter Jefferson wrote to Bishop Madison of William and Mary College about the land being common stock and his remark that all should have a little portion of it. And it was at Madison that we met with Mayor Willard Whitaker, then seventy years old, who had presided over this largely black community for thirteen years. It was, he told us, not so hard to get elected, since he had managed to survive the bullets in a Ku Klux Klan raid (Forrest City being the place of the Klan's birth), but there was some difficulty in getting into the mayor's office after the election. The former officials (white) would not give him the key, letting him in only after he threatened to go to the attorney general. Mayor Whitaker told it as a funny story, but when I looked at Calvin he wasn't laughing.

The town hall of Madison, an incorporated municipality of twenty-three hundred people with as many dirt roads as paved ones, was a concrete block building, set on its own spacious lot, next to the firehouse. It was perhaps symbolic, perhaps not, that the mayor's office was at the center of it, windowless, small, secure. From this Delta version of a castle keep, Whitaker dreamed big dreams about self-sufficiency for his people, based on agriculture. He wanted, he said, the local integration of production, processing, distribution, and sales of food products. "If you've got sense enough to grow it," he said, "you've got sense enough to can it. Then small farming would survive."

The trouble was, though the town was black, all the land around it was owned by white farmers. It was not easy for blacks to crack this Caucasian curtain of landownership, said Calvin. "One man who wanted to buy property didn't go to a bank because he didn't want anybody to know that a black man was going to buy land. What happens is, if they find out, the loan application is delayed, and then a white person comes in and buys it."

"This is America," Mayor Whitaker said bitterly, "where they're supposed to give you a chance." Then he paused for a moment. The mayor had a dramatic aspect about him, with a great square face and resonant voice, a kind of stage presence common to actors and politicians. A former casket carpenter, he had left his village to get an education and then returned to help lead it. "The irony of it," he said, referring to Calvin King's story, "is that we fought to get the vote, and we fought to get an education, and yet we let them beat us on the land. Black people owned the land here, but were starving to death on it. They were being so badly treated by whites, they had to leave. They could make an honest living only up North. But after the Civil Rights Act, and the improvements that followed, they should have come back."

What was left in the South then were the very old—a seventy-year-old mayor, say—and those who were the age of his grandchildren. No bridging generation, as Butch Wright had put it. Calvin, the exception, was somewhere in between. He had the optimism of a young man, but was experienced enough in the ways of the Old South to know what to expect in the New. Indeed, he and Whitaker made a good combination, there in the windowless office. King and the mayor told story after story about all the lawyers' tricks to get land away from blacks. As agents of most of the bad things that happen to black landowners, white lawyers have become symbolic of the forces ranged against them. "Is all this a completely *conscious* conspiracy against black farmers?" I asked at one point, because they were telling their stories allusively, roundabout, as black people have learned to do after centuries of practice in the presence of a white person. Then Calvin and the mayor both put their heads back and laughed and laughed.

"You might say that," said Mayor Willard Whitaker, pulling a face and dabbing at his eyes with a huge white handkerchief. "You might just say that!"

It was good to see Calvin laugh this time, even at my expense. I was pretty sure he didn't laugh a whole hell of a lot.

———————

One of the "bridging" landowners who didn't leave—or at least came back soon enough to hang on to the family farm—was Ephron Lewis, who, Calvin said, farmed two thousand acres, of which he owned fifteen hundred. Lewis was, by any account, what is called a big producer—wheat, soybeans, rice. After leaving Madison, Calvin and I drove to Lewis's place, finding him on a farm road that traversed a wide, flat, newly cultivated field. He was messing with a tractor, which was idling loudly and unevenly, and in discussion with its driver, so Calvin had a hard time getting his attention from the distance where we parked. When Lewis spotted us, he waved in a way that meant we were to wait for a minute, and turned back to the tractor and its driver. They fiddled with the tractor some more, and then the driver climbed back on and sped down the road.

It was clear by his deliberate, unhurried gait as he came toward us that Ephron Lewis was a man with self-confidence and a sense of his own achievement. He reminded me of certain master sergeants in the army whose commanding presence could awe not only raw recruits but officers up to and beyond field grade.

As it turned out, Lewis was not a rough-talking sergeant, but a pleasant-voiced businessman farmer, of about my own age, and like me putting on weight. Ephron Lewis and his farm were the necessary exception in the Delta, showing others that a black farmer could be a big operator, although Calvin said later that he might be the only really sizeable black producer left in the state.

Lewis told me that he had left home to work for Boeing, but his mother had implored him to take over the farm; and over the years, starting in 1959, he was not only able to make a go of it on the original acreage, but added more land to it. These days, he said, it was important to own a majority of land you farmed, if you were black. "They don't want to rent to a black man," he said. Moreover, "if a black farmer wants to buy land, he'd have to pay two or three times as much as a white farmer would, and you can't get a loan for that." Calvin nodded in agreement.

"Once you leave the land, you can't get back," Lewis said. "If you're black. There's going to have to be a change in attitude for black farmers to come back into this business."

I wondered out loud if it had always been this way. Lewis replied that it was not. He said he used to rent land from whites, and buy it too. And then farmland became valuable. "You know, for about ten years, up to 1980 or so, farming was a pretty good business. You could really do well."

Lewis said, "When I started out, it used to be that the Farmers Home Administration served blacks and low-income whites. Now they have no maximum loan, so now they tend to deal only with the big white owners. It's left a void. All it takes is two hundred acres to have a going farm. If a man owns his own land, he can make a good living on two hundred acres."

We walked up and down along the rutty farm road as we talked, Lewis kicking at the clods at the edge of a newly plowed field. "We've had a marketing swing of 33 percent on soybeans," he said. "I don't know how you are supposed to deal with that. Farmers have a new occupational disease. It's called 'farmer's stress syndrome.' You can't sleep, you don't eat right."

He told me his son was getting his degree from an agricultural college, and he was hoping he would take over the farm. When he said that, it seemed to me that Ephron Lewis would be a pretty hard act to follow. How many could do what Lewis had done? We fell silent, and Lewis kept kicking at the gray clods turned up by the cultivator. "We call that 'gumbo,'" he muttered. "Lotta gumbo around here."

After we said good-bye and I had climbed back into Calvin's car, we drove along the narrow flat road between Ephron Lewis's fields. As we pulled out onto I-40, the six-lane interstate that knifes through the big flat farm country of Arkansas's Delta region, Calvin said, in the saddest voice I have ever heard: "When this is all passed over, when the storm has all gone by, the land will still be there, the farms will still be there. But there will be no black farmers among them. And the kind of people who worry about such things will not know anything about what happened. Everyone will soon forget."

Thomas Jefferson argued that the land was ours—yours and mine—common stock. And that there are certain inalienable rights that, once abridged, diminish us all. I have no idea how most people feel about the abridgement of the civil rights of black landowners in the South—

or of Chicanos in California, or Appalachian poor whites, or young farmers trying to get started in the Dakotas. The young, the poor, and the minorities are for one reason or another being discriminated against. For some—such as those who can't qualify for a loan—the discrimination may be institutional, an adverse effect of wrongheaded policy. For others—those known to Calvin King and Butch Wright and Willard Whitaker and Ephron Lewis—the discrimination is vicious and personal. And in this case, it seems to me that the problem transcends inappropriate economic policy, and enters the area of basic human rights.

It is not as though the issues of equitable landownership have never been raised. From the Free Soilers of the early 1800s to the distribution of land to former slaves after the Civil War, from the Homestead Act of 1862 to the Resettlement Administration of the 1930s, there has been a long history of the democratic distribution of land to those who could and would work it. And yet the distribution hasn't stuck; instead, it just invites the major and minor chiseling that has accompanied much of the sordid history of land dealing in the United States. Paul Wallace Gates, the Cornell University historian of U.S. public land policy, asked an apt question at a 1976 Senate hearing: "This country once had opportunities of landownership that attracted populations from lands of great estates owned by an aristocracy and worked by landless peasants. Are we now coming full circle?"

It is, I suppose, no longer fashionable to be a bleeding heart liberal of the kind that held our attention during the 1960s, when many marched for civil rights and many others cheered from the sidelines. In time, black separatism and white "realism" called the marching and the cheering into question. People now say that our concern was hypocritical and insincere. But even acknowledging a good dose of that, perhaps the common cause was at least sometimes genuinely felt as we all stood there, holding hands and singing "We Shall Overcome." The diminishment of civil liberties for one was understood, at least for a moment, as a diminishment for all.

The black people a generation ago taught the rest of the country an important lesson, and reforms followed. Calvin King and his colleagues are still teaching, as did Martin Luther King before him. And their effort to achieve a true democracy of the land in our nation is as crucial a civil rights issue as any, and should be seen as one.

I'll tell you what I think of Calvin. I think he is doing the Lord's work, and Tom Jefferson's too.

DUSTY OLD DUST

At first they thought it might be a great underground river. Later it was called a lake—and sometimes still is, the "Sixth" Great Lake, with as much water as Huron or Erie, a quadrillion gallons. Only it isn't a lake either. It is an *aquifer*, or more exactly a formation of water-saturated sand, gravel, clay, and caliche, the bottom of it a thousand feet deep in some places, only twenty feet in others. This is the Ogallala, named for a Sioux Indian tribe that once roamed the High Plains that lie above it.

Nothing of the Ogallala's vastness shows on the surface. But if you are far above the land, watching the movie on a coast-to-coast airline flight, take a moment to lift the shade when you are over the flatlands of New Mexico, Colorado, or Kansas, or the sandhills of Nebraska, or the panhandles of Texas or Oklahoma. Then you will "see" the Ogallala—in giant green circles, stretching to the horizon, the work of center-pivot irrigation rigs sucking up the waters at a thousand gallons a minute. In just a single generation, these center pivots converted millions of acres of former High Plains shortgrass prairie into lush, row-crop agriculture and pushed the Corn Belt westward into the heart of the Great American Desert.

Consisting of a long pipe—over a thousand feet long—supported by wheeled A-frame towers, tall as a house, the center-pivot system requires no manual relocation. You just start the pump motor—typically an automobile engine converted to use natural gas—and the center pivot, powered by the flow of the water itself, moves around in a slow circle, taking twelve hours or more to do so. With stately progress, it inundates, in one roaring sweep, a quarter-section of land—a quarter of one square mile—at a time. The first center pivot was patented by Frank Zyback in 1952. There are now over a hundred thousand of them, of various design, in the High Plains.

Climate-free agriculture this is called. But it was not always so. On April 14, 1935, a young plains drifter and political activist from Pampa, Texas—a hard, dry Panhandle town even in the best of times—watched a towering black airborne tidal wave sweep down from the north. It consisted of thousands upon thousands of tons of dust from farms as far away as the Dakotas, and as near as the next county. When the cloud enveloped the little town, visibility went from blinking bright to zero. On that day, all across the Panhandle, animals died of asphyxiation, as did babies and small children whose mouths and noses became clogged with the dust—that is, with somebody's topsoil.

So Woody Guthrie wrote his song, "Dusty Old Dust," later retitled "So Long, It's Been Good to Know You," and like tens of thousands of others picked up and left the land that had been so fecklessly plowed and plowed and plowed to death. In a desperate attempt to keep up with falling commodity prices during the 1920s and 1930s, farmers had pushed farther and farther westward into the hot prairie, plowing under the matted native grasses of the fragile lands that for eons had held the soil in place. "Rain follows the plow," they said. Only it didn't, and the land turned to dust. I was four years old when this happened. Woody was twenty-three. Most Americans weren't even born. Domestically, the great dust storms were, next to the Civil War, America's single most vivid historical event. The Dust Bowl. But oddly, few Americans know what happened next.

What happened next was the deep-well turbine pump, the center-pivot irrigation system, and the energy to run them, which was supplied courtesy of the Rural Electrification Administration and the new natural-gas pipelines. In short order, thanks to these remarkable technologies, agriculture in the High Plains tapped the riches of the Ogallala and went from dusty disaster to astonishing wealth. But now it is on its way back to disaster again, at least in some parts. In recent times, the Ogallala's waters have been pumped out so fast that some farmers have had to redrill their wells every year. Many of them just go broke. In a sizeable area, the Ogallala's "overdraft" has reached 95 percent, which is to say for every gallon of water pumped out only a teacupful is restored by the natural processes of aquifer recharge.

But let us begin at the beginning, at a time a billion years past, when the American tableland began to take shape under the sea. As the oceans slowly withdrew, the flat layers of sediment hardened into bedrock. Then, some seventy to ninety million years ago, the Rockies began to rise from a trench left behind by the oceans. As the mountains grew, the rains coursed down their flanks to the east, creating what author Russell McKee calls "river-clawed badlands sloping for hundreds of miles to the Mississippi." But then the rains decreased in force and frequency, and the channels, no longer scoured clean by regularly running rivers, began to fill up with stones, sand, and silt. Afterwards, when the seasonal torrents *did* come, the blocked riverbeds forced the water out of the old channels and created a complex of overlapping deltas. In time, a mantle of saturated debris, hundreds of feet deep, spread over some 150,000 square miles of the old bedrock base.

The whole process—to build the mantle of water-saturated geological debris that is the Ogallala formation, and then to overlay it with more hundreds of feet of soil from "the perishing rivers," as historian Walter Prescott Webb puts it—took about ten million years to complete. Now it would seem that in parts of the High Plains the Ogallala's waters may be all used up in scarcely more than a hundred years.

According to a 1982 government report, five million acres of irrigated land will, by the year 2020, be irrigated no more. This obtains because the aquifer cannot be recharged from its original source, the east-flowing runoff from the Rocky Mountains, for the High Plains are now geologically separate from the larger matrix of the Great Plains, which run from the 100th meridian west to the Rockies. Indeed, the Ogallala's only source of recharge is the local rain, and to a minor degree the associated rain-swollen rivers—the Platte, the Arkansas, the Canadian—which are few in the High Plains of modern geological times. Sometimes, however, these rivers can *lower* the water table, for their channels cut below it, and when the rains stop, the Ogallala feeds the rivers, rather than the reverse.

In the northern part of the High Plains, in Nebraska, a good rain can go a fair way to recharging the aquifer, for the overlying soil is sandy and porous, letting the rainwater through to the formation beneath. But in other areas, especially in Texas, there is a layer of "caprock" between the surface strata and the Ogallala formation below. When a Texas farmer pumps water from a deep well, the deficit is permanent. In Colorado and Kansas the problem is almost as bad, with water tables dropping routinely two or three feet a year, sometimes as much as ten in some places in a dry season. The rule of thumb is this: for every acre of land irrigated to an aggregate depth of twelve inches in a year, the water table will drop five to six feet.

The rule of thumb has kept the High Plains in a state of anxiety for decades. In some areas, the "saturated thickness" is three hundred feet or more, and a drop of maybe five or six feet a year doesn't mean much. In others, where the thickness is one hundred feet or less, a farmer might expect to be out of irrigation agriculture pretty soon. In Texas, some farmers sink small wells in various places on their land for the sole purpose of transferring water to a big center-pivot well no longer able to operate a sprinkler on its own.

To irrigation farmers running out of water, the obvious solution is to get some from elsewhere. At first, hydrologists thought they might recharge the drying Ogallala by putting water *into* the deep wells from seasonal playa lakes. The trouble was, the silt from the playas fouled the turbines when the water was pumped out again. Moreover, environmentalists raised the issue of pollution. The pure, million-year-old water from the aquifer would become laced with last season's persistent pesticides.

What really captured the imagination of High Plains irrigators were the water transfer schemes, the most astonishing of which (though taken quite seriously at the time) was the so-called North American Water and Power Alliance. NAWAPA would tap into the Yukon and other far-north freshwater sources—mostly in Canada—and pipe the waters southward, with a significant percentage going to the High Plains and from there down into Mexico. In all, NAWAPA water would exceed the flow of the Mississippi. The price tag would be upwards of $100 billion. Wrote Texas Congressman Jim Wright at the time (1966): "NAWAPA has an almost limitless potential if we possess the courage and foresight to grasp it."

Luckily, we didn't, and after that more limited plans were advanced. But these days, even the most modest "interbasin" water-transfer proposals (the most recent envisions pumping water from Arkansas, Missouri, and South Dakota into the High Plains) are thought to be without a chance of implementation. And so, today, farmers are beginning to ponder what they should have been pondering all along—ways to conserve the water they have left. For one thing, they can turn the sprinklers on the center pivots upside down, thus reducing the amount of water lost to evaporation. Many are installing sophisticated "drip-irrigation" systems the Israelis made famous which require only a tiny fraction of the water once used. Some others are planting less-thirsty crops: milo and sunflowers instead of corn and beans.

For a good many farmers, though, the new water conservation techniques have come too late. There has been, according to Bob Raschke of the National Association of Conservation Districts, a "positive correlation" between farm bankruptcy and center-pivot irrigation on the High Plains. Moreover, High Plains irrigation farmers have flocked to a "Conservation Reserve Program," established by Congress in 1985. The CRP offered to pay farmers between $40 and $50 per acre per year to retire "highly erodible" land from active agriculture for a period of ten years, and required them to plant cover crops or trees to hold the soil in place. After the ten years, farmers could return the land to agriculture, but it would be ineligible forever for any crop subsidy payment. According to Mack Gray of USDA's Soil Conservation Service, there were forty-three counties nationwide in which farmers retired agricultural land up to the limit allowed by the program (25 percent of total county land area) within a year or two after it began. Of those forty-three counties twenty-eight of them, or nearly two thirds, were in the Ogallala–High Plains area.

As it happens, the Conservation Reserve Program may point the way to a more permanent approach to the stewardship of the ravaged landscapes of the High Plains—however plowed up and sucked dry they might be. They can, ecologically, make a comeback. During the 1930s, the National Resources Planning Board recommended buying up seventy-five million acres of devastated Dust Bowl land and returning it permanently to native grasses. In the end, reserves totaling only eleven million acres were bought, becoming, as University of Oklahoma geographer Brett Wallach has put it, "the orphans of the federal estate." But after being transferred from agency to agency for twenty-five years they finally came to rest in the U.S. Forest Service in 1961 as designated "National Grasslands." They are in fact heavy in grass, says Wallach, "while on the private side of the fence the land is nearly denuded." In Kansas's 107,000-acre Cimarron National Grassland, for example, buffalo once again roam, chewing on the native bluestem. Grazing-rights leases to local cattle ranchers bring in enough revenues to pay for administration and range maintenance. Given the overdraft crisis of the Ogallala plus the farm failures throughout the Plains, Wallach has recommended that the National Grasslands concept be dusted off and significant additional acreage of dried-out land be acquired by the Forest Service without delay.

As everyone knows, the politically conservative High Plains farmer would just as soon invite Karl Marx to a barbecue as even *think* about conveying land to the federal government. At the same time, a mechanism of some sort may be necessary, after the Conservation Reserve Program is over, to return affected lands to economic use, as well as to arrive at some sort of economic and ecological equilibrium in the High Plains as a whole. Clearly, a sustainable balance between irrigation, dryland farming, and the restoration and management of rangeland is needed.

The key to balanced land use is, many believe, the return of a significant portion of the High Plains to managed rangeland— something approximating the original shortgrass prairie. However, according to SCS official Mack Gray, the lands retired under the Conservation Reserve Program are extensively "checkerboarded," intermixed with cropland to such an extent that the parcels would not be large enough for livestock range. Fencing costs alone, Gray has estimated— a single quarter-section parcel would, for example, run some $3,000— could make grazing economically impractical for an individual farmer.

The double whammy set up by the Conservation Reserve Program—the discouragement of cropping retired land ever again for lack of crop subsidy eligibility, plus the checkerboarding that can keep the land from being economically used for grazing on an individual basis—might, however, make a National Grasslands-type buyout much more feasible politically after the CRP has run its course. Existing National Grasslands are themselves checkerboarded, but the basic mechanism nevertheless created large areas of leasable range through land trades and linkages as well as through economies of scale in land restoration, including fencing. From an ecological, wildlife, and soil- and water-conservation standpoint, as well as an economic one, "the sensible thing," according to Oklahoma's Brett Wallach, is to return the plowed-out, dried-out land of the High Plains to "the open prairie the settlers found. That way, at least, we would get something of value from the land; . . . we would have grazed parkland with recreational elbowroom—a prairie equivalent of the national forests."

A less intrusive governmental approach, one that would leave the land in private hands, can be found even farther back in history. In 1878 John Wesley Powell, founder of the U.S. Geological Survey, Colorado River explorer, and prescient philosopher of the Great American Desert, made a recommendation that might now work. In his classic *Report on the Lands of the Arid Region of the United States*, Powell suggested the establishment of large, multifamily-owned "grazing districts" as a means to avoid overtaxing the fragile grasslands. The districts, set up with government assistance, would in effect be cooperative "commons," where use and management could be controlled for the commonweal.

Rutgers University land-use planner Frank J. Popper, Jr., holds the view that it will first take a wholesale economic disaster—which is surely coming, he says—for us to recognize that the "true architect of the Plains has never been governmental, private, or even human—it has been the desert, its immense expansions and contractions, its pitiless resistance to cultivation." In fact, Popper and his wife, Deborah, a geographer, have gained a fair amount of notoriety on the High Plains with their notion of a "Buffalo Commons." Part prediction and part proposal, the idea would simply allow those areas undergoing population loss as well as decreasing groundwater supply to move into public ownership as a cheaper alternative for the government than continued agricultural subsidy. The Buffalo Commons would consist of a somewhat discontinuous stretch of land totaling some 139,000 square miles in a north-south strip from Canada to Mexico, between the 98th meridian and the Rocky Mountain front range. Aggregated, the total amount of land would be roughly the size of a couple of western states.

"We tried to force waterless, treeless steppes to behave like Ohio," Frank Popper told *New York Times Magazine* writer Anne Matthews, "and got three or four boom-and-bust episodes for our trouble. Now the classic Plains cycle of drought, financial woe, and depopulation is rolling again, and this time it may go all the way. Thirty years of water-table depletion, S & Ls collapsing right and left, whole rural counties voting with their feet—and still no one's thinking ahead."

Such views are something for the policymakers to consider, and I hope they do, though I am not holding my breath. For myself, I went in 1985 to take a look at the place where, exactly fifty years before, Woody Guthrie watched the towering clouds of dust descend on a Texas town. I asked my brother-in-law, Bob Fixsen, who lives in that part of the Panhandle, to drive me out to an irrigated farm he knew.

The center pivot was quiet on this hot afternoon, so we walked into a field. Bob had given me a farmer's cap that read, hopefully, "Greenbelt Irrigation." A good ol' boy Ogallala cap it was, providing me a protective disguise in these precincts. The sun was low so I tilted the visor to keep the hot, punishing rays off my face as I knelt to examine the gray silty soil we were walking over. The earth was dry and cracked, and the corn seedlings pushing up through it were wilted already. "They don't look so good," said Bob, probably wondering what in the world was on my mind. Actually, it was to pick a handful of dust and let it sift slowly through my fingers. When I did so, a light evening breeze caught the fine particles and blew them eastward. Such innocent dust, I was thinking. Is it possible that one day the dust might *not* fall to earth a few yards away but gather more dust to it, and then more, and more still, until once again it would grow into something vast and terrible? Woody's insistent tune ran over and over in my mind: "So long, it's been good to know ya."

Now the sun was turning orange. "Let's get on down the road," said Bob in his gentle Texas way. And as we walked back to the car, little plumes of soil from the dry field spurted up from the sides of our shoes.

OLD FARMS,
NEW LIVES

There is plenty of bad news having to do with agriculture in our rural places. Despite the radically increasing levels of financial support to farming during the 1980s—typically $25 billion annually in the Reagan years, a whole order of magnitude greater than it was during the 1970s—farming has found itself in as deep and persistent a depression as any since the Dust Bowl 1930s. World commodity prices have been dramatically below the cost of U.S. production, and the shrinking export trade will, according to many experts, stay shrunk as European and Third World nations increase their agricultural production. Nations that were just yesterday at or near the point of famine have become self-sufficient in grain—even Bangladesh, despite its tragedies. Given the low "target prices" set by our government in order to meet the new low-price international competition, a good many farmers have thought that they had better push to the limit the land they crop, even as they collect federal payments for not cultivating other land. One result is that erosion levels have risen to a point somewhere between serious and tragic, and, as chemical use increases (regardless of recent blandishments about "low input sustainable agriculture"—LISA—from Washington), synthetic compounds that interact in untold ways with one another are running off into streams and polluting groundwater to a greater degree than ever before. The "pure countryside" has become, in places, no better environmentally than a subdivision of huddled terrace houses in the industrial flats of a poisonous city.

The result? Farm population is down to just two percent of our total population. The vitality drains away from the working landscape and its small towns and villages. The land might well be returned to the public estate, though that thought, at least when voiced by Frank Popper (as I described), brings only howls of dismay. But the fact is that in a single generation literally hundreds of thousands of farms have gone into bankruptcy and many more have been sold off, abandoned for taxes, or just sit there, awaiting the next development of condos if they're close to a city or within a popular vacation area. This is not exactly what Thomas Jefferson had in mind.

Since Europeans arrived, there have been two kinds of agriculture in America. The first was the agriculture of settlement and subsistence, which was not only the agriculture of colonists who clung to the edge of the continent, but of those who pushed on into the hinterlands— the pioneers and homesteaders, especially those of the nineteenth century who, with John Deere's mass-produced moldboard plow and a stout team, could turn the heavy bottomland loams along the rivers of the Middle West and zip open the primeval sod out where the buffalo roamed on the native shortgrass prairies beyond the Mississippi. This was the agriculture of those who got on the land soonest—as in the Oklahoma "Sooners." To survive was to succeed. Those who failed literally "starved to death on a government claim," as the folk song has it, or they succumbed to disease, exposure, or calamity.

This agriculture outlived its time. It was, as historian Walter Ebeling puts it, an *extensive* agriculture, based on the availability of endless quantities of land, rather than an *intensive* one, based on the careful husbandry of limited land resources, as in Europe. The saying—during the period we might call "Agriculture I"—that "rain follows the plow" was, like many aspects of "moon farming" (the phrase is Liberty Hyde Bailey's, a reference to planting superstitions based on phases of the moon), tragically wrong. When the farm depression of the 1920s set in, farmers took their plows into dry prairies in order to maintain an income in the face of falling prices. They plowed and plowed, and it did rain; 1929 and 1930 were good, wet years. Then in 1931 and 1932, the first warnings came in Kansas and eastern Colorado as the dust devils kicked up after the dry spells. A few years later, the dry spells became a drought, and the drought became pandemic, and dust storms blackened the middays throughout the Plains. The cataclysm triggered the greatest migration in U.S. history, and before it was over one hundred million acres of cropland had been ravaged.

And so "Agriculture II" was introduced: the planned industrialization of farming. FDR's Agricultural Adjustment Act of 1933 and subsequent programs were based on a policy of establishing a certain amount of financial stability (via "adjustments" of prices and production levels), increasing yields per acre, and, most significantly, reducing the number of farms. Brain Truster Rexford Tugwell, the brilliant assistant secretary of agriculture, wrote in 1936 that the most important part of New Deal farm policy was "partly the effort to make 'two blades of grass grow where one grew before,' but only partly that. Most significant has been the making of more blades of grass grow for one farmer."

Our present difficulties stem from the irony that Agriculture II succeeded too well—it grossly overshot the mark. The subsidies entrained by the Agricultural Adjustment Act, together with the advances in mechanized and chemical agriculture on larger and larger farms, have created a farm economy so financially attenuated that it cannot adjust downward without such dire results that the impacts, like the crisis in the steel industry, reverberate throughout the whole society. Agriculture II is oversimplified and therefore vulnerable; it lacks the strength of diversity. It has outlived its time and the limits of its resources as surely as did Agriculture I.

What could an Agriculture III be like? Let me tell you about some people I met on my country-road travels who may have a good deal to do with the future of American agriculture.

In Banks, Alabama, I met Jerrell Harden, who farms about nine hundred acres of the hard, red, gritty soil characteristic of the southeastern coastal plain. Harden is a studious-looking man, which he comes by naturally, though not from any excess of formal education. According to Dr. Albert Trouse, a respected soils scientist recently retired from Auburn University, Jerrell Harden is quite possibly a genius.

Harden is in fact a self-taught mechanical engineer who has invented a device called a "Ro-Till." Long a soil and water conservationist, Harden cosponsored a demonstration of "no-till" agriculture on his farm in the early 1970s. The idea of no-till is to reduce soil erosion by seeding directly into the stubble from a previous crop, without "plowing down." Herbicides are applied to eliminate cover crops but can be "banded" to control weeds after planting, letting the mulch do most of the work. The technique has been in use on a commercial scale since the early 1960s, and today about fifteen million acres of U.S. cropland are "no-tilled."

The catch is that in the Southeast, with its extremely compactible soils, no-till often doesn't work. The hardpan created by years of moldboard plowing together with the surface compaction from heavy farm machinery keeps rainwater from penetrating beyond a few inches and serves as a barrier to roots seeking moisture and nutrients in the permeable subsoil below. This effect was clear-cut in the field that Harden had devoted to his own test of no-till. The resulting crop was a disappointment. However, in one corner of the test field, Harden had used a "subsoiler" prior to the no-till planting. A subsoiler is a steel shank, about twenty inches long and shaped like an old-fashioned anchor fluke, which is pulled through the soil to break up hardpan. There the effect was fabulous. In the part of the no-till field where Harden had run his subsoiler earlier in the season, the crop was better than any he had ever seen before.

An inveterate tinkerer, Harden hurried to his shop, fired up an acetylene torch, and fashioned a no-till planter with subsoiler shanks attached. A modest idea, but no one had thought of it before. He called his gadget a "Ro-Till" because unlike a plow it did not till all over, but only in the planted row. The beneficial residues of prior crops would be left in place between the rows, as in no-till, but moisture and plant roots would have a way to get past the hardpan and into the loose subsoil where the shank penetrated the pan. Harden licensed the Bush Hog manufacturing company to produce and market the Ro-Till, which guarantees that it will increase yields over any conventional tillage equipment it replaces.

Another farmer I visited was Morton Swanson, whose story is not unlike that of Jerrell Harden. Swanson farms twelve hundred acres of wheat land in the starkly beautiful Palouse country of eastern Washington. The Palouse is sui generis geologically, a region about half the size of New Jersey that is made up of dunelike deposits of aeolian loess, "aeolian" meaning windborne (volcanic ash blowing in from the predecessors of Mount St. Helens) and "loess" from the German word for "loose." So loose in fact that the erosion rates on the steep hillsides of the Palouse are among the highest in the nation. It is a prairie built like a roller coaster.

Swanson told me that the techniques of no-till agriculture were essential for the steep, dry lands of the Palouse if it were to continue to be agriculturally productive. The land could not sustain much more erosion, because of a vicious circle of erosion leading to reduced soil moisture (since the harder subsoils were less permeable), which led to increasing amounts of plowing (to break up the soil so that moisture could penetrate), which led to increasing rates of erosion. And so on.

Mort Swanson was a compact, wiry man who not only farmed a lot of land but owned one of the largest shops I have ever seen. It was a hangar-sized six thousand square feet. Adjoining it was a small office, with a professional drafting table tucked into a corner. Many a late night was spent here on shop drawings for "Old Yellow," Swanson said, which was a prototype no-till seed drill specially designed for big acreage wheat farming, capable of holding up while being pulled by a tractor through the punishing steeps of the Palouse.

Unlike Jerrell Harden, who licensed his invention to an existing manufacturer, Swanson, plus some family members and a few close friends, created a new corporation—the Yielder Drill Company—to manufacture a production version of Old Yellow. (To drill a seed is to plant it mechanically at the proper depth.) Swanson set up an interview for me with the staff, whom I found to be so enthusiastic about the potentials of their machine that they seemed almost messianic. As one of the executives—Greg Schmick, an agronomist and the firm's best sales rep—told me: "Do you realize that for the first time in ten thousand years people can grow crops without destroying the land?"

And then there are Carl and Rosemary Eppley, who farm 550 acres of corn and soybeans in northern Indiana, near Wabash. The Eppleys use a technique called "ridge till," which looked to be a field scale version of a raised-bed victory garden. Permanent planting ridges are created with special machinery for this purpose (the Eppleys' was made by the Fleischer Manufacturing Company of Nebraska). This method can cut erosion rates because residues (corn stalks, for example) would be left in the spaces between the ridges. It can reduce compaction and require fewer chemicals—both fertilizer and herbicides—than other methods. The raised ridges warm up quickly in the spring, getting the crop off to an early start. And the proprietors of the farm make more money, with less work, than they did before. The Eppleys told me they did not need or want a larger farm, or more land. That would be uneconomical and less enjoyable.

Said Rosemary: "Have you ever picked up a handful of earth and considered what you were holding? Within your hand is life. Just as individuals are stressed, and families are stressed, so too is the land being stressed by misuse. Don't you think it's time we stopped abusing ourselves and our land? After all, there's nothing quite like working together and with the land: planting, nurturing, preserving, and using this good earth, making the world a better place to live, and to enjoy each other."

The fishworms were coming back in the Eppley's cornfields, Carl said. He confessed to me, just as I was about to leave, that he thought he might be edging in on some kind of organic agriculture. He said he didn't need nearly as much nitrogen as he used to, or herbicides or insecticides either.

In Maryland, in the far suburbs of Washington, D.C., I visited Todd Greenstone, father of two young children, who then owned no land at all but made a whole living nevertheless for himself and his family from land rented from estate owners and retired farmers. He used a combination of no-till (though quite unlike that of Morton Swanson) and chisel-plowing, which he said was gentler on the land than the old-fashioned moldboard plow. Greenstone seemed like a yuppie farmer, striding through the fields in chinos and sport shirt. He said that the way to succeed is to "farm the desk," not ride a tractor. He had a degree in agriculture from the University of Maryland, and he was a farmer because he wanted to be one, not because he was born on a farm or because he inherited a farm or because other options were limited.

Indeed, the reason that Greenstone could make a go of it without the family-land subsidy many other farmers require was directly and specifically because of advances in tillage technique. And it seemed to me that was good for him and good for the rest of us too. Good because he liked the look and feel of the land; he liked growing things; and he was expert at it—I later learned from the county agent that Todd was one of the best farmers in his county. We need more farmers like Todd Greenstone, I thought. He fine-tunes his cultural practices on each of the half-dozen fields he crops. He uses the land well and carefully. He is a professional.

———————

If Agriculture I is the agriculture of self-sufficiency, the mixed-farm agriculture of the eighteenth and nineteenth centuries, which, taken to extremes in the twentieth, led from depression to dust; and if Agriculture II is the industrial agriculture introduced by New Deal technocrats in the 1930s, which, taken to extremes in the 1980s and into the 1990s, has shaken the very foundations of the American economy; then some new form, made up of elements of the old but different from it, is, as all good Hegelians would argue, inevitable. That is why

I wondered if the kind of farmers I visited might be prelusive of that synthesis: Agriculture III.

At the most superficial level, conservation tillage was what Jerrell Harden, Morton Swanson, Carl and Rosemary Eppley, and Todd Greenstone had in common. This technical term may sound like an oxymoron to some, but it's nevertheless useful and accurate, for it describes a collection of what are actually quite different ways to till the soil and yet conserve its organic content, moisture, and nutriment, rather than deplete it. Conservation tillage, broadly defined, is now in use on about a third of U.S. cropland.

In 1987 I published a book about conservation tillage—how it works, how it came to be, what its environmental implications are, and so on. But the more I think about it now, the more I am convinced that the most important thing these people have in common is an extremely intelligent, quite independent approach to farming as a technology, as a way of life, as a profession. The technical strategies (loosely called "conservation tillage") they independently developed, based on their particular crops and soils, were a *result* of their intelligence and independence, not, obviously, a cause of it.

And so, on a deeper level, my investigation of conservation tillage set me to thinking about the long-term future of agriculture—what it could be like if farm policies would encourage the individualistic approach to farming that conservation tillage illustrates. In the era of Agriculture III, for example, scientific inquiry would be conducted by farmers themselves, people like Jerrell Harden and Mort Swanson, instead of left to government and industry "experts" who push technology, not science. Farmers would write the articles in journals, not bureaucrats and academics who are on the agribusiness payroll. Further, with Agriculture III, the reward structure in agriculture could be based on how well you farmed rather than how many acres you planted, how much horsepower you required, or which chemicals you used—as the Eppleys had found in making a comfortable living on a modest-sized farm with low "inputs." Indeed, Agriculture III might well bring a greatly reduced capital requirement for entry into farming, permitting more "elective" professionals like Todd Greenstone to participate.

And Agriculture III also would produce a more relaxed and creative life on the land, with a sufficiency of discretionary time. The Eppleys had plenty of time to lecture all over the country. Agriculture III would also automatically confer an improved social status on farming. America has never gone in for a peasantry anyway. The normative farmer-proprietors would never again be thought of as hayseeds, but would be middle-class "statesmen," as they were called in England, of culture, learning, community responsibility, even privilege.

——————

If it were up to me, I'd call a great meeting of thousands of people from the Palouse and the southern Coastal Plain and the corn and soybean country of the Middle West, and from all the other places where farming is done, from Vermont and Arkansas and Maryland and talk this out for maybe a week or two, to decide that we can actually have Agriculture III, and *how* we can have it. I should not want us to wait too long for this to happen. Twenty-five billion—or any number followed by nine zeros, for that matter—is a lot of dollars to prop up a set of policies that perpetuate a misery.

The strength of the working landscape, and of those who work upon it, is still out there. I know this because I have seen it. And it is worth the effort to make it right. We owe this much to the memory of Deane Hoisington, to the founding vision of Thomas Jefferson, to the good works of Calvin King, and to a song by Woody Guthrie. Those modern agronomists who are the precursors of Agriculture III may be showing us something important: how new lives can be created on the old farms, how to nourish and preserve a rural heritage.

THE GREAT AMERICAN WILDERNESS

Arthur Carhart, a landscape architect for the U.S. Forest Service (he was scornfully called "the beauty engineer" by his colleagues), is generally given credit for the idea of protecting designated areas of the public lands as permanent wilderness. As he wrote in a 1919 memorandum to his superiors, "The scenic spots where nature has been allowed to remain unmarred will become some of the most highly prized scenic features of our country." A young forester stationed in New Mexico, Aldo Leopold, learned of Carhart's idea and the two of them began a campaign for the U.S. Forest Service to set aside certain areas that would be spared from logging or development. The first of these, in Gila National Forest, was so designated in 1927.

In the 1930s, the wilderness preservation idea got a major boost from Robert Marshall, the socialist son of a wealthy New York attorney. Marshall joined the Forest Service and from that vantage point, among other government posts, militated for a much stronger set of wilderness preservation policies. In 1935 he collaborated with Aldo Leopold, TVA regional planner Benton MacKaye (founder of the Appalachian Trail), editor and national park publicist Sterling Yard, and several others to create the Wilderness Society, which gave the nascent wilderness movement a permanent voice. At length, the society, along with other conservation groups, managed to persuade Congress to give wilderness areas on the federal public lands (forests, parks, wildlife refuges) statutory protection as well as a formal procedure for their selection. The result was the Wilderness Act, which was signed into law by President Lyndon Johnson in 1964.

Today, the statutory wilderness system is approaching one hundred million acres in size. But have we "saved" the wilderness? For the most part, the organizations that seem to have succeeded so well now fear that the modern-day economic pressures that encroach on designated wilderness *areas have made them extremely vulnerable ecologically—isolated "islands" in seas of clear-cuts, recreational development, and the whatnots of urbanization. The result of the island effect is slow ecological death, where plant and animal species, needful of far-flung genetic interchange, weaken and sometimes die out.*

The conservation leadership in the U.S. is now, accordingly, giving a good deal of emphasis not just to individual wilderness tracts, but to the preservation of whole ecosystems of natural resource lands so that their wilderness "cores," and the wildlife and native plants they sustain and protect, can and will continue to prosper. In the Lower 48 there remain, remarkably, a good many areas where large-scale ecosystem management is not only possible but vitally necessary. Five that the Wilderness Society has identified include the old-growth forests of the Northwest, the California Desert, the Southern Appalachian Highlands, the South Florida Everglades, and what is called "the Greater Yellowstone Ecosystem."

Of all the regions where ecosystem planning is needed to protect the wilderness, the highest priority as well as the most paradigmatic is Greater Yellowstone, which is the subject of this chapter. The issues that are developing there, and the responses to them by the conservation community, can, one hopes, serve as a model for ecosystem thinking elsewhere in the coterminous states as well as in Alaska.

ORIGINS OF AN IDEA

Suddenly, outside your tiny plexiglass window in the airliner that has for hours droned above the patterned fields of the Great Plains, there appears, just opposite a wingtip, a looming vision: the bright massif of the Absorokas, a towering curtain of folded mountains so magically high they are scarcely to be believed.

And beyond them, more mountains rise, and mountains upon mountains, creating a complex of ranges and plateaus dimming into the cerulean distance of the afternoon. So abruptly, so decisively, does this place emerge from the American flatlands; so vast and unexpected is it that it might be a different country, a walled arcanum holding unimaginable secrets.

And that is true; it is, and it does.

This is a country called Yellowstone, so named after a river that rises at its approximate geographical center. It has, besides the Absorokas, many other mountain ranges—the Gallatins, the Centennials, the Grand Tetons, the Gros Ventres, the Madisons, the Palisades. And a dozen rivers, depending on what you call a river, and what a creek. Many have the same name as the mountains that feed them; others—the Green, the Snake, the Wood, the Shoshone, and the Yellowstone itself—do not.

Here too is the largest high mountain lake on the continent. Also a great, flat caldera with a crust so thin that the seething core of the earth itself is revealed in spouting geysers, hundreds of pools of boiling water, a thousand vents of sulfurous steam. And all around, the vast forests and limitless meadows hold animals so large their weight may be calculated by the ton; birds so big their wingspread is a matter of yards, not feet or inches; and in the rivers heavy-bodied trout skim and surge and dance jewel-bright on their tails. It took fifty years for the wonder of this country to be believed by the outside world. Many do not believe it yet.

Let me be clear about one thing at this point. The country of Yellowstone should not be confused with the national park that bears the same name. It is true that the park is quite a fine one, centrally located, and comprises one-sixth the land area of the country as a whole. But to grasp the importance of the place you must forget about the park for a minute. The mountains and valleys and lakes and forests that surround the park are not like suburbs to a central city. The country is all of a piece. It includes not one, but *two* national parks (the other is Grand Teton), three wildlife refuges, substantial parts of seven national forests, and various tracts of public and private land. To locate it, find a map that has on it the states of Montana, Wyoming, and Idaho. Now, take a marking pen and draw a slightly lopsided oval, tilted to the northwest. The line—make it a heavy one and more important than all other lines on the map—should start at Bozeman, Montana; arc down to Cody, Wyoming; it should cut across south of Pinedale, Wyoming; swing up just to the east of Idaho Falls, Idaho; and then it should curve back around to Bozeman again.

And there you are. Within the oval is the country of Yellowstone, a place that many now call, with reason, the "Greater Yellowstone Ecosystem," for it is topographically distinguishable from other parts of the Rocky Mountain chain and, astonishingly, turns out to be one of the largest relatively intact areas of wild nature left in the temperate zone of the world. I would ask the reader to pause a moment to consider the implications of that description.

Taken together, the GYE is, at twenty-one thousand square miles, a third again larger than the country of Switzerland, and like it it is landlocked. It is entirely surrounded by the United States of America, which believes it has sovereignty over all. It does not. What is truly sovereign in the Greater Yellowstone Ecosystem is the state of nature.

———

In natural America, myriad species of wildlife abound—panthers, salmon, eagles, to name one each from the realms of beast, fish, and fowl—but perhaps no creature is so fundamentally expressive of the state of nature than the bear. Indeed, bears and humans get along so badly that a sound assumption can be made that where the bear survives, nature still has the upper hand. The assumption no doubt dates to grunted campfire narratives of preliterate societies, but perhaps nowhere in literature has the image of the bear as symbol of the American wilderness been made so vivid as in William Faulkner's short story, "The Bear," in which a young boy instinctively under-

ORIGINS OF AN IDEA

stands the connection. The boy is only ten, yet the bear, writes Faulkner, "ran in his knowledge before ever he saw it. It loomed and towered in his dreams before he even saw the unaxed woods where it left its crooked print ..."

Of all the bears, perhaps the grizzly, old silvertip, *Ursus arctos horribilis*, has the greatest claim on our imagination. In 1800, when the frontier was still east of the Great Plains, there were estimated to be a hundred thousand grizzlies in the United States. In 1909, when wildlife conservationist and Wilderness Society cofounder Aldo Leopold explored the West, he said that grizzlies could be found "in every mountain mass." But today the wild grizzlies left in the coterminous states wouldn't be enough to provide a pair each to public zoological parks. Most grizzly bears are in Alaska and Canada. Of those few hundreds that remain below, relentlessly driven into the Rocky Mountain fastness by stockmen and settlers, there are but two significant populations. One lives in wildland areas along the Canadian border, the other in the Yellowstone region, where there are two hundred animals left—perhaps a few more, perhaps a few less.

Bear stories are a special art form in the lore of the settling of the continent, and especially of the Old West—part of its mythos. They persist for two reasons. First, because they speak to "the epitome and apotheosis of the old wild life," as Faulkner puts it. And second, because there is instruction in them. Accordingly, let us consider a story, and attend to its lessons, about Barbara Pettinga, who is a lover of bears and of the unaxed wilderness they need in order to survive.

Mrs. Pettinga is an attractive, self-effacing woman of middle age and mother of grown children, articulate, and exudes an air of quiet strength. She has been a seasonal ranger at Yellowstone National Park for many years. Winters, she is an art teacher in Vermont and a quilt-maker with a growing national reputation. Like many seasonals, a group that routinely includes academics, artists, and writers, even U.S. congressmen, Mrs. Pettinga is dedicated, bright, and knows her business. After joining the National Park Service, she took an advanced degree in natural science teaching.

As an interpretive ranger, one of Mrs. Pettinga's duties is to lead nature walks. Bear walks she calls them, though only *signs* of bear are in evidence—tracks, scat, tufts of hair—no real live bears. Barely 5 percent of visitors, she says, actually see a grizzly during their stay at Yellowstone. She sees only a very few herself each season.

One summer, the usual area where she led her walks was closed by the bear management people—a routine precaution when bear activity increases in a given locale. At the time, her husband Robert was visiting, so the two of them set out to find a new place for her to reveal the bear as the essential symbol of the old wild life in the greater Yellowstone region.

The Pettingas decided to explore the Sulphur Springs section of Hayden Valley, just north of populous Yellowstone Lake with its manifold hotels and campsites. They drove to a loop-road parking lot, then hiked in a mile or so. Cutting cross-country, the breeze in their faces, they scrambled up a wooded slope into a meadow. At once, Mrs. Pettinga signaled her husband to stop. She had spotted a bison carcass, and that meant the likelihood of a bear nearby. They were to find out almost immediately just how near, for less than a hundred feet away Robert Pettinga saw that a female grizzly was bedded down, tending two cubs.

Mr. Pettinga knew this was a dangerous situation, but he had established eye contact with the bear, whose neck fur was fluffed and ears erect. These were signs of peaceableness, though a grizzly's mood can change quickly. Female grizzlies with cubs are especially intemperate and unpredictable when surprised by humans, as was the case this time. With the wind against them, the Pettingas had given no scent warning of their presence, or sound warning either, for the noise they made was also carried away in the wind. They were, moreover, off the trail, where a bear would not expect them to be. And then there was the matter of the bison carcass. No one should get anywhere near a grizzly's kill. Everything was wrong. Mrs. Pettinga had given lectures about this and now it was happening.

Bear people know some other things as well: that a grizzly, even though it may weigh a quarter ton or more, can charge at speeds of up to forty miles an hour. But at this point Mrs. Pettinga was not considering these facts, for only her husband knew of the bear. She was taking a look at the newly dead bison carcass through her field glasses so that she could report its presence to the bear management people. She knew the carcass would soon draw bears to it, if it had not already. If so, this area too might have to be closed off, with a posted official warning: "Closed. Dangerous Bear Frequenting Area."

But just as she was focusing her field glasses on the bison, she heard her husband snap out a short, awful warning: "Barb, Barb, Look out!" When Barbara Pettinga turned, she saw a bear whose fur was no longer ruffed, ears no longer erect. The beast was charging at top speed, fully stretched out, ears and fur laid back smooth as a torpedo. She knew she could not outrun the bear, which might then consider her to be, in effect, a prey animal. Another option was for her to fall down, pulling herself into what is called a "cannonball" position to protect her face and vitals. Yet another was for her to stand her ground, facing down the bear. This is what she did, for quite often a bear will not complete its charge under these circumstances.

But the bear charged on unchecked and Mrs. Pettinga, terrified, saw the bear's head get very very large; then the jaws closed on her left thigh. She fell to the ground, landing face down, and immediately felt an incredible weight on her back. "Oh, no!" she heard herself cry over and over again, for it seemed so inappropriate, so inopportune that her pleasant life should end this way, in this elemental instinctive violent rage.

Then, unbidden, a sudden clarity came to her mind. The only possible way to live, she thought, was to convince the bear that she was already dead. With an enormous effort of will, Barbara Pettinga stopped her crying and went limp. The bear paused. Then released her. The grizzly then turned on Mr. Pettinga, who moments before had in powerless frustration thrown his canteen at the beast. Robert Pettinga was standing behind a fallen tree, and as the bear reared he was able to duck behind the tree, so the bear could only graze his face with her teeth. As he went down the grizzly bit him above the knee, then it retreated to the edge of the wooded slope.

It was not yet over. Again without warning, the grizzly charged back to get at Barbara, running right over her husband to do so. As if to assure itself that Barbara were really dead, or at least no longer a threat, the bear hooked Barbara's body with a claw, flipping her over on her back. But Barbara kept her eyes closed, and, using the momentum, rolled over downhill onto her stomach again. It was almost automatic, almost instinctive, and yet calculated somehow through the red film of semiconsciousness.

Three times the great claw pulled her over. Three times Barbara rolled over with it. Then the bear stopped and there was silence. The Pettingas lay still at the edge of the wood, faces buried in the meadow grass. The minutes passing seemed like hours. There was no sound save the soughing of the afternoon breeze through the valley.

"It was all so very fortunate," said Mrs. Pettinga of the encounter later. "Nothing happened to the bear." It was indeed a remarkable outcome, for this was a so-called grizzly-human conflict of the kind that often leads to the destruction of the grizzly by park authorities.

Somehow the Pettingas managed to get to the hospital, and while Robert was not seriously injured Barbara Pettinga's scalp was torn from the side of her head, her upper left thigh was laid open in two places by deep wounds from the initial bite. One claw had swept, mercifully not too deeply, across her face. A pattern of puncture wounds dotted her midsection and there were severe abdominal contusions. Thanks to modern surgical techniques, there were no permanent disabilities, and the disfigurement from the mauling doesn't show or is covered by clothing. As for the bear and her cubs, they melted into the wilderness. No sure sighting of the she-bear has been made since, and no effort has been made to find her. "She behaved correctly and in accordance with her nature," Mrs. Pettinga says.

She still leads her bear walks. "I say to my classes, 'Can't you just *feel* the presence of the bears?'" And of course they can. Who would not?—in this place, with this incredible woman who loves the bear that mauled her. She obtained a grizzly skull from the bear management people to use in her lectures, and she held it out for me to inspect, caressing the jawbone gently as she did so, a *memento mori.* She said: "You see, this is an old female. Look how worn the teeth are. She probably had a natural death. Isn't that wonderful?" Indeed it was. In the Greater Yellowstone Ecosystem, 80 percent do not. Over half are killed by hunters, stockmen, or landowners; 20 percent die from official "management control"; and 10 percent are struck by vehicles or die from other unnatural causes.

Though "ecology," a neologism of the late nineteenth century, has always been a part of the study and appreciation of the Yellowstone region, the idea of a "greater Yellowstone ecosystem," in so many words, is quite recent. And it has everything to do with the bear. According to Tim W. Clark, an ecologist based in Jackson, Wyoming, the term "Greater Yellowstone Ecosystem" was first used by Frank Craighead in his 1979 book, *Track of the Grizzly Bear.* Craighead, Clark told me, "recognized that Yellowstone grizzly bears used about 5 million acres, of which only 2.2 million were in the park. He concluded that grizzly bear conservation required proper management throughout the entire grizzly bear ecosystem."

To an outsider, such a conclusion may seem so painfully obvious that it would scarcely need to be stated. Grizzly bears, though quite smart, do not know, or care, where the boundaries of Yellowstone National Park are. Moreover, the human managers of the park and other public lands in the region are not so stupid as to think that an island population of bears can survive when they are fully protected only in a small fraction of the "island" they inhabit. Some scientists estimate that each grizzly bear may need as much as one hundred square miles of range to survive. Yellowstone Park, even with nearby Grand Teton Park added to it, contains scarcely more than four thousand square miles, hardly enough for a self-sustaining population even under the most favorable circumstance.

But of course these propositions are wrong. Bears, at least for a while, *did* know the boundaries of the park, more or less, and park authorities had no concern about their survival. The reason? The grizzly and black bear population was semidomesticated through daily feedings of garbage. In fact, this practice became so popular that grandstands were built next to garbage dumps so that visitors could watch the grizzlies scarfing up the unspeakable wastes from the kitchens of the lodges and the refuse cans of the campsites. Naturally, the bears got fat and prospered and hung out where the people were.

Accordingly, the popular image of a national park bear, mostly blacks but grizzlies too, made it out to be a sort of oversized raccoon, a nearly suburban-type animal that in *New Yorker* cartoons stood erect along car-choked park roads and had droll things to say to the tourists. In time, with the emergence of a more finely tuned ecological consciousness during the greening-of-America 1960s, this was not thought to be funny any more by those who cared about the survival of wildlife. So the park service commissioned a major study of park management, led by Aldo Leopold's son Starker, a distinguished scientist and author in his own right. The large natural parks, the Leopold report recommended in 1963, should be ecologically restored as "vignettes of wild America." Since the feeding of bears at Yellowstone was hardly consonant with this finding, the park officials decided the dumps ought to be closed as soon as possible.

However, Frank Craighead and his brother John, then and now the preeminent experts on grizzlies, warned that an abrupt closing of the dumps would require the bears to range out of the park in search of food and thus become a danger to people and to themselves in the process, since in most "human-bear" conflicts the bear usually loses, with a thirty-aught-six bullet in its brain. Government authorities nevertheless disregarded the Craigheads' pleas for a slow weaning from the garbage pits, together with a close watch on bear movement through the use of radio collars. Neither would be natural, said park officials. "We are not running a zoo." And so scores of garbage-addicted grizzlies became "problems," and had to be killed by authorities in the park. Outside the boundaries, where most of the killing still takes place, unofficial riflemen often did the job, authorized or not.

Today, the two hundred or so grizzlies left are hanging on, thanks to a number of techniques, including a "bear lift" which tries to remove (sometimes by helicopter) potential problem bears to unvisited areas before a "conflict" takes place. Possibly the strategy is working. According to bear expert Stephen Mealey, who was the supervisor of the Shoshone National Forest for many years, there has been a decrease in bear killings and an increase (though slight) of breeding female grizzlies in the ecosystem as a whole. But whether the Yellowstone grizzlies are making a comeback or are on the verge of extinction depends on whom you ask. The government experts tend toward an optimistic outlook, but a good many nongovernmental wildlife scientists are not so sure.

This particular argument rages on. The Craighead-garbage story is told and retold in the literature, and surely its participants are always angered, for different reasons, at the simplified accounts. But the bear became a wild creature again. And its return to wildness created—or perhaps demanded—the sense of urgency that the Yellowstone region be considered a single ecosystem, not only by Frank and John Craighead, but by a growing tribe of believers. Their doctrine, now widely accepted in scientific and official circles, is that if policies to manage the Yellowstone region as a whole can be created which are good for the grizzly—with its need for old-growth forest unsegmented by logging roads, broad, open meadows, and undeveloped riparian habitat uncluttered by tourists and teeming with delicious cutthroat trout in the spring—it follows that the integrity of the ecosystem as a whole can be maintained.

In fact some progress has been made in this direction. Although an effort at management coordination in behalf of protecting the threatened grizzly population had long been made by the managers of the public lands in the Yellowstone region, the work is now given official structure via an "Interagency Grizzly Bear Committee" made up of representatives of all the Yellowstone public land agencies. The committee has developed various regionwide programs to help the bear recover, including the designation of land into three grizzly bear habitat areas. In "Management Situation I," where there is the greatest grizzly bear population and the most ideal habitat, all land uses must be compatible with the needs of the grizzly, or the uses—whether logging, camping, or development—must be changed. In "Situation II," management decisions must accommodate the grizzly if at all possible. In "Situtation III," where grizzly sightings are rare and habitat quality is not especially remarkable, management decisions do not give any particular weight to the grizzly's needs, but do strive to minimize "human-bear conflicts."

Many conservationists feel that the existence of the Grizzly Bear Committee, however imperfect its operation, is a significant step in the overall effort to establish ecosystemwide management principles that can take precedence over too-narrow interpretations of existing agency missions—"multiple use" and "sustained yield" for the forests, and preservation and public enjoyment for the parks. Other interagency committees have subsequently been established—for bald eagles, swans, and elk, for example—on a species-by-species basis. What remains, of course, is finally to integrate the management of all the species into the coherent management of the whole ecosystem. This is a big step, but perhaps a possible one some day, thanks to the grizzly bear.

Barbara Pettinga puts the ecosystem idea in terms that are for her quite personal. "You cannot ask people to support what they cannot grasp," she told me, "but if you truly understand the bear you can begin to understand the concept of the ecosystem." And so Faulkner's mythic connection between the grizzly and the wilderness—"the old wild life"—is given substance: in the work of a government committee, in the nature walks of a seasonal ranger who loves the bears.

THE SHIFTING VALUES
OF THE FOREST

East of Livingston, Montana, lies the 63 Ranch, at the end of a ten-mile-long dirt road that winds into the foothills of the Absorokas. I had been invited to the ranch by its proprietor, Sandy Cahill, who wanted to tell me about an impending "timber sale" on a few hundred acres of Forest Service land in the Tie Creek area of the Absorokas. This is, of course, one of the things the Forest Service does, hold timber sales, but the Tie Creek cut, which was on land adjoining the 63 Ranch, would affect the livelihood of Sandy Cahill and her family, for it could to a significant degree vitiate the back-country experience of the "dudes" who visit her ranch every year. At issue was a little sliver of "timber management" land between 63 Ranch and the wilderness area where the ranch takes its guests on horse treks. The sliver probably should have been included in an original wilderness designation for this part of the Absoroka range, but wasn't.

Despite extraordinary efforts on the part of Sandy Cahill—including a costly trip to Washington, D.C.—to fight off the Forest Service and to get the area made a part of the Absoroka–Beartooth Wilderness, this outcome was not to be. And so, at 63 Ranch, the chainsaw's snarl and rattle would soon shatter the stillness of the forests. Then, afterwards, an unwonted flood of rifle-rack, pickup-truck recreationists would come to the area via the forest road, drawn thither by an improved habitat for elk, a consequence of clear-cutting, which increases edge and the vegetation that ungulates like to eat. Mrs. Cahill told a congressional committee at the wilderness hearings that not only would her livelihood, and the quality of her guests' wilderness experience, be affected; she also anticipated that the new forest road, needed to get the equipment in and the logs out, would produce significant erosion that would silt up a trout stream that runs through her ranch property.

The forest would probably regenerate, of course, but Sandy Cahill told me that she would probably never live to see it, for the trees—lodgepole pine, mainly—take two lifetimes to reach maturity here. Part of the area was burned over in 1907 and the replanted pines still haven't reached maturity. "Right now, after eighty years, they're still only corral-pole size," she said.

Mrs. Cahill was heartbroken. "The Forest Service people contend that cutting trees gives people good jobs," she said, "as opposed to the low-paying summer work we provide here at the ranch. But we have been employing people year after year since 1929. The timber jobs will disappear after all the timber is cut." She told me that she had been so outspoken against the Forest Service it had cost her many friendships in town. Livingston had earlier lost a thousand jobs when the Burlington Northern Railroad closed its operations there, and so townspeople found it hard to support any wilderness-protection effort that might cost additional jobs, even though the amount of logging work would be modest for the small Tie Creek cut.

Still, feelings ran high. Mrs. Cahill said that she figured the district ranger had it in for her when he arranged for a group of local hunters to come in and clear a forest road whose ownership was in fact in contention, since it was considered to be part of the original 63 Ranch homestead deed. She thought the road work was a form of harassment, and so fearful was she of a confrontation with the hunters that she began carrying a rifle. On another occasion, the Forest Service demanded that an old spring house built by her father on national forest land be painted the official Forest Service colors. "It was a constant hassle to figure out what they were going to be up to next," she said.

Sandy Cahill is a tall, slender woman with graying hair. The people who come to the ten-cabin ranch—at the height of the season they have only thirty guests—are like family. They return year after year, usually for a week or ten days. There are a lot of children at 63 Ranch, and they have a happy time. The cost is $75 a day for lodging, three squares, the horseback riding, the works. This is no profiteering outfit. Mrs. Cahill is active and highly regarded in dude ranch and outfitters' associations. She is, everyone agrees, an extremely decent person.

Sandy Cahill told me that the lumber mill that would most likely contract for the Tie Creek cut would be the Brand S Corporation.

And so that is where I went next—to the Brand S stud mill located right off I-90 just south of Livingston. It was managed by Doug Crandall, son-in-law of the owner and a forestry graduate of Oregon State University. Crandall—young, polite, yet sure of his ground—told me that the tree growing in the forest near 63 Ranch, the lodgepole pine, *Pinus contorta,* is a first-rate kind of tree. For studs. Not many foresters from Oregon would agree. Compared to Douglas fir, which can produce great timbers, wide planks, and plywood as well as studs, lodgepole pine is a "weed" good only for two by fours or two by sixes, and a slow-grower in these parts as well. In fact, a southern hard pine can reach maturity up to five times faster than a Yellowstone lodgepole.

Never mind that. Brand S mills tens of millions of board feet of logs every year, most of it lodgepole, and Doug Crandall was looking forward to those kinds of years for a long time to come. "When there was a depression in the timber industry in the early '80s, we took that opportunity to automate our plant," Crandall said. "When everybody was not spending, we were. We're automated and computerized; we are in for the long haul. What we've got here is just about as efficient as you can get for a stud mill."

He was right about that. The long, skinny lodgepole logs come in at one end of the plant, are debarked, rough cut, culled, finished, graded, and palleted with a very few employees (120 at the time of my visit), considering the number of trees they process—an average of forty-five truckloads of logs a day. When Crandall took me for a tour, I noticed that the employees all wore hard hats and most were young and strapping, but few actually handled any wood. A good many worked in glass-walled cubicles that contained an array of levers and buttons and monitor screens to control various operations. They were a happy crew, giving the boss a thumbs-up sign and a grin when he clapped them on the shoulder, shouting a wisecrack above the whines and roars and crashings of the logs moving through the mill. The boss, Doug Crandall, was then thirty. The logs were between 90 and 120 years of age.

In the storage yard, the pallets of finished two by fours and two by sixes towered in long rows. Crandall was clearly pleased with the look and feel of his product. "Lodgepole from here makes a straight and tight-grained board," he said, pointing to the white, close grain of a palleted stud. "People really like it, so we've been able to beat the southern pine market." In fact, according to Crandall, 97 percent of what his mill produces is shipped out of state: to Middle Western cities, to New York, Phoenix, Denver, even Florida—with an increasing portion of it sold directly to retail outlets in these areas, the hardware stores and do-it-yourself emporia in the shopping malls of suburbia. The "over-the-shoulder market," Crandall called it. There was even a bit of historical symmetry here, I reflected, for *Pinus contorta* was named "lodgepole" because Indians had used the long, thin trunks to make poles for their lodges and teepees. Today the lodges where the lodgepole is used are split-levels, ranchers, and townhouse subdivisions, but the tree is favored for the same reasons. (The Latin name *contorta* refers to a characteristic of the tree in coastal areas and other exposed places where the shape is "contorted" by wind and weather.)

Brand S Corporation was, Crandall told me, privately owned, a midsized Oregon firm which had two operations in that state—a plywood mill and resin plant—plus the mill in Livingston, Montana. The Livingston mill, founded seventeen years ago, was, he said, almost wholly dependent on the national forests for its supply of trees, and the Brand S Corporation, given the rapidly decreasing market for Oregon plywood, was increasingly dependent on Livingston. "About 70 percent of our volume comes from Forest Service timber sales," said Crandall. "We draw from about a 130-mile working circle—as far as West Yellowstone. We're logging there right now." He said that Brand S contracted with some thirty-five loggers—they had only about ten company people who actually worked in the forest. Some of the contract loggers could produce up to twelve truckloads a day.

The forest is a dangerous place, and tree cutting and hauling a dangerous business, still dominated by free-lance professionals. But the logger doesn't "buy the timber sale" from the Forest Service, the mills do, and they supervise the cuts as well, usually carefully designed clear-cuts of about eighteen acres apiece in a sale area. A typical acre contains six hundred to seven hundred trees. Crandall maintained that selective logging isn't possible with lodgepole if it's old growth, for the lodgepole is such a tall, skinny, weak-rooted species that the trees left standing, unprotected by neighbors, would likely fall in a storm. Indeed there are frequent "blow-downs" of large uncut areas of old-growth lodgepole forest when a high wind follows a heavy rain.

Doug Crandall's office was in a trailerlike prefab building, with a picture window framing a scene of the Yellowstone River. Here the water runs swiftly, with smooth, deep power as it moves northeastward out of the mountains and into the flatlands of Montana. Crandall confessed that he occasionally casts a trout fly at this bend in the river, for these are perhaps the most productive trout waters of the world. He's a wilderness hiker as well and is glad there is wilderness left to hike in. Still, he made it clear that he believes that there's wilderness enough.

With his associate, Brand S timber manager Michael Atwood, Crandall had built a presentation map, doubtless to persuade conservationists, citizen groups, officials, and visiting writers of the need to clear-cut lodgepole pine from the public lands. The map, which looked like a giant Colorforms project, showed the 1.7-million-acre Gallatin National Forest, where most of the Brand S logs came from. "The black areas," Crandall explained, smoothly pointing to the massive hunks of that ominous color on the map, "are wilderness." I wondered to myself whether he believed any significance was conveyed by the color choice. "The orange," he went on, "is where there is no timber harvesting by administrative decision of the Forest Service, for habitat protection or recreational-use reasons. In the dark blue areas, timbering is okay, but the Forest Service manages these areas primarily for nontimbering purposes. In fact," Crandall concluded, pointing to the the tiny scattered pieces of green, "only 4 percent of the entire Gallatin is managed for timber."

Clearly, Crandall's map put the worst possible face on it, in terms of cuttable land versus the noncuttable. A third of the Gallatin National Forest is not forested at all and so ought not to be counted as if it were land made unavailable on purpose. And while 700,000 acres are designated wilderness, much of the land remaining that Crandall said was administratively withdrawn or managed for nonlogging values was not necessarily off limits to cutting forever. According to Bob Dennee, information officer for the Gallatin, whom I asked about this later at the Forest Service office in Bozeman, some 17 percent of the land was managed for timber, not 4 percent. Forty-three percent was designated wilderness. Some 30,000 acres were recommended for additional wilderness by the Gallatin officials, although environmentalists would like that figure to be closer to 300,000 acres.

But these were only numbers. In fact, between Crandall, Dennee, Mike Scott of the Wilderness Society (who had briefed me earlier), and a good many others I talked to, I was being numbered to death. It was true that there was a diminishing amount of national forest left to be cut—partly because of wilderness designation, partly because the forest takes so long to regenerate. There are cut-over places where the forest will never regenerate, especially on slopes where the topsoil needed by new roots to get a purchase is severely eroded. As for the privately owned woodlands, they were either not available to Brand S, belonging to the giant Plum Creek Corporation, the forest-products subsidiary of Burlington Northern, or they had been logged already, especially during the 1970s agriculture boom when so much land was cleared for grazing.

(The Yellowstone fires of 1988 had not struck at the time of my visit. But in any case, virtually all the burned forest was confined to Yellowstone National Park. Taken together, the surrounding national forests—many of which had been cut over and highly flammable deadfalls and snags had not accumulated to the degree that they had in the park—were not as seriously affected.)

Because Brand S Corporation had invested heavily in a modern plant and equipment, Crandall and Atwood understandably sounded beleaguered in their explanation of the economic necessities of lodgepole clear-cutting. Crandall said he had reduced the payroll somewhat in anticipation of a reduced allowable cut (an irony, considering Sandy Cahill's argument with the Forest Service about employment); but to amortize the investment, those forty-five logging trucks had to keep pulling into the mill every day.

Crandall was no good ol' boy snapping his galluses and fulminating against the "suede-o conservationists." But he did complain: "I have a tough time with people saying the only way to manage the Greater Yellowstone Ecosystem is to lock it up. They used to log twice as much in this area as they log now. Blue-ribbon trout streams are still blue-ribbon trout streams. In some places there was no elk population at all. Now there is an incredible elk herd because of the logging. To me it's management versus nonmanagement—that's the argument. I do believe in wilderness, the only question is, how much is enough? We're on the line here. There's very little forest left that we can use, and they want to take more away." He was earnest in these views, and I was sympathetic. Like Sandy Cahill, he too was an extremely decent person.

I later learned that Doug Crandall and Sandy Cahill had never met face to face, but they were locked in a true Old West battle over resources—like the open-range cattlemen versus the nesters a hundred years ago. But unfortunately, they were both going to lose, I felt sure. Cahill in the short run, because it was too late to save her bit of forest. Crandall in the long run, because the economics of logging vis-à-vis other elements of the economic mix in the region were changing rapidly. Actually, they had changed already, though there are many—from both sides of the dispute over forest use—who have difficulty accepting the fact.

———

In 1986 the Greater Yellowstone Coalition—an association of conservation-oriented organizations and individuals—asked a resource economics consulting firm called CHEC (Cascade Holistic Economic Consultants) to take a look at the plans being prepared for the national forests of the greater Yellowstone area and to evaluate them in terms of the shifting values that both Sandy Cahill and Doug Crandall were struggling with. CHEC's findings after looking at these plans must surely astonish even those who have long harbored suspicions about the economic viability of the timber industry in Yellowstone. Here is a summary of some of its salient points.

1. The Yellowstone forest is among the least productive of all national forest areas. Compared to the most productive forest, the Siuslaw in Oregon, between six and fifteen acres of forest land must be cut over in the Yellowstone forest to equal one acre of the Siuslaw. Most forests (the exception is Shoshone) of the Yellowstone region would have to sell timber for at least $200 per thousand board feet to break even on timber sales. (Doug Crandall of Brand S told me he paid between $35 and $40 per thousand board feet.)

2. Of the direct nongovernment jobs created by the Yellowstone national forests, timber accounts for 609, which is 12 percent of the total jobs provided by timber, grazing, and recreation taken together. Each private timber job in the Yellowstone forests requires a taxpayer subsidy of between $5,000 and $70,000 per year, depending on the forest.

3. Timber produces 5 percent of the economic benefits of the forest—from logging, recreation, and grazing—but receives 59 percent of the money expended on these three resources by the Forest Service. Recreation produces 81 percent of the aggregate benefits, but receives only 18 percent of the money spent on the three resources in the Yellowstone forests.

4. Net returns to the Treasury from timber management on the Yellowstone national forests in 1986 was *minus* $21,634,000. This figure reflects timber sale receipts less timber management and road costs.

Numbers again. There are, let it be said, infinite ways to manipulate Forest Service statistics, for they are plentiful and diverse. Just as these were organized by CHEC to show the relatively low economic value of the forest for logging, as opposed to recreation, others can be gotten up no doubt to defend the timber industry's continued economic preeminence in the region. But the proponents of that preeminence are becoming less persuasive.

I found this to be particularly true in the Bridger-Teton, a double-forest that is administered as a single unit out of Jackson, Wyoming. At 2.7 million acres, Bridger-Teton is the largest of the Yellowstone region's Forest Service holdings. According to Ernie Nunn, the deputy forest supervisor I interviewed at the B-T's capacious headquarters building, the plan was to reduce the B-T's allowable cut by one third. (Nunn sometimes called it, cowboy-style, "the B-bar-T.") Moreover, they had already eliminated sizeable areas from oil and gas exploration. The reason, Nunn said flatly, was that "new values are coming to the fore." By this he meant that the commercial logging values of the forest were being replaced by environmental values.

The allowable cut reduction for the B-T was still not enough to suit many environmentalists, especially those knowledgeable about forest economics. Even Nunn admitted that the most economical level of timber output would probably be around two to three million board feet. "Anything beyond that," he said, "would be a below-cost sale."

On the other side of the argument, the forest products industry had stated emphatically that the reduction would be disastrous for them and for the logging communities their industry supports. Nunn said that industry had demanded an *increase* of 50 percent in the allowable cut, which he considered to be utterly impossible. "If we had to supply that demand," he said, "we'd be harvesting timber in areas that are simply not suitable. In the steep terrain of the Gros Ventre area we have a lot of soil and water problems, for example. We might be able to get a road in there, but the roads would last only three months. Our soils scientists say they'd be sloughing off down the hillsides into the creek bottoms in no time. A lot of folks don't realize that this forest has harvested over six hundred million board feet of timber since 1962. Why we used to push about thirty-eight million board feet of timber a year out of here. The point is, we have already cut over the easy country."

And of course the country shows it. Because forest regeneration is so slow, there are parts of the Bridger-Teton where the clear-cuts connect, one to another, making a skein of ravaged forest land stretching as far as the eye can see.

So the question arises, why did the Forest Service want to sell any more timber at all? Reducing the CHEC findings to their most elemental level, the taxpayer subsidy for logging in the Yellowstone forests works out to something like nine dollars a tree. The catch, it would appear, is that there is a traditional logging infrastructure embedded in the localities of the Yellowstone region. I for one would not want to holler too loudly about a subsidy of nine dollars a tree in the coffee shops and saloons of almost any town within the Greater Yellowstone Ecosystem, for the fellow on the next stool might very well depend, directly or indirectly, on the forests to provide a stable job for him on a logging crew or in a mill.

In the town of DuBois, Wyoming, for example—once described in a magazine article as "the most isolated" community in the Lower 48—some of the citizens became so exercised over the loss of timbering jobs in the Bridger-Teton that they established a group called "Citizens for Multiple Use" and threatened to boycott any local businessman who did not join them in a militant effort to keep the local Louisiana Pacific stud mill well stocked with national forest sawtimber. Said a 1986 study commissioned by the Forest Service: "The topic of timber and the Louisiana Pacific mill [so] firmly divides the community, some people can't talk about timber without getting red in the face or leaving the room. It should be talked about. It is an important resource. But 'to be L-P or not to be L-P' has become . . . a stumbling block."

The stumbling block, it turned out, was not all that big. In fact, according to an economic impact assessment conducted by the Bridger-Teton, the actual job loss due to a reduced timber cut was estimated to be only 15 percent of total employment, thirty-seven people, about a third of the number of jobs associated with the L-P mill and the production of studs. The challenge for DuBois seemed to be how to replace those jobs through diversification rather than fight an unwinnable battle against a forest ecology that just wouldn't cooperate by growing trees any faster than in increments of one hundred years, and by an emerging proclivity of Forest Service planners (such as those of the B-T) to emphasize "other values"—wildlife, recreation, aesthetics, historic preservation, and the like.

According to James Kent, head of a Denver, Colorado, think tank specializing in small-town economic recovery, DuBois had already begun to diversify its economy, despite the militancy of some of its citizens. Two new enterprises, he told me, had recently been started in town—a fur business and a textile manufacturer—and plans were afoot to improve the dollar volume (and therefore jobs) of existing tourism and recreation-oriented businesses, especially those featuring the spectacular local population of bighorn sheep. A museum was planned to interpret these and other features. In addition, said Kent, the Shoshone National Forest, which also affects the town's economy, had detailed a forest-products consultant to work full time with the town officials to figure out wood-product alternatives to studs—"small round wood" products that would require less wood (and less subsidy) and would provide more "added value" than studs, a great many of which, as Doug Crandall at Brand S up in Livingston had shown, can be produced with a relatively small work force. The handsome, close-grained white wood of the lodgepole pine could be made into other, quite appealing products—a beautifully finished mantlepiece clock case, for example.

Ernie Nunn was clearly pleased about the direction DuBois had taken to fight its way out of its presumed dependence on lodgepole two by fours. "No local economy should be tied to one sawmill," he said. "A museum, for example, may only employ five people, but if you get five people here and five people there, pretty soon you've made up for the lost jobs." Still, he added, "I would hate to see all the woods work go out of DuBois. That too is part of the diversity, after all. And it's important to the forest. We need commercial operations to help us manage this resource."

Of course the forest-products industry is not going to be interested in that kind of low-level talk. Louisiana Pacific, Brand S, and the others around Yellowstone are running big stud mills, not craft shops. And as the pendulum of public opinion swings toward a more balanced approach to forest use, they are beginning to act a bit panicky. "If you go back a few years," Ernie Nunn said, "it was the environmental groups that a lot of times would refuse to compromise. Now it's just the opposite. Industry are the folks not willing to compromise on this national forest. In closed-door meetings we've experienced a real hard-line approach."

I observed that it always seemed to me that the noise level in conflicts over resources is often the inverse of the level of power. That in the old days, when the environmental groups did a lot of screaming, they did so because they were powerless. Perhaps, I ventured, the reason timbering companies were stonewalling in the conference room of the B-bar-T was that they feared they were losing their power. Ernie Nunn did not answer, of course, being a canny bureaucrat; he just smiled.

THE TENUOUSNESS
OF VALLEYS

There is a secret valley in the Greater Yellowstone Ecosystem. Semisecret anyway. When top-of-the-season tourists are standing hip to haunch at nearby Yellowstone National Park waiting for the next ebullition of Old Faithful, or are foregathered in knots of station wagons and Winnebagos at park laybys to view a roadside moose, here in the secret valley you will find a landscape of lonely dirt roads unstrung with electrical or telephone lines, long, long vistas beneath the uncomplicated sky, and an overwhelming sense that you have stepped back a century in time.

The valley, first settled only a hundred years ago, has never been settled very much. Once you get just a few miles off the busy highways that pass it by, the few cattle ranches, all of them sizeable, only add to the sense that here is the Old West as it used to be, of grasslands and mountain range and strange wild creatures—bounding pronghorn, and pairs of sandhill cranes with their red-dotted heads atop long necks visible in the tall-grass distance uttering their primordial cry of welcome and warning. Above a defile leading from the mountains, an eagle soars.

This is the Centennial Valley, named after the year of its settlement, 1876. It is bounded on the south side by the Centennial Mountains, an unusual east-west range that rises abruptly from the valley floor in a near-escarpment some three thousand feet from bottom to top. Along the ridge, which is the continental divide as well as the Idaho-Montana state line, the occasional grizzly roams, as does the more plentiful black bear; there is, in addition, a resident population of three hundred to five hundred elk, lesser numbers of moose and mule deer, lynx, wolverine.

For reasons of geology and wildlife, the mountains are unusual enough, but the valley is more unusual still, and not only for its isolation or its antelopes, eagles, and sandhill cranes. Also resident is the largest remnant population of the trumpeter swan south of the Canadian line. This is the great white bird whose three-yard wingspan made such an easy target for the gunner that the species was very nearly shot into extinction during the eighteenth and nineteenth centuries to furnish swansdown for milady's quilts and pillows in the bedchambers of Belgravia. Species have been extinguished for lesser reasons, perhaps, but the trumpeter was—and only barely still is—the world's largest waterfowl. This is a bird to be reckoned with. Its nest is eight feet across; an egg weighs nearly a pound. A cranky cob can lash out with his wing and break an arm. And yes, they trumpet: neck upstretched, bill partly open, "ko-hoh, ko-hoh," calling for a mate in the valley of the swans.

In 1935, when there were thought to be no more than two hundred trumpeters left in the United States and Canada (an Alaskan population was discovered later), the U.S. Department of the Interior established what is now known as the Red Rock Lakes National Wildlife Refuge to save the stateside swans from sure extinction. While trumpeters ordinarily migrate, flying south to winter feeding areas, here is open water for a wintering ground that requires no commute. The Red Rock lakes, together with other waters in the Yellowstone region warmed by geothermal activity, is ideal summer and winter.

It was a lucky thing the swans discovered this area and adapted to a nonmigratory pattern. "Greater Yellowstone," biologist and swan expert Ruth Gale told me, "was about the only region available that could provide both the critical ice-free winter habitat and the remoteness necessary to save the trumpeter swan."

While the Red Rock Lakes trumpeters are now augmented in the winter by a sizeable migrating group that comes down from Canada each year, the population of the local, nonmigrating swans has always been perilously thin, despite the presence of the wildlife refuge. In 1985 trumpeter population took a nosedive, plummeting from 499 birds to 392, the lowest count since 1950. Alarmed, biologist Gale sought a grant to study historical population fluctuations over the long term at Red Rock and other areas and to try to correlate changes in management policy with the rise and fall of the population. Although there are many reasons for swan mortality, what she discovered was that over the past fifty years the numbers of swans lost related clearly to the amount of supplementary feeding provided by the refuge. According to refuge manager Barry Reiswig, who took me on a tour of the swan habitat in his charge, swan feeding had historically been quite irregular. In fact, some biologists had concluded that supplementary feeding wasn't strictly necessary.

"The recent data we collected here at the refuge didn't tell us much," Reiswig said. "It wasn't until Ruth analyzed the population in the whole region on a fifty-year basis that we began to understand." Accordingly, he instituted a regular feeding program in which results are carefully monitored. The next step, according to Ruth Gale, was to figure out some way for the nonresident population to teach the locals how to migrate, a learned behavior. Once this could be achieved—probably the work of the *next* fifty years—then the trumpeter might be said to have returned to a truly wild state, as opposed, as Gale pointed out, to the last fifty, when the birds survived only because they remained in intensive care.

While nonmigration saved the Yellowstone swans from extinction (presuming supplementary feeding, as Ruth Gale found), that characteristic also makes the birds extremely vulnerable to the external stresses of human disturbance. The Yellowstone region, though remote, is not the same as the wilds of Canada. So sensitive are the birds during the crucial nesting period that refuge authorities ask visitors not to approach nesting swans closer than four hundred yards, warning that should the birds' privacy be infringed upon they may abandon their nests and even the cygnets. At Red Rock there were only twenty-four nests in the spring of 1987; even a single nest abandoned could have a significant population impact. According to the Fish and Wildlife Service, "The continued existence of trumpeter swans in the Yellowstone Region depends in large part on the willingness of people to forego development in important swan habitat." But how do you manage that? It is one thing to keep the tourists away; developers are another matter.

The Red Rock Lakes refuge, at 40,330 acres, takes up less than a third of the Centennial Valley. There are some other public land holdings, administered by the Forest Service and Bureau of Land Management, but for the most part the valley is privately owned. The refuge has been able to engineer a 1,700-acre addition to its holdings, but there are still approximately 100,000 acres left of private land. This is why refuge manager Barry Reiswig confessed to me that he was as concerned about the use of the land that surrounds Red Rock Lakes as he was about the swans that live in them. Ecological management of high-elevation areas of the GYE is one thing, for the land there is publicly owned. But in the *valleys* of this wilderness ecosystem the problems are complicated—potentially even rendered intractable—because so much of the land is in private hands.

At the moment, Reiswig told me, he had no objection to the present ownership pattern in the Centennial Valley. "Ranching interests are very compatible with the current mission of the refuge," he said. The only present difficulty he is having is with cattle, which, being of a modern breed (as opposed, say, to longhorns, whose grazing patterns are much like the bison's), tend to cluster, browsing off the range unevenly and causing erosion along the stream banks. Reiswig said he could crudely replicate bison grazing by shifting the cattle from area to area through manipulation of grazing rights on refuge land.

The ranchers grumble about this, he said, but so far his manipulations had not affected ranchers' productivity. The old ranch-owning families seemed to be hanging on, despite the agricultural crisis that has afflicted farms and ranches throughout the nation. "Most ranchers don't want to subdivide, but pass along land to their children," Reiswig said, adding, however, that "if our ranchers are constantly stressed economically there will come a point when they *have* to sell out. Then real estate development becomes likely."

To understand what might happen in the Centennial Valley, it is necessary only to take a look at the other valleys of the Yellowstone region. Perhaps the most vivid example is Jackson Hole, a valley just south of Grand Teton National Park, where conservationists have been struggling for years to keep ranchland from converting to second-home subdivisions. During the 1970s, citizens hoped to persuade Congress to vote funds to purchase conservation easements over the private land—land which was crucial to the aesthetics of the valley, setting off the magnificence of the Tetons and serving as wintering ground for elk, not all of whom confine themselves in the Fish and Wildlife Service's National Elk Refuge. But the energy crisis, the Ayatollah, and a national economic slump intervened at the crucial moment in the effort to enlist the help of Congress, and no federal funding for the purchase of easements to forestall development was forthcoming. Since then, the Jackson Hole Land Trust has protected several thousand acres, but ten times as much is as yet unprotected.

Another worrisome privately owned area in Greater Yellowstone is Paradise Valley, a fifty-mile stretch of grassland, rolling foothills, and

Yellowstone River floodplain that pierces to the very heart of the ecosystem—from Livingston, Montana, southward nearly to the boundary of Yellowstone National Park. Here, the protection of a substantial portion of what the park's research director John Varley calls "lower elevational habitat" may be too late.

I visited Varley at the park's headquarters at Mammoth Hot Springs, not far from the lower end of Paradise Valley, to get the full story. He was greatly concerned, he said, with an outfit called "Church Universal and Triumphant," or CUT for short. The church—an authoritarian, apocalyptic-survivalist, neo-Manichaean sect that would make your average suburban Presbyterian extremely uncomfortable—had bought a twelve-thousand-acre ranch from publishing tycoon Malcolm Forbes in the early 1980s and had since augmented this holding with additional land purchases elsewhere in the valley. The total acreage owned by CUT in Paradise Valley is thirty-three thousand acres, according to Edward L. Francis, whom I also visited. Francis was vice-president and business manager of CUT and husband of its "spiritual leader," Elizabeth L. Prophet.

Since their arrival in the GYE, CUT and the National Park Service have increasingly come into conflict. One of these conflicts concerned the La Duke Hot Springs, part of the complex of geothermal features that the park's boundaries do not entirely enclose. Geologists warn that any tampering with underground strata might seriously affect the geothermal features of the park, of which Old Faithful is only the most famous. There are more than a thousand others. "Once you turn a geyser off by tampering with its underground system," say the scientists, "you can never turn it on again." Indeed, so concerned were federal authorities about this prospect, in connection with oil and gas exploration in the Island Park area outside the west entrance to Yellowstone Park, that a law was passed severely limiting any exploration in the future.

While all this was going on, however, CUT quietly tapped into the strata feeding La Duke, to the consternation of John Varley and everyone else. "They took us totally by surprise," said Varley. "We'd been battling over geothermal issues on the west side of the park for fifteen years, but literally while our backs were turned, Francis punches one through on the north side. We have no idea what the adverse effects might be." When I relayed this to Francis he told me that CUT would definitely not pump water out of their hot springs well if any adverse effects showed up. But of course, by then it might be too late. "The park people are just ideologues," Francis said, complaining that CUT had had difficulty with park authorities at their earlier establishment in the Santa Monica mountains near Los Angeles. Said Francis, "The Park Service targeted our property for park acquisition, they attempted to downzone our land, they urged county officials and the California Coastal Commission to deny us permission to build on it, they threatened condemnation, they compiled an extensive dossier on our organization . . . and they continually made false and slanderous statements about us."

There is more. Not the least of the issues is that CUT owns roughly 60 percent of the winter range of Yellowstone Park's pronghorn antelope population. "They are our antelope for nine months of the year," Varley told me. "And they are Francis's for three months. If they are not allowed to use that range during those three months, then we've lost 'em. The trouble is, the wilderness areas, where the animals are safe, have always been created above eight or nine thousand feet. Nobody has dealt with the key connections between that alpine and subalpine country and lower elevational lands. We just give the lower lands to industry, private landowners, whatever. If you ask me, that's what is going to kill this area in the long run—not having enough of the low-elevation lands to perpetuate the region's ecological attributes."

"Look at the grizzly bear situation," Varley went on. "Two thirds of the problems that we have with human-bear conflicts last year occurred on private lands. Everywhere you see a population sink for grizzly bears—with the exception of Fishing Bridge, which is in the park and which we're desperately trying to resolve—is outside the park in areas of predominantly private lands. And it's not just bears. CUT brought in domestic sheep to graze on the bighorn winter range, but the bighorn can't deal with the diseases and parasites that domestic sheep carry." (CUT's Ed Francis countered later that the park's surplus of bison, which carry, but do not suffer from, brucellosis, had been encroaching on his grazing land and might infect his cattle.)

The disagreements between Varley and the Church Universal and Triumphant were not small matters for which an eventual accommodation could be worked out. Instead, there were all the makings of an awesome political confrontation and I wondered whether the National Park Service could win. In the West, the rights of the private landowner are zealously guarded, not only by the owners themselves but by organizations formed for the express purpose of reducing federal influence. One of these is the American Land Alliance. This group, headed by militant lawyer Joe Gughemetti, apparently did not find CUT to be too extreme to be an ally. When interviewed by Spiritual Leader Elizabeth Prophet for an article in a CUT publication, Gughemetti came up with anecdote after anecdote showing how the Park Service could be expected brutally to dispossess private citizens in its insatiable grab for land. In one passage, after describing how the Park Service wiped out entire towns in Yosemite and the Cuyahoga Valley, Gughemetti described efforts by the Rockefeller family to determine the future use of all the private land in America:

> PROPHET: "So it's population control through zoning."
> GUGHEMETTI: "I think so."
> PROPHET: "I know you have compared this to what happened in Nazi Germany."
> GUGHEMETTI: "There is a frightening comparison."

Back in the Centennial Valley, in the valley of the swans, some folks were trying to avoid a CUT-style confrontation by dealing with the private land problem privately before any ugliness started. Using techniques pioneered by the Jackson Hole Land Trust, three land-saving organizations were working diligently in the valley—the Montana Land Reliance, the Nature Conservancy, and the Conservation Endowment Fund. The key figure in these nongovernment efforts to protect the valley floor was John Taft, a retired Southern California businessman who had a summer place in the Centennial Valley. Refuge manager Barry Reiswig couldn't have been more pleased about Taft's work. "He's the one," Reiswig told me, "who got the ball rolling."

The approach commonly used by land-saving organizations in these situations is to seek development-limiting conservation easements from local landowners by gift or purchase. Sometimes the sale of development rights can help ranchers over a temporary financial crisis, for it puts money in their pocket without limiting the uses of their land for ranching. If an easement cannot be secured this way, conservation organizations can purchase a property when it comes up for sale and either donate the property to a public agency or manage it themselves for conservation purposes. Often, such groups, in order to restore some or all of their capital, resell the land to a public agency when and if public acquisition funds become available. Otherwise, the organization can resell the land to a private owner, subject to permanent deeded restrictions limiting subdivision and use so that the land remains an asset to the functioning of the ecosystem rather than a potential destroyer of it.

Luckily, the swans of the Centennial Valley do not know of all these machinations. They are nervous enough as it is. Anyway, the trumpeter's knowledge is of more basic things and, we hope, more eternal. If you doubt this, read (or reread) the beloved E. B. White's beautiful and wonderfully droll children's book *The Trumpet of the Swan*. White writes about Louis, the trumpeter swan who could not, like his parents and his brothers and sisters, trumpet "ko-hoh, ko-hoh." So Louis winds up *wearing* a trumpet around his neck and has many adventures, as bugler in a summer camp, soloist for the Swan Ride in the Boston Public Garden, and member of a jazz ensemble at Lucky Lucas's Club Nemo in Philadelphia. Then, after a close call with authorities at the Philadelphia Zoo, Louis returns home with his bride Selena to Red Rock Lakes, to rejoin his family after many years of absence—those lakes, as Louis's slightly orotund father opines, "which nature has designed especially for swans."

The lovely, serene Centennial Valley. It is the only place, as E. B. White says, "where all Trumpeter Swans feel safe and unafraid." May it ever be so.

RETURN OF THE WOLF

I am staring at Monte Dolack's twilight painting of a mother wolf and three cubs going "yip yip yiparoo" at a new moon over Yellowstone, the new moon that holds the old moon in her arms, as Coleridge would say. They are standing on a rock outcrop, these painted wolves, and below them a wide alluvial valley spreads from canvas edge to canvas edge, steam rising here and there from the hot springs that seethe just below the thin crust of this caldera. The river, which stands for all rivers of the region, meanders peacefully into the distance, with a moose posed in the foreground shallows and a dozen buffalo agraze on the far bank. Dusk is gathering quickly, the last light catching the high clouds over the mountains. Yellowstone dreams. Primal. Whole. Complete.

The painting, whose unapologetically sentimental style might not be to everyone's taste, was commissioned by Defenders of Wildlife, the conservation organization that has spearheaded the drive to get wolves back into the Greater Yellowstone Ecosystem and improve their chances for survival in two other large wilderness ecosystems, in northern Montana and central Idaho. The Defenders published the work as a poster in order to raise money to pay off ranchers who can show they have lost livestock to wolf predation—or "depredation" as some call it, using a more freighted word, as if the wolves were acting out of malice.

I will return to these matters after a bit. They are important, but are in many ways less important than what this painting actually depicts, however well or badly. It depicts a wolf family in Yellowstone, where no wolf family has existed for half a century. The painting is of the time when the wolves will have been *put* there, in Yellowstone, by human beings. Not by God, or accident, or outcome of evolutionary dynamics, but by men and women who have consciously decided, probably for the first time in three million years, to reintroduce a

major big-game predator into a range from which it had been extir-
pated and banished forever.

When the reintroduction comes about, and there is no doubt in the
minds of most that it will, the event will signify in a way that few
other environmental reform actions of this century have. Perhaps the
only truly comparable achievements, from a purely ethical point of
view, are the establishment of the national park system itself and later
the Wilderness Act—both of which transcend ordinarily ratiocinated
public policy and move into a realm scarcely touched by legislators, or
even fully understood by them: a kind of uncomplicated reverence for
what Faulkner calls "the old wild life."

Let us be clear. The reintroduced wolf will be as elusive as the
mountain lion and the grizzly bear. As a reinstated member of the
triumvirate of Rocky Mountain big-game predators, the wolf will be
rarely seen (though sometimes heard) by visitors to the park and its
surrounding hiking areas and camping grounds. Why then bother
with the wolf in Yellowstone? Could it be that by reintroducing the
wolves, those old enemies, we hope paradoxically that we will become
more fully human?

———

The story begins (at least as I imagine it) one fall afternoon in the
mid-1930s when a Yellowstone park ranger astride his favorite chest-
nut mare—a good trail horse, good for tracking—spotted a paw print
in the first snow of the season. He dismounted to take a closer look.
No doubt about it, it was a wolf. You hardly saw them anymore, but
by golly there it was. Probably denning hereabouts. He knew something of wolf denning, too, this ranger. Why, in the old days they'd
find the dens in the spring and shoot the pups right then and there,
kick the dirt over 'em, and that was that. And that was the law, too.
The very law that set up the the U.S. National Park Service made it
clear: to destroy any "detrimental" animals and plants in the parks.
And what was more detrimental than a wolf?

The ranger followed the tracks, now plain, now obscured, over
rocky ground until at last, with the sun low, glinting beneath the
scudding clouds, something entered the corner of his eye. Could it be
the neck ruff of a gray wolf? He guessed that whatever he saw was
perhaps two hundred yards across a swale. He dismounted quickly,
pulled his Springfield thirty-aught-six from its scabbard, chambered a
round quietly, and crept into an aspen thicket. He held his position
for a moment, testing the wind. It was in his face, praise be. Then he

climbed softly up a slope that concealed him and would put him above the wolf and maybe fifty yards closer at the same time. Some minutes later, he came out into an open grove of lodgepole and, looking down, saw the wolf, its fur thickened up for winter, tinted orange by the lowering sun. The wolf was poised with one foot off the ground, exquisitely balanced and muscle-ready, staring hard at the place the ranger had been, as if to begin a dash the moment it saw any motion. If the wolf were startled, the ranger knew sure enough he'd lose it. Even an old wolf could run all day at twenty or twenty-five miles an hour if it had to, could outrun any critter there was except maybe a griz over short distances. Wolves were about as scared of bears as he was.

As the wolf stood, frozen in indecision, the ranger laid his rifle stock against the rough bark of a lodgepole. He adjusted for windage and elevation, clicked off the safety, sighted at the wolf's shoulder down the blue barrel, and squeezed the trigger. After the rifle crack, the wolf leapt up and a split second later came the shrieking bark. It was a fair shot, a solid shot. The wolf fell to the ground squirming, unable to run. Hit the backbone, most likely, paralyzing the animal. The ranger ran down the slope, splashed across a stream, and found his quarry. Turned out to be an old female, about eighty pounds, now just lying still, looking at him approach out of her yellow eyes. She thumped her tail, her head lifted slightly, watchful. Without pausing, the ranger, now half a dozen yards away, took aim and mercifully put a bullet into the wily old brain, just behind the ears. The head jerked, lowered, and the yellow light went out.

When the ranger rode back into his station, long after sundown, he gave a whoop. The wolf carcass was strapped on behind the saddle and everyone came out to admire what he had done, examining the old gray female by flashlight. They did not know it then, nor did he, but none of them would ever see a gray wolf in Yellowstone Park again.

———————

In a 1944 review of a book about wolves, Aldo Leopold, who by then had changed his mind about these and other predators, provided a capsule history of gray wolf extirpation in the United States. They were "incredibly abundant in buffalo days," he wrote, but then in the 1870s were decimated by the demand for their fur, just at the time Yellowstone was established as the first national park. "It appears that the Russian army at that time used wolfskins for part of its winter uniform, and thus levied tribute on all the world's wolfpacks"—including the packs of the big gray wolf that roamed throughout the northern Rockies. The fur-trade wolvers used poison, not wishing to puncture the pelts with bullet holes.

After the white man killed all the buffalo and had vanquished the Plains Indians whose economy depended upon them, the wolf might have been in almost as much trouble as the Sioux. As it was, the buffalo were rather quickly replaced by cattle and sheep as a food source for the wolf. And so they held their own, even though they were avidly hunted for bounty. In 1914 the U.S. Biological Survey, predecessor agency of the Fish and Wildlife Service, dispersed with federal bounties (though others remained) in favor of salaried trappers in an all-out effort to control predators. After that the wolves were all but "wiped off the map," said Professor Leopold. "I personally believed, at least in 1914 when predator control began, that there could not be too much horned game, and that the extirpation of predators was a reasonable price to pay for better big game hunting." But, as he had written elsewhere, "I was young then, and full of trigger-itch."

So, it took fifty years to wipe the old devil gray wolf off the map of the Yellowstone country. And then fifty years, so it would seem, to decide to put the wolf back. A long time, but not as long as it might have been, for wolf-fear and wolf-hatred is close to the surface in many of us. And yet, the salient and scientifically accepted facts of the case are these:

- Wolves are about as harmless a species of large wildlife as there is, certainly safer to be around than a bison or a moose or a black bear, never mind a grizzly. There has been not one documented case of any human being in North America ever having been seriously attacked by a healthy (that is, nonrabid) wild wolf. When a wolf encounters a human, it flees.
- Wolves, at least in the Rockies, do not come down like an Abyssinian horde and feast on sheep. Or cows or calves. They much prefer elk and deer. In northern Minnesota, where wolves have lived interspersed with livestock since the time of settlement, the average loss has been five cows per ten thousand (one twentieth of one percent) and twelve sheep per ten thousand (a bit over one tenth of one percent).
- Wolves do not multiply to the degree that they deplete their natural food supply. Their numbers are governed by the prey base, not the reverse. Therefore they do not eliminate a prey such as elk, which is also the prey of hunters.

Nevertheless, even Aldo Leopold, during the trigger-itch days, killed wolves every chance he got. (Indeed, his famous description of the dimming light in the eyes of a dying wolf inspired my own tale of the last wolf in Yellowstone.) His mentor, the great William Temple Hornaday, father of scientific wildlife management, wrote in 1914: "Wherever found, the proper course with a wild gray wolf is to kill it as quickly as possible." In the distinguished eleventh edition of the *Encyclopaedia Britannica* (the last "scholarly" edition, published in 1910–1911), we learn that from time immemorial the wolf has been "the devastator of sheep flocks" and that, "as is well known, children and even full-grown people are not infrequently the objects of their attack."

Given the unimpeachable misinformation of the experts early in this century, it is something close to a miracle that the wolf has survived at all in the United States. In England, gamekeepers and shepherds succeeded in extirpating wolves during the reign of Henry VII (1485–1509). In the view of some, the mythic wolf—the ravenous, vicious beast of fables ranging from the Werewolf to the Three Little Pigs—has come down from the Middle Ages when starving wolves roamed the countryside during the time of the Black Plague.

——————

After the gray wolf had been cleaned out of Yellowstone, a long wolfless era ensued when the elk multiplied, unpreyed upon, and (as Leopold later came to understand) degraded their range to the point of near catastrophe in some areas. Coyotes, once relatively rare, multiplied too, partially filling the niche left by the wolf, which kills the competing coyote whenever it can. And so, by the 1970s, with the bear population greatly reduced and the wolf gone entirely, only the mountain lion, among the big three predators (though never very plentiful) seemingly had a chance to survive in the region.

But an agent of change—a legislative *deus ex machina*—was at hand: the Endangered Species Act of 1973.

The Endangered Species Act says that when a species is listed as endangered (or threatened, which means likely to be in danger of extinction if present trends continue), you've got to do something to get it *off* the list. Among the remedies: ban (or restrict) hunting and killing, protect and improve the habitat, reintroduce the species into suitable former range. From its earliest version, the act has listed the Rocky Mountain gray wolf as endangered. And since the Greater Yellowstone Ecosystem, a former habitat for the wolf, was practically perfect for the purpose ("The place cries out for the wolf," said the renowned wolf biologist David Mech), the reintroduction of the gray wolf to Yellowstone would seem virtually mandatory.

Yet, as many will remember during those early days of implementing the Endangered Species Act, the desert pupfish and the furbish lousewort were most often in the news. The wolf, though mentioned, became no *cause célèbre*. Perhaps even those conservationists who proclaimed a solidly scientific, coolly rational view could not fully escape from the layers of acculturated wolf-aversion. Indeed, the gray wolf originally roamed everywhere in North America save the Southeast (home of the red wolf, a different species, extinct in the wild but experimentally reintroduced into North Carolina in 1987) and the coastal Southwest. The four major subspecies south of the Canadian border are *Canis lupus irremotus*, the Rocky Mountain gray wolf, which ranged not only throughout the Rockies, but a good part of the intermountain West; *C. l. lycoan*, the eastern timber wolf, which is now restricted to northern Minnesota, Michigan, and Wisconsin; *C. l. monstrabilis*, the Texas gray wolf, probably extinct; and *C. l. baileyi*, the Mexican wolf, extinct in the United States but still found in the Sierra Madre mountains in Chihuahua and Sonora.

Over the years, we have had no compunctions about overt expressions of fear and loathing for the wolf anywhere it might be found in America. Ethologist Roger Peters, in his book *Dance of the Wolves* (1985), which recounts his studies of wolf behavior in northern Michigan (*C. l. lycoan*), found human behavior to be equally fascinating, and vile. He tells of a pair of fishermen who, discovering a female wolf near a favored spot, returned to their jeep, excitedly grabbed a rifle, and killed it. They drove back to town with the dead animal, and once arrived trussed the carcass with rope, tying one end of the rope to the rear bumper of the jeep. "All that evening," writes Peters, "they dragged it up and down the main street of Axe, until nothing was left but a dust and blood-caked swatch of black fur. They stopped at every bar but could not pay for their drinks. They were men of the hour; they had killed a wolf."

Wrote David Mech in his 1970 book, *The Wolf:* "If the wolf is to survive, the wolf haters must be outnumbered. They must be outshouted, outfinanced and outvoted. Their narrow and biased attitude must be outweighed by an attitude based on an understanding of natural processes."

———

According to Hank Fischer, the Rocky Mountain representative of Defenders of Wildlife and the point man for the wolf recovery movement, the recent turnaround in attitudes about the wolf in Yellowstone has been nothing short of astonishing. The first official effort to comply with the mandates of the Endangered Species Act was begun reluctantly and with a palpable lack of enthusiasm when the federal government belatedly assembled the first team of biologists in 1977 to take a crack at a recovery plan. The draft of the plan issued the next year was so vague about the whole business of reintroduction that it might have seemed to be a hurried term paper, not a blueprint for resolute action. But the plan was nevertheless approved (in 1980), though its weaknesses were so obvious that conservation organizations, scientists, and others demanded that it be immediately revised, with the missing details of reintroduction included. The federal authorities agreed and, amid growing controversy, began working on a revised recovery plan in 1982, having just completed an ecosystem-oriented plan for the grizzly bear.

Now that government agencies seemed to be taking wolf reintroduction seriously—at least as seriously as the grizzly bear—stockmen, hunters, and doctrinaire antienvironmentalists enlisted powerful members of Congress from the three affected states—Wyoming, Montana, and Idaho—in an antiwolf campaign designed to reach deeply into unconscious wolf-fears. So effective was the campaign that Russell Dickenson, then the director of the National Park Service, denied that any effort was being made to restore the wolf to Yellowstone.

It was then that the prowolf groups—a growing number that by this time included not only Defenders of Wildlife but also the Wilderness Society, the Greater Yellowstone Coalition, and the National Audubon Society, among others—realized that, if there were no strong countermeasures from the conservation community, any hope that the wolf could soon be returned to Yellowstone would be dashed. Fischer then paid a call on Yellowstone Park Superintendent Robert Barbee, who had dutifully supported the views of Director Dickenson but whom Fischer found to be a sympathetic listener. He was able to convince Barbee to permit Defenders of Wildlife to mount an exhibit in the park called "Wolves and Humans." Created by the Science Museum of Minnesota, the exhibit was seen by an estimated 250,000 Yellowstone visitors during the summer of 1985. Among the most impressed were Park Service employees themselves who, along with other government officials, saw that people were genuinely fascinated by the idea of wolf reintroduction. Nearly three-quarters of the visitors polled in Yellowstone during the summer when the exhibition took place said they would favor the return of the gray wolf.

Fischer believes that the great shift in attitude about the wolf, at least insofar as *C. l. irremotus* was concerned, began with this exhibition. But more political troubles still lay ahead. The revised plan was quite specific about where wolf recovery should take place—in the Selway-Bitterroot wilderness of Idaho, the Glacier Park-Bob Marshall wilderness area of northern Montana, and in Yellowstone. It called for the introduction of ten breeding pairs of wolves (imported from Canada) into each of the three areas, presuming that these pairs would then create ten packs of five to ten animals each. Under the Endangered Species Act, the northern Montana and Idaho animals, as existing endangered species, were automatically protected from hunting and killing—no administrative decisions or legislative acts were necessarily required to affirm that status. But in Yellowstone, where reintroduction was needed, three different habitat *zones* (also called for in the grizzly bear recovery plan) would be established so that management problems could be dealt with. In Zone I, prime habitat, the wolf's welfare would be paramount. In Zone II, a so-called buffer area, wildlife managers would remove problem wolves or take other steps to assure that the animals did not unduly interfere with livestock operations. In Zone III, wolves could be rather more freely controlled (that is, killed), but only by employees of responsible government agencies.

The National Park Service approved the plan, but the Fish and Wildlife Service refused to release it. At length, and after much wrangling, the FWS finally acquiesced, agreeing to the recovery scheme in 1987. Immediately, William Penn Mott, as the newly appointed director of the National Park Service, ordered an environmental impact statement (EIS) for the Yellowstone reintroduction as a means to move the schedule along as quickly as possible.

But the antiwolf forces were still well organized. Senators Malcolm Wallop, Steve Symms, Alan Simpson, and James McClure inveighed against the plan, as expected, along with many members of the House representing affected areas in the three states. Stockmen and hunters' groups were able to convince the legislators that the wolves would cause great economic hardship to the region, even though conservationists could produce scientific evidence that the impact would surely be negligible. Moreover, state wildlife agencies were opposed because they were given only a minor role in the management of the imported wolves.

Perhaps the most effective opponent of the recovery plan was the highly respected congressman Richard Cheney of Wyoming (who became secretary of defense in the Bush administration), who sent a blunt letter to Interior Secretary Donald Hodel. "I just wanted you to know," wrote Cheney, "that I am every bit as committed to preventing government introduction of wolves to Yellowstone as Bill Mott is to put them there. If he wants to fight, I'm ready." Whereupon Director Mott announced that the recovery plan would be delayed while further educational efforts took place.

This turn of events introduced a new phase in wolf politics. In 1988, annoyed at bureaucratic inaction and the ability of wolf opponents to thwart the provisions of the ESA, a Utah congressman named Wayne Owens offered a bill, quite off his own bat, that cut through all the nonsense and required simply that the wolf be reintroduced forthwith. Owens did not believe that his idea would simply sail through Congress, become law, and solve all the problems. He did hope that it might somehow get the reintroduction process started again. And in this respect, he succeeded. Hank Fischer of Defenders, and a good many others who were impressed with Owens's initiative, convinced the congressman to revise his bill so that instead of mandating reintroduction it would call for the now-postponed environmental impact study as Mott had suggested as the more politically palatable approach.

After making the rounds on Capitol Hill, Fischer and the other prowolf lobbyists were able to convince the House to appropriate the money needed to carry out an EIS, but when it came to the other body they bumped into what might be called the Rocky Mountain Curtain of antienvironmentalist senators—Symms, Simpson, Wallop, and McClure. In his meeting with McClure, whose environmental record was generally abysmal, Fischer found that although the senator was unwilling to support the EIS approach, he *would* back a special appropriation of an equivalent amount for what came to be called the "Yellowstone Congressional Studies." On the one hand, it would appear that McClure had cleverly introduced a stalling tactic. On the other, the congressional studies might be a way to lay to rest the old notion that a hundred wolves in Yellowstone would wipe out all livestock operations in three states, demolish the sport-hunting business, and reduce the region to a condition of economic collapse.

As it turned out, the possibility of compromise, via McClure, was significantly enhanced by Montana Congressman Ron Marlenee, whose vituperative ravings against the wolf made a moderate prowolf position, toward which both Fischer and McClure were working, appear sweetly reasonable. In a sense, if Marlenee did not exist, Fischer and his colleagues would have had to invent him. "Montana needs wolves like we need another drought," said Marlenee. He compared wolves to "cockroaches in your attic," which would breed madly and fan out across the countryside devouring sheep and cattle by the thousands.

When the congressional studies were completed, the antagonism lessened somewhat (except for Marlenee and a few others). Moreover, Defenders mounted a new PR initiative to follow up on their successful "Wolves and Humans" exhibit. This was the creation of a Wolf Compensation Fund that would reimburse any rancher who had lost livestock to wolves. The program was started in northern Montana as a kind of test. After three years of operation in Montana, the Defenders have paid out some $9,000 for five cows, fourteen calves, nine sheep, and one electric fence. The fund gets its money from the sale of the Monte Dolack poster described earlier.

In 1990 McClure introduced his own bill, suggesting a very limited program of wolf release at Yellowstone and considerable latitude on the part of state-level wildlife agencies to limit the population. Defenders and others opposed this bill, but they did not miss the implications of McClure's willingness to provide leadership in the Senate for some sort of compromise action. Meantime, the House approved the money for an EIS study, but once again McClure blocked the initiative. Then, as part of an Interior Department appropriations bill, wolf proponents tried another tactic, this time suggesting that money be set aside for a "Wolf Management Committee," made up of representatives of the National Park Service, the Fish and Wildlife Service, state wildlife management agencies, commercial stock-growing interests, hunting interests, and conservation organizations. Hank Fischer was named as one of the ten members.

Ron Marlenee, true to form, complained in his own curious idiom that "the committee has been stacked with a predetermined bias to reintroduce the wolf"; that "the Secretary (Lujan, of Interior) has been sold down the river"; that "the environmental activists have eaten his lunch"; and that "if Hollywood made a movie of what's been going on . . . they'd have to title it 'Dunces with Wolves.'" The committee nevertheless got down to work to determine the exact details of how (not whether) the wolf would be restored in Yellowstone and in the two other Rocky Mountain areas.

"When do you think the first wolves will be released in Yellowstone?" I asked Hank Fischer.

"In the spring of 1993," he answered.

"Really?"

"Well, I really do hope so."

Now for a bit of ecological symmetry. On the one hand, the gray wolf has been the beneficiary of a new kind of thinking about wilderness areas in general and Yellowstone in particular that has emerged largely because of a better understanding of the ecology of the grizzly bear. Although conservationists are unsatisfied with the bear recovery program, the fact remains that it did lead to an ability of the public land managers to think about the Greater Yellowstone Ecosystem as a whole and therefore the need to restore nature's original wildlife balances, in which the wolf plays a significant role.

On the other hand, though there's no great scientific agreement on the point, maybe the reintroduced wolves can, for their part, help out a bit in grizzly recovery. Although the bear will kill other animals, it is only a sometime predator, preferring berries and other vegetation much of the year, and often settling for the kills of other animals rather than going it alone when the hunger for flesh is upon it. The trouble in Yellowstone, of course, is that few other animals can provide kills for the bears to eat—the occasional mountain lion or an especially accomplished pack of coyotes in rare instances, but not often. Once some wolf packs get established in the back country, however (as Olaus Murie found in his 1944 study of wolves in Alaska), some of the wolf-kill—of elk, deer, moose—can feed the griz, who'll chase the wolves off a carcass any chance they get.

Doug Peacock, in his marvelous book *Grizzly Years* (1990), describes how he observed this phenomenon in the wolf pack at Glacier National Park (made up of migrating Canadian wolves). "I saw the remains of seven deer carcasses," he writes, "in the immediate vicinity of sweetvetch patches used by bears. Grizzlies had visited every single wolf-killed deer at some point. Deer hair was in nearly every bear scat. Something symbiotic was going on there with wolves and griz. Reintroducing wolves to a place like Yellowstone might make for a lot of extra grizzly food."

That's the way the old wild life is supposed to work, of course. The ecological vision that people such as Hank Fischer and Doug Peacock hold for Yellowstone is of something symbiotic going on, a predatory loop that simply does not include *Homo sapiens*, except perhaps as an observer of outcomes.

"A deep, chesty bawl echoes from rimrock to rimrock," wrote Aldo Leopold, "rolls down the mountain, and fades into the far blackness of the night. It is an outburst of wild, defiant sorrow, and of contempt for all the adversities of the world. . . . Only the mountain has lived long enough to listen objectively to the howl of the wolf."

Doubtless true. But we are trying, Professor Leopold. Perhaps one day a tiny bit of the mountain's wisdom will find its way into our flawed plans and policies to help get the bears and wolves together again—as they have lived naturally for eons. And then the healing may truly begin in a great and wonderful wilderness ecosystem where, as Monte Dolack's painting suggests, a new moon hovers on the horizon.

SOME QUESTIONS
OF POLICY

The trouble with *Homo sapiens* is that he thinks too much. Our species has the capacity, as a self-conscious organism, to separate itself intellectually from its surroundings in order to plan for the future, and the plans don't always turn out well. When somebody says, "This is the Greater Yellowstone Ecosystem, seven national forests, two national parks, three wildlife refuges, and some very crucial private land," the next question is: "Well, what are we going to do about it?" And so you wind up talking policy, even if all you had set out to do was enjoy the scenery.

But policy must be talked, to deal not only with the future of the Greater Yellowstone Ecosystem, but with the remaining wilderness ecosystems elsewhere in the United States. Can the various missions of the public land agencies be coordinated, which is clearly needed not only for the management of the public land but as a means to deal effectively with private ownerships as well? And how can these agencies fulfill the *scientific* demands of ecosystem management in areas as vast as the Yellowstone region? This last point was thought to be the most crucial issue for the first of several Yellowstone conservation leaders with whom I talked policy.

There is an old saying in the advertising business that half of all advertising is effective. The only trouble is, which half? That was what bothered Alston Chase about managing the Yellowstone ecosystem. Chase, a philosopher with a doctorate from Oxford who gave up the academic life to live and work as a writer in rural Montana, is the author of an important and controversial book entitled *Playing God at Yellowstone*, published in 1986. At one level the book, unfairly some believe, attacks the National Park Service for perversely failing to undertake even rudimentarily competent research at Yellowstone on matters of wildlife ecology. But at a deeper level it raises an important question pertaining to whether and how an entire ecosystem can ever be managed coherently.

In Chase's view, the Park Service's approach to ecological management has been so deeply flawed that the extent to which its ideas might tend to dominate regionwide, multiagency ecological management of the Greater Yellowstone Ecosystem is worrisome to contemplate. Chase specifically objects to what he believes is the Park Service's hidebound adherence to the principle of "natural regulation"—meaning that the ecology of the region will regulate itself if you just leave it alone. As we have seen, the principle arose in the 1960s as an antidote to a game-management approach at Yellowstone that led to exterminating the gray wolf and feeding garbage to the bears. More recently, natural regulation affected the wildfire policy within Yellowstone Park. Here natural regulation was expressed in the "let it burn" strategy that, given the buildup of dry tinder in the park's forests, produced wildfires in 1988 that simply could not be controlled. While many thought that the fire-scarring would be the end of Yellowstone as we know it, another outcome has obtained—the ecological renewal has become an object of fascination for visitors and scientists alike. Yellowstone's chief scientist, John Varley, is often seen on television happily leading camera crews to visit fields of new wildflowers in the regenerating forest.

It would seem that, notwithstanding Chase's criticism and even before the fire, the Park Service had greatly improved its research agenda, which perhaps suggests somewhat greater flexibility in its viewpoint on natural regulation. But even granting an increased quantity of research—of the kind that might lead to "proactive" management, such as swan feeding at Red Rock Lakes—Chase believes that natural regulation is so bureaucratically safe it may be impossible to dislodge. Following a natural-regulation policy, should a species become locally extinct, bureaucrats can simply shrug their shoulders and explain that they are not to blame, for they have let "nature take its course."

I met with Chase in his modern ranch house in Paradise Valley, with its picture window framing the looming Absorokas. "If the greater Yellowstone area had been managed by the Park Service for the last twenty years," he told me flatly, by way of example of the follies of natural regulation, "there would, without question, be no bighorn sheep left. Most of those remaining are along the boundary between Yellowstone and Montana. That population suffered a crash in 1961 and 1962, but was allowed to continue to decline into the 1980s under the policy of natural regulation. The Montana Fish and Game Department people undertook their own research on their side of the line, finding a reproductive rate of only fourteen lambs per one hundred ewes, well below maintainance level. They found that the incidence of lungworm in this population was over 80 percent, the result of nutritional stress due to food competition with elk. So the state of Montana opened up that area to an enormous amount of harvesting of elk by hunters and in one year brought the lamb-ewe ratio up to forty per one hundred. The point of the story is that a different management philosophy on the part of Montana was needed to compensate for the policy of the Park Service. It's not that Montana is always right of course. In fact, with grizzly bears these days, it might be the other way around. But if you want to have a coordinated policy in the greater Yellowstone area, then the question is, 'whose and what kind?'"

I also visited geologist J. D. (Dave) Love in Jackson, Wyoming, a scientist emeritus of the U.S. Geological Survey, and the subject of an admiring book by author John McPhee, *Rising from the Plains.* Love agreed with Chase that better research is essential, but he did not view past failures as a deterrent to coherent ecosystem management in the Yellowstone region. It was a positive inducement for it, he said. Morever, he thought that great strides have been made already. "A lot of research is already being done," he said. "Botany in landslide areas, pelicans, the ancient shore beneath Jackson Lake." In fact, according to John Varley, in the prefire year of 1987, there were some 170 research projects in Yellowstone Park alone. The postfire era has escalated that level of effort mightily.

Regardless of the amount of research, Love said he was a great deal more concerned about *communicating* scientific findings. He cited the example of radiation research as related to the region's geothermal activity, which he said might very well have been suppressed. "At Senator Malcolm Wallop's hearing on geothermal proposals at Island Park," Love explained, "I raised the question, 'What are you going to do about the water tests at nearby Huckleberry Hot Springs, Crawfish Creek, and Gray's Lake, which show a lot of radium?' That question never got in the hearing record."

In the Yellowstone region generally, Love said, background radiation is usually about forty clicks per second on a Geiger counter. At Huckleberry Hot Springs, near the south entrance to Yellowstone

Park, the count is nine thousand. In fact, said Love, "lupine, an annual plant, takes up so much radium around there they can take their own picture on photographic film."

Besides high radium content in some of the region's waters there's the question of radon. Love thought the presence of radon might persuade the people at the Church Universal and Triumphant to move on, for La Duke Hot Springs, their favorite project, is in an area with extremely high quantities of this deadly poison.

Even though Chase and Love may have disagreed about the imperatives of policy, their examples did suggest that a major pulling-together of the ecological facts would be a necessity if policy were to be firmly grounded in science—as clearly it must be if the objective is to manage a world-class ecosystem larger than a good many nations, and if Yellowstone is to serve as the planning-and-policy model for other U.S. wilderness ecosystems.

As it happens, this pulling-together process has already started, at least in a rudimentary way. The effort, undertaken by the Greater Yellowstone Coordinating Committee and consisting of the heads of the national parks and forests in the region, is called simply "the aggregation." The idea for the project arose in connection with a 1985 congressional hearing on the Yellowstone ecosystem that while producing a seven-hundred-page hearing record, showed that no one had any clear idea of what was really going on ecologically in the ecosystem as a whole. Accordingly, the twelve-member coordinating committee began to "aggregate" current park and forest plans and to plan research that for the first time could provide a statistical and conceptual basis for carrying out the Greater Yellowstone Ecosystem idea. As Red Rock Lakes Refuge manager Barry Reiswig said of it, "For the first time, we have a chance to look at timber cuts of the Targee, for example, as compared to the Shoshone or the Beaverhead. Or how many moose Bridger-Teton has compared to Red Rocks. It may be a crude resource, but it's the first opportunity we've had to see what is where in this ecosystem."

For Robert Barbee, superintendent of Yellowstone National Park, the best thing about the aggregation was that it demanded a next step, although he was hard put to describe it. I would guess that the problems he and his colleague John Varley were having with CUT (among other "low-elevational" issues) may well have been in his mind. "It seems to me," he told me, "that we've got to go beyond the glittering generality that we should maintain the 'integrity of the ecosystem.'

That's like saying, 'I'm for wise use.' There have to be sovereign conditions in the ecosystem that we can all agree to—that go beyond our agency missions and mandates—in order to insure this integrity."

The implication here of course is *statutory* policy, as opposed to the soft-edged policy-of-principle. I asked John Good, a nationally known and highly respected Park Service naturalist now living in Jackson, Wyoming, whether he thought Congress needed to produce some coordinating legislation. Actually he did not. "There's good strong research that's taking us in the right direction without any new federal policies," he said. In fact, this view was shared by many—especially those in the Forest Service who were obliged to create elaborate long-range forest plans for the resource areas in their care. At the time of my visit, one of these was just nearing completion at the B-bar-T. "No new plans!" wailed Ernie Nunn. Who can blame him? The Bridger-Teton plan turned out to be fifteen hundred pages long and weigh twelve pounds.

Ed Lewis, executive director of the militant Greater Yellowstone Coalition, told me that if you take care of the problems the policy will take care of itself—it would emerge naturally, as naturally as the park's lodgepole forests are emerging after the fire. Accordingly, the Coalition publishes an "issue book," a recent edition of which provided 198 different cases in point. When I asked local park and forest officials about this tactic, most agreed that it was necessary, even though they sometimes weary of the constant criticism of the conservation community.

Ecologist Tim Clark agreed that policy could follow action (rather than the reverse), but only partly. When I put the policy question to him, he said: "As far as tinkering with policy is concerned, there's a lot of administrative latitude in the Forest Service and other agencies to make things better. But I have a sense that this latitude is not enough.

"At the very least," Clark suggested, "we're going to need some federal legislation stating that this piece of geography is unique in a national and global sense, and that says 'we expect you guys out there—Forest Service, National Park Service, and so forth—to come up with specific management principles that recognize this uniqueness, applied through rigorous implementation, plus monitoring and evaluation.' That's the kind of broad 'umbrella' policy that is needed."

If such a policy "umbrella" could be put in place by Congress, Clark said, the effort to protect the Greater Yellowstone Ecosystem over the long pull could be "a major conservation success story—so long as the conservation community does not let up on the pressure."

IV

THE LIVING LANDSCAPE

In any broad-scale discussion of planning and conservation in the U.S., it is hard to resist organizing the material into the three primary categories of land use: the land that is used for settlement; the land that is used for agriculture; and the land that is left alone, as wilderness. This book, thus far, has held to these traditional divisions. But I have not yet run out of categories. Indeed, I believe there ought to be a fourth primary land-use category—areas that may be called the living landscape. Such landscapes often have elements of the three main types, but are not really a subset of any of them.

As we shall see, what seems to distinguish an outstanding living landscape from other places has to do with aesthetic qualities and cultural values that relate, usually, to some sort of unique, or at least special, geomorphology that sets the landscape apart. There is one other criterion—sheer size. The living landscapes this chapter discusses range from thousands of acres to the millions.

The first of these is the Pine Barrens of New Jersey (one million), followed by a short essay on the Lake District of England (half a million) as a kind of model for managing such areas, followed by the Adirondacks of New York State (six million), whose planning and management policies are very much like those of the British national "parks." I have also included an essay—"Greenlining"—occasioned by legislation to protect the Santa Monica Mountains of California (two hundred thousand) but goes on to summarize planning and regulatory techniques that can be applied generally. I think we ought to be protecting living landscapes everywhere in the United States, not just in a few places.

The chapter concludes with my adventures in "Dime Country," which goes to show that quite small living landscapes can be found in surprising places and in surprising ways.

IN THE PINES:
NATURE AND CULTURE

Here's how to catch a snapping turtle the "Piney" way. It is called "progging." First, take off your shoes and roll up your trousers. Now, wade into the shallow water of a pond where the turtles are and poke around with a long pole. You'll be able to tell when you've hit a turtle's back; the thick shell of a twenty-five or thirty pound snapper makes an unmistakable thunk. Then, as progger Herb "Snapper" Misner of Medford, New Jersey, describes the process, "Just step your foot on him. Give a couple of pushes to see which way he's gonna move—he always moves forward, he won't come back—and then just grab the tail." And there you are. You've got the makings of some fine snapper soup, or you can sell the cooked meat to a local restaurant for a dollar a pound or more.

Progging is most often carried out during the fall of the year in this place, the Pine Barrens of southern New Jersey, a remarkably remote and unspoiled area. Other seasons, Pineys (as they are called, not always derisively) are inclined to use a snapper fyke—a baited trap-net held open by a series of hoops and set horizontally in shallow water—or simply a hook and line. In any case, catching snappers is part of a Piney's "seasonal round" of subsistence occupations with the expertise handed down through the generations, such as the demonstrated truth that, under water, snappers are unperturbable. On dry land, according to Misner, the snapper king, "They're mad all the time." Even after a snapper's head is cut off, the head will keep on biting, he says, just as a snapper heart will keep on beating. "You can clean all his insides out, and lay his heart in your hand, and it's still pumpin'. They say if you swallow a snapper's heart, you'll never be ascared, while it's still beatin'."

The Pine Barrens ("barrens" because they were originally thought to be unsuitable for agriculture; they are now also called the "Pinelands") comprise a fifth of the state of New Jersey. This one-million-acre rural region contains a number of ecological marvels. There is the famed "pygmy forest" in the center of it, for example, twelve thousand acres of full-grown pine trees reaching no higher than a man's shoulder—an adaptation to the frequent forest fires. The rare Pine Barrens tree frog and curly grass fern attract naturalists from the world over. The surface waters of the Pinelands range from the tea-colored creeks and wetlands of the interior, stained by bog-iron once smelted here, to the blue riffling waters of the biologically rich Barnegat Bay, shielded from the Atlantic by barrier dunes. Sand is everywhere, from the surface of the ground down to bedrock—the incredible Cohansey aquifer with seventeen trillion gallons of some of the purest water on earth.

It was because of these attributes (which became newsworthy in the 1960s when a massive jetport was proposed to be located here, and again in the 1970s when legalized gambling in Atlantic City threatened to create new development corridors to New York City and Philadelphia) that the federal government, in concert with the state of New Jersey, established the "Pinelands National Reserve" in 1978. Significantly, the legislation called for the protection not only of Pinelands ecology but of the Piney culture as well. As a consequence, unlike a typical national or state park project in which land is purchased and local residents are replaced by tourists and campers, here in the Pines the land uses are strictly regulated by an intergovernmental commission, but landownership remains in the hands of the local people.

This is a land-management concept called "greenlining," and is meant to provide a way to protect treasured landscapes that are inappropriate candidates for national parks (which would be colored a solid green on a map) but yet cannot be allowed simply to deteriorate with random development debasing their natural and cultural integrity. And so they would be designated with a *green line*, to indicate special planning and management.

In the case of the Pine Barrens, the airport scheme was beaten back, with much credit for this going not only to the conservation organizations that opposed it, but to author John McPhee, whose 1967 *New Yorker* story (later a book) on the plight of the pinelands galvanized the conservation conscience of the State of New Jersey—and persuaded it as well that something ought to be done to save the Pines permanently. Yet clearly it was impossible to make the whole of the Pine Barrens a national park. The cost would have been ludicrous and would have preserved "nature" but destroyed the "place," which was a cultural landscape as well as a natural one.

Even so, many proposed the national park solution, at least for part of the region, for lack of an alternative. The dim prospect for the Pines brightened considerably, however, when James Florio, then a congressman and later governor, advanced the idea that only a small (and affordable) amount of land be purchased, but that the remainder of the Pine Barrens be protected by a variety of land-management devices that would limit development but permit residents to own and live on their property. These devices included environmental regulations that would protect shoreline areas and riparian corridors; subdivision regulations that would maintain the water quality of the Cohansey aquifer, which was overlain by soil so porous that pollutants could travel for miles unmodified by their journey underground; and a number of means to preserve and protect the resource-based economy, for the area produced more cranberries than any other in the United States, was among the top three in blueberries, and, thanks to Barnegat Bay, a prime shellfishing area as well.

To save the unique pygmy forest and other natural areas that could sustain little or no development without losing their integrity, the Pinelands Commission used an approach called "transfer of development rights" (TDR) as opposed to wholesale land purchase. Pioneered in New Jersey, this device permits landowners to retain the right to develop *a* piece of property, but not *their* piece of property if it is located in a preservation area. In such a case, the rights can be transferred to land more suitable for development—either through the sale of rights directly to a developer or in some cases indirectly by "depositing" the rights in a "bank" established by a planning authority. This way the Pinelands Commission could avoid the constitutional problem of "taking without just compensation," permitting the owner to profit economically from the development of other land. In the summer of 1991, the New Jersey Supreme Court affirmed the legitimacy of the Pinelands approach to land-use regulation.

As might be expected, these newfangled approaches created controversy and were difficult to administer. With so many parties at interest there was a land-use policy commotion of epic proportions in New Jersey: big developers wanting to cash in on the Atlantic City boom, local governments protective of their home-rule prerogatives, landowners beset by regulation and hollering about "property rights," farmers expecting to retire on the revenues generated by the sale of land for development, state officials concerned with the intrusion of the federal government in local planning, and the federal government (represented by the National Park Service on the commission) wondering what in the world they were doing here trying to deal with a place that was not a park. And yet, somehow, good planning has made the effort at greenlining work out. No one had to be dispossessed, but the landscape is safe. As Terrence Moore, executive director of the New Jersey Pinelands Commission, wrote in a professional journal article in 1987, "It is, perhaps, time to suggest that the Pinelands experiment . . . [has] proved successful."

And so the life of the country beats on, like the snapper's heart, in the Piney's seasonal round—pulling pine cones to sell in the winter, for example, or trapping snapping turtles beginning in early spring, clamming in the summer, and working the cranberry bogs in the fall. There's fox hunting, huckleberry knocking, and at every time of the year, there's watching out for the "Jersey Devil," an apparition whose actuality is doubted no less (or no more) than the Loch Ness monster of the Scottish Highlands or the Abominable Snowman in the Himalayas.

There was a time when this cultural richness was scorned by outsiders as well as the Pineys themselves. A Piney, according to Janice Sherwood of Forked River, New Jersey, founder of the Pinelands Cultural Society, was typically described as "someone who is a little bit deeper in the woods than you are." There is a story about an anthropologist who in the 1930s started at the north end of the Pine Barrens and asked all he encountered where the Pineys were. Each time he was told, "go farther south," until finally he got to a place where they said, "go north."

Now all of that is decisively changed, for the work of the Pinelands Commission has succeeded not only in regulating land uses, but in helping to preserve thereby the culture of the Pinelands, such as progging for snapping turtles while managing to retain all ten toes. In fact, the cultural richness of the Pines has now been captured through thousands of recordings and photographs and interviews, sorted and indexed and archived, and then transmitted back to the Pineys themselves in publications and exhibits by a team of top professional folklorists from the American Folklife Center, a division of the Library of Congress in Washington, D.C. Beginning in 1984, the Center undertook a three-year project to collect perhaps the most comprehensive record of a contemporary rural culture ever. According to folklorist Mary Hufford, director of the Center's Pinelands project, she and six associates collected "seventeen hundred pages of field notes, three hundred hours of sound recordings, and fifteen thousand still photographic images."

Now the lore of the Pines will never be lost. Unless, perchance, it's kept secret on purpose. For example, the only way to make a true "Barnegat Bay sneakbox," a tiny duck-hunting skiff built with Jersey cedar, is to use techniques handed down through the generations in a family. The craft is small, with a draft so shallow that it should be able to "follow a mule as it sweats up a dusty road." So it's tricky to make and the designs are jealously guarded. Piney George Heinrichs told Mary Hufford, "I made a promise to my father that if I didn't build boats and my brother didn't, that I'd cut up the patterns and destroy them, because it's his pattern and no one has ever copied it." But folklorists are patient. Chances are the Heinrichs design will wind up in the archives sooner or later.

So it is that in the New Jersey Pine Barrens the human ecology of the landscape is now seen as every bit as important—and rare—as the pygmy forests, the ferns, and the tree frogs that characterize the ecology of nature. Says Alan Jabbour, director of the American Folklife Center: "We are dealing with 'cultural conservation' here—the whole culture in a comprehensive way. In the Pinelands, we wanted to see how it all fitted together, nature *and* culture, as inseparable elements to create a true sense of place." Jabbour—a deep-voiced, courtly academic from the rural South (the name is Syrian, from his father's side)—sees the project as a model that can provide tested techniques for collecting, evaluating, and communicating folklife data in other outstanding natural landscapes such as the Pine Barrens. To this end, the Center has published an excellent how-to booklet on the subject, "Folklife and Fieldwork: A Layman's Introduction to Field Techniques," and issues a first-rate quarterly newsletter, free for the asking, to keep folklife aficionados, amateur and professional, up to date on developments in the field and on new Center projects.

In the end, as the Pinelands project has shown, the *process* of monitoring the folklife of the country may be as important as the folk materials that are collected and archived. For it creates not only a record, but a sense of pride that can come to any community that values not only its natural landscape, but its cultural heritage as well. Right down to the turtle soup.

HOME AT GRASMERE

I am reliably informed that during the time the poet William Wordsworth lived in and around Grasmere, Cumbria, in the Lake District of northern England, which is to say from 1799 to 1850, he walked, on the average, twelve miles a day. By my reckoning, that's 223,380 miles for those fifty years, plus a few extra thrown in for leap years. (Thomas DeQuincey, Wordsworth's protégé, estimated 170,000. Either way, it's a lot of shoe leather.) And rugged miles they are too in the Lake District, where the mountains rise to three thousand feet from near sea level: up fells, pikes, knobs, and crags; across gills and becks; around forces, rivers, and tarns; down dales and cloughs; through crofts, closes, and nooks; and then back again.

These terms, mostly from Old Norse, are actually in use in the Lake District. A fell is a mountain, usually the high part of a mountain, and a pike is a sharp peak; a gill is a cascading stream in a rocky ravine and a beck is a small brook; a force is a waterfall and a tarn a mountain pond; a clough is a narrow defile, a croft a farm, and closes and nooks are farm fields, which are small in lakeland.

I know about this at first hand because I am an alumnus of possibly the most *strenuous* scholarly conference in the realm of English letters. Now the planners of your average academic conclave tend to favor concurrent panels, with a few optional "field" trips (museums, galleries, etc.) thrown in. The Wordsworth Summer Conference, held at Grasmere every year, turns that notion on its head. The "outings" are held daily—actually several times a day—run concurrently ("A" walk, "B" walk, "C" walk, depending on degree of difficulty) and are all but obligatory. Only the seriously blistered and those with no moral character to begin with fail to sign up for the walks (Americans would call them "hikes"; sometimes they are more like forced marches). As for lectures, they are rigorous too, but are held at hours less convenient than for walking. The conferees attend them in hiking garb, anoraks at the ready (this is England's wettest corner), Vibram-soled boots tightly laced, eager to get on the trail. You may fall asleep at lectures, if you wish, but there is to be no lollygagging around during the walks.

The reason for this approach is that the conference director, one Richard Wordsworth, who is in his early seventies and a great-great-grandson of "the poet," has an understanding of William Wordsworth's true greatness that could come only through the genes. Richard is a scholar, albeit not a formally trained one, and an actor, often in productions of Shakespeare's plays. He sports a trim Shakespearean beard, along with the longest legs and strongest lungs in the North of England. As a chip off a chip off a chip off a chip off the old block, he knows that just as you need a stage to understand Shakespeare you need mountain trails to understand Wordsworth. The participants evidently agree, for the conference attracts a distinguished group of world-class academics.

The topography of the Lake District—about 850 square miles of uplands—is palmate, with the lakes radiating outward as fingers from a hand. Between the lakes are the high fells, which rise quite steeply from the U-shaped valley bottoms, characteristic of a glaciated highland. The valleys—dales they are called—provide the land for crops and dairying while the fellsides pasture the sheep: Herdwick and Swaledale mainly, which are original Norse breeds brought to the region over a thousand years ago and in modern times "bred back" to their original characteristics. They now breed true to type. Indeed, the Herdwick appears truly primordial, shaggy and goatlike, with wool so filled with lanolin that a Herdwick cap I own has remained perfectly waterproof after ten years of wear.

At the confluences of Lake District dales, where the gills and becks run together thence to run into the lakes themselves, the settlements are located. Quite often these hamlets are not on main thoroughfares, but up narrow roads that dead-end at a dale head. Thus, only rarely is the highway the shortest distance between the villages. More often, the footpaths (which are also public rights-of-way) provide a much shorter route. In Wordsworth's time it was often quicker to go afoot—up one dale, over the high fells, and down another—rather than by carriage on more level ground to get from settlement to settlement.

Using the dale-to-dale footpath shortcuts is also Richard Wordsworth's inclination. One memorable afternoon found his "A Walk" group rambling from Borrowdale, which runs into Derwent Water,

one of the largest lakes, across the fells to Grasmere via Far Easedale—
a distance of about fourteen miles, which by road would be well over
thirty. Characteristically, within a half-hour of setting out, the A-walk
scholars—about twenty of us—were strung out along the trail over a
distance of a quarter mile, Richard in the lead, chatting animatedly
with anyone who could keep up with him, usually junior scholars with
grandparents scarcely older (if at all) than their pace-setting guide.

We hiked alongside Greenup Gill ("up" is a corruption of Old
Norse "hop"—a valley) until it disappeared as a single stream, whereupon we arrived at a steep, ending in a lung-busting five-hundred-foot
scramble up a rocky scree to the top of Eagle Crag, where a view of the
valley behind us was breathtaking, for those who had any breath left
to take. I was among the last of the last group, and Richard greeted me
with mock delight. "Didn't you just hate it," he said, "when you were
a little boy on walks with your parents and couldn't keep up?" Whereupon, with a wave of his hand, he set off himself, with his claque of
young hikers in tow.

But all could be forgiven as we gained the tops of the Borrowdale
Fells. Now the A-groupers were widely separated. With only a solitary
Herdwick in sight, one could wander lonely as a cloud through the
high boggy commons (as indeed they are, even to this day, having
escaped enclosure). Here on the treeless moor is white cotton grass,
yellow Asphodel, the green rushes that are gathered at this time of year
by the children of St. Oswald's Parish (which was Wordsworth's) for
the Rush Bearing, a ceremony whose origins are pre-Christian.

The felltops seem almost rolling, once you are up there, a complex
of grassy mountain intersections. The possibility of picking the wrong
dalehead to descend is high, and in fact a Harvard scholar did just that
during one of the conferences, causing Richard and his "tutors"—
freshly minted Ph.D.s who moderate some workshop discussions and
occasionally handle subgroups of walkers—no end of consternation
and roaming about the Borrowdale Fells and hallooing, or whatever
appropriate noise one makes in such a circumstance.

I had not fallen so far behind that I lost my way, but I was not just
about to go loping thoughtlessly down the footpath paralleling Far
Easedale Gill from the scarp at Greenup Edge, for here in a succession
of gillside tableaus was the most perfectly beautiful mountain landscape I had ever seen. I am not talking about wide-angle views across
the dale to distant peaks—though there was plenty of that. But little

streamside nooks, no bigger than a room, tucked among the rocks beside the tumbling water, each place carpeted with tufts of soft grass, alight with wildflowers, butterflies in attendance—meadow browns, painted ladies, green-veined whites—protected from the wind by the sheltering outcrops of warm-gray granite and shaded by orange-berried rowan trees, the tree we Americans call mountain ash.

Such scenes as these are among the reasons that the British do such a good job at protecting their landscapes, especially in the national parks, such as the Lake District. National parks (there are ten in England and Wales) are not publicly owned as in the United States, but the private lands within them are stringently regulated. The British are unashamed by their love of landscape and have upheld, through Labor and Tory governments alike, the 1947 law (the so-called Town and Country Planning Act) which effectively nationalized the right of landowners to change the use of their land. Accordingly, the decision to build a row of terrace houses, say, is not a private one, but public, via a planning council that would keep the aesthetic protection of a place such as the Lake District uppermost among their permission-granting criteria. A parallel statute, the National Parks and Access to the Countryside Act of 1949, established the national parks, "Areas of Outstanding Natural Beauty," and the long-distance footpaths, providing for a commission and a set of standards for their protection and use.

I don't suppose these matters much concerned the literary scholars in attendance at the Wordsworth Summer Conference. But they should, for I believe the British are as good at land-use policy as they are at landscape poetry, and that the former has a great deal to do with the latter. Indeed, on the footpath down Far Easedale Gill toward Grasmere, I felt great kinship to the man who actually *invented* the idea of preserving large natural and cultural landscapes such as this. For it was he—William Wordsworth—who wrote in 1810 that the Lake District should be deemed "a sort of national property, in which every man has a right and interest who has an eye to perceive and a heart to enjoy."

In a poem called "Home at Grasmere," Wordsworth recounts walking homeward to Cockermouth, a small city northwest of the lake country. He was just a youngster returning from his boarding school at Hawkshead (afoot as usual on a dale-to-dale route). After a long upward climb, he reached the crest of a fell, and suddenly before him lay a valley he had not seen before from this perspective. It was the vale of Grasmere, and he decided then and there that this rural region would be his home for the length of his days—and they were many indeed, for he lived to the age of eighty. In fact, not only would this place be his home, it would provide the inspiration for a body of work that compares with that of Milton and Shakespeare and very few others in the pantheon of English literature.

As for me, I first saw Wordsworth's landscape after a nightmarishly delayed flight from New York, and a long, scary drive up the M-6 in the smallish hours of a wet, dark morning. I too surmounted a hill in a rented car, and before me was revealed a similar valley, smoothly green, dotted with sheep, laced with ancient stone walls, the small fields sloping to a stream bordered by stout oaks. When I stopped the car and got out, a broad shaft of sunlight lit the scene, and joy quite literally lifted my heart.

Only a very few times in my life can I recall experiencing just that emotion. Perhaps the first was on the vestibule platform of a Pullman car rolling through California on a very early December morning in 1947. I had been away at school, the first time away, and I was so eager to return that I had opened the top half of the car door so I could lean out in the gray light of early morning and face into the wind, as if physically to impress into my permanent memory the dark rushing of the orange trees, the pastures of the small stock ranches, the warm, brown, plowed fields of the farms, the lush arroyos and the dry hills, the little agricultural towns in the California valleys. Then as the sun rose, I saw the green leaves of the orange groves become tinted with gold. And the brightness of a fine California day crept up the sides of the dusky San Gabriel mountains—my mountains. I had come home, and the thought filled me with such happiness that I shouted, "Heya, heya, heya," until the porter came to hush me up.

There have been sunrises over many landscapes since the one viewed from the Pullman vestibule, often with an infusing sense of gladness. The infusion obtains, I think, whenever we encounter what might be called a "homecoming" landscape, not because they actually *are* home (as the vale of Grasmere was not for Wordsworth until he reached the age of twenty-nine), but because they produce the sense of rightness that home brings. As I have written, I felt it in Vermont the very first time I visited there. And now, on a footpath along Far Easedale Gill, I felt it again. Had I too, with some mysterious land-consciousness, come "home" to Grasmere?

William Wordsworth wrote:

> Paradise, and groves
> Elysian, Fortunate Fields—like those of old
> Sought in the Atlantic Main—why should they be
> A history only of departed things,
> Or a mere fiction of what never was?

For me, that is the main question, and one I ask each time I consider the salvation of living landscapes, in which we all have a right and interest. I think of Richard striding along the lakeland footpaths as if the centuries distancing him from his forebear were no more than an instant. And, I have concluded, the thousands of miles between the place I live and that nook of English ground is but a step across a tuft of grass.

A DIFFERENT KIND OF PARK

Not many natural resource planners get to go back and do their plans over again fifteen years later. As F. Scott Fitzgerald put it, "there are no second acts in American lives." But Fitzgerald didn't reckon on my friend George D. Davis, who, as executive director of New York's Commission on the Adirondacks in the Twenty-first Century, was given a second shot at saving his beloved Adirondack Park, a huge, six-million-acre hunk of northwoods landscape that is larger than the entire state of New Jersey.

The commission was established in 1989 to eliminate the loopholes in laws created in 1973—with Davis playing a key role then too—that many thought would forever protect this vast assemblage of scattered public forest preserve lands (2.3 million acres) and private ownerships (3.7 million acres), and confine development to its thirteen villages and seventy unincorporated hamlets scattered amid the magnificent lakes and forests.

But nobody figured on leveraged buy-outs weakening the grasp of giant forest-products companies on their holdings. Nobody figured that foreign investors would think that Adirondack land would be cheap at five times its asking price for jet-set recreational development. Nobody knew how suburban condomania could metastasize into the far-north backcountry. Nobody (although Davis warned of it fifteen years ago) knew how easily the primeval ambiance of this last vast northeastern forest could be shattered by roadside zoos, roaring speedboats on the lakes, doublewide trailers along the highways, tacky advertising signs, and all the other whatnots of recreation-mad America the Ugly.

Now, if Davis and his colleagues have their way, new laws and regulations will snap the loopholes shut. The key elements of what the commission—which counts among its membership the cream of New York state conservation, civic, and business leadership—has recommended relates to strengthening the state's hand in protecting the natural areas and the aesthetics of the mountains as well as nurturing an indigenous Adirondack economy and way of life.

Regarding the preservation of natural areas, the commission has called for the creation, from existing public lands, of the largest true wilderness area in the northeast. In fact, at 400,000 acres the Oswagatchie Great Wilderness, as it would be called, would be the third largest east of the Mississippi and managed much more stringently than any federally designated wilderness area. In addition, Davis and his commission recommended that the state government be given the authority to purchase development rights over the years on as much privately owned resource land as possible—theoretically all of it—to guarantee in perpetuity that the land will never be developed and to provide for recreational access as needed.

To protect the "sense of wilderness" that most visitors to the Adirondacks find so remarkable, shoreline development along the many lakes, ponds, and rivers would not be permitted any closer than 650 feet in backcountry areas, and 200 feet *anywhere* in the park; nor would owners be allowed to disturb vegetation, except for a 5-foot path that must be designed so that no structure would be visible from the water.

In built-up areas, off-premise outdoor advertising would be eliminated with on-premise signs allowed only on a permit basis. To protect the view from the road in undeveloped areas, no buildings would be allowed within 200 feet of a roadway unless fully screened by vegetation; preexisting eyesores would be purchased by a nonprofit authority when land comes on the market, torn down, and land transferred to state ownership or resold.

Development would be permitted, however, in already-settled parts of villages and hamlets, though not allowed to sprawl into the surrounding landscape. To guard against gentrification that might drive out existing subsistence residents, the commissioners recommended that an "Adirondack Park Community Development Corporation" be established to provide for appropriate and affordable housing and public facilities.

"This time," George Davis said when he briefed me on these tough new recommendations (nearly 250 in all), "I hope we got it right."

157

Actually he got it right last time. It's just that times change—and almost any change in this environmentally and aesthetically fragile northern forest brings new perils. And Davis, a forester trained at the State University of New York College of Forestry in Syracuse, is as sensitive to this fact as anyone could be. For this is more than your typical, lightly developed forested mountain region. The Adirondack Mountains are, in fact, one of the biggest, possibly most beautiful, most varied natural landscapes anywhere in the United States.

Within the Adirondack's six million acres there are twenty-three hundred lakes and ponds, one thousand miles of rivers fed by thirty thousand miles of brooks and streams. Forty-six of the mountain peaks exceed four thousand feet in elevation. On the flanks of the highest one, Mount Marcy (5,344 feet), the Hudson River begins. Birdwatchers can find 220 species here. Hunters come in the winter for black bear and deer. Indeed, the Adirondacks present a combination of lakes and peaks and big trees and animals that combine in a unique way to make the Adirondack Park an aesthetic treasure the likes of which exists nowhere else. "It is a landscape of infinite variety," writes Courtney Jones, a north country author. "It has millions of acres of forests, thousands of acres of wetlands. It has high waterfalls, deep gorges, rolling countryside, alpine summits. It houses both endangered and abundant species of plants and wildlife. It has names that linger in the ear, names like Noonmark, Boreas Pond, Tahawas, Lake Tear-of-the-Clouds. Its images linger in the mind. It is, in short, a natural pageant of unusual richness, a feast for the eye and spirit in a time of unusual needs."

Such was not always the case in the Adirondacks. In fact, during the nineteenth century these mountains were ruthlessly cut over by unprincipled loggers who in complicity with corrupt officials would buy land from the state, sometimes for as little as fifteen cents an acre, fell every tree in sight to build the tenements of Manhattan and the rowhouses of Flatbush, and then move on, letting the land revert to state ownership for nonpayment of taxes. The devastation was so pervasive that in 1857 a journalist by the name of S. H. Hammond complained, "Where shall we go to find the woods, the wild things, the old forests?"

"Had I my way," Hammond suggested, "I would make out a circle of a hundred miles in diameter and throw around it the protecting aegis of the constitution. I would make it a forest forever."

Such a plan would have produced a reserve of some five million acres, surely a romantic journalist's impractical fantasy. And yet, in time, the state of New York actually followed Hammond's advice. First, the legislature prohibited, in an 1883 law, the sale of state-owned forest lands; henceforth, the cutover land reverting to the state for back taxes could not be resold and would be designated as part of a "forest preserve." Then in 1892 the legislature established the Adirondack Park with a "blue line" encompassing all the bits and pieces of state-owned forest preserve land thus far accumulated, with the hope that more would be acquired. Then, finally, in 1894 the protective aegis of the constitution was indeed invoked by an amendment that would make these forest preserve parcels "forever wild." The famous words of this constitutional provision have ever since been a kind of talisman for New York State conservationists.

The lands of the State, now owned or hereafter acquired, constituting the forest preserve as fixed by law, shall be forever kept as wild forest lands. They shall not be leased, sold, or exchanged, or be taken by any corporation, public or private, nor shall the timber thereon be sold, removed or destroyed.

There was only one problem. As the twentieth century unfolded, the rate of tax-reversion land coming into state ownership (effectively at no cost) slowed and then finally stopped. One hundred years after Hammond first made his suggestion, the "forever wild" forest preserve parcels in the park aggregated only a bit more than a third of the six million acres within the blue-line boundary. The rest of it was privately owned forest. (Today the ratio is 42 percent public, 58 percent private.)

Despite the imbalance of public to private land in a region designated as a "park," a period of stability ensued in the Adirondacks. The forest-products industry, which owned most of the private land (as it does today), went about its business but now with modern and more responsible forestry practices. The wealthy enjoyed their elaborate Adirondack "camps" around the lakeshores in holdings often totaling thousands of acres. Vacationers from the underclasses who managed to straggle into the park erected their tents in the public woods and could fish and hunt with as much freedom as could the millionaires on their private preserves. The conservationists—the latter-day S. H.

159

Hammonds, which included the "father" of the American wilderness movement, Bob Marshall—were concerned about the divided ownership of the park during the first half of the twentieth century, but were by no means panicky. Recreational development pressure was light—wars and depressions saw to that—and anyway the mountains were remote, well removed from the urban moil of the coastal cities of the Northeast.

And then something happened. During the 1950s, postwar prosperity encouraged Americans to see the U.S.A. in the Chevrolet, and President Dwight David Eisenhower made it easy with the 1956 National Defense Highway Act. Ten years later, the gleeful highway builders produced a plan for an interstate from New York City to Montreal—I-87—that would skirt the edges of the park and instantly put fifty million people within a day's drive of the Adirondacks. That's when the privately owned land became a ticking time bomb in the bosom of the woods. Resource planners like George Davis knew it was only a matter of a few years before the checkerboarded tracts of private land throughout the mountains and around the lakes would be inundated with cabins and trailer courts and tourist-oriented commerce that would turn the great north woods into a tacky recreational suburb of the whole Atlantic urban region. Roadside viper exhibits, peepshows, miniature golf courses, and souvenir emporia with wooden Canada geese whose wings paddle in the breeze would prove beyond all doubt H. L. Mencken's assertion that nobody ever went broke underestimating the level of American taste.

This horrible prospect led conservationist Laurance Rockefeller (brother Nelson was then governor of the state) to conduct a study of whether and how the vulnerable, checkerboarded Adirondack State Park could become a *national* park. It seemed to Rockefeller and his staff that to have something called the Adirondack "Park" consist only of chunks of forest preserve land scattered around the north country was a misnomer and a misbegotten idea, given the likelihood that the uncontrolled and vulnerable insterstices, at 62 percent of the total, could, if developed, turn the entire landscape into a piece of Swiss cheese. The study was published in 1967, just before the Northway of I-87 was to open and the developers' assault would begin.

In sum, what the Laurance Rockefeller study proposed was the creation of a national park in the central, "high peaks" area of the Adirondacks that would involve a little less than a third of the land within the state park's "blue line." Some 1.1 million acres of state-owned forest preserve would be transferred to the federal government, and 600,000 acres of private land would be acquired in order to produce a wholly owned national park on the standard model, somewhat like the Great Smoky Mountains National Park in Tennessee. It would be a park for outdoor recreation and the "interpretation" of natural features, but no longer a living landscape in which the interleaving of public and private land uses would remain. Outside the boundaries of the new national park, presumably on the remaining two-thirds of the original state park, commercial tourist riches were promised. The plan projected increased "visitor days" and computed the vast economic benefits stemming from them. (The authors did not mention any drawbacks of this kind of development, as is evidenced in the tawdry "gateway communities" outside many national parks, especially the garish commercial strip at the Gatlinburg, Tennessee, entrance to Great Smoky.) The staff plan also suggested, gently, that the National Park Service was much better at the job of administering an area such as the Adirondacks than state-level bureaucrats, especially when they were so hampered by the rigidities of the constitutional "forever wild" provision on forest preserve lands. And, it further suggested, New York State could never get the money to complete the acquisition of significant tracts within the blue line anyway.

The key finding was this: "Laudable as the Adirondack Mountains State Park program today may be, continuation of it under present authorization, procedure, and funding provides no guarantee of ultimate success in consolidating the public land holdings and *actually creating a park*" (emphasis added). Clearly Laurance Rockefeller's experts, having never studied the British national park system, could only conceive of a public park in terms of a real estate transaction to achieve fee-simple ownership, followed by the removal of residences and businesses, bulldozing areas for parking lots and campsites, contracting with concessionaires to provide log hotels and stores and gas stations, and an advertising campaign to attract the tourists.

At last here was a proposal for the Adirondacks about which everybody could agree: it was a lousy idea. The Rockefeller report not only insulted long-established hegemonies, but was also thought to be utterly without merit throughout the state by conservationists, loggers, developers, state and local officials, and very nearly everyone else. Laurance Rockefeller backpedaled quickly. Three months after his plan came out he said, "I now wish we had made it more clear just what this proposal is. It is a study by a group of citizens with no official standing. It was prepared and released to stimulate thinking on an important issue—not to railroad anyone into anything." Such a statement was of course disingenuous. The power of the Rockefeller family in the state of New York over the generations, the fact that brother Nelson was now governor, and the almost dictatorial influence that Laurance Rockefeller and his family had on the Department of the Interior as the donor of a great deal of national park land suggested a railroading effort, whether fully intended or not, of epic power and potential.

But the outcry seemed to work—not only to scotch the Rockefeller plan, but to coalesce the conservation forces in the state (and nation, for that matter) to figure out a way to keep the six-million-acre Adirondack aggregation of forest preserve land, timber industry land, private, noncommercial holdings, and villages and towns whole and well protected in the bargain—to make it into a different kind of park than anyone had ever seen before in the United States.

This vision is what persuaded the then-governor Nelson Rockefeller (who understood a political typhoon when he saw one) to establish in 1968 a Temporary Study Commission on the Future of the Adirondacks. The two-year study concluded (in 1970) that the Adirondack Park needed regional land-use regulations and the firm hand of a state-level planning authority to implement them so that ill-planned development on the private lands would not destroy the entire region or vitiate the public values of the forest preserve lands accumulated over the past one hundred years.

Specifically the commission recommended that

• an independent, bipartisan Adirondack Park Agency be created by statute with general power over the use of private and public land in the park (as defined by the blue line);

• the agency should prepare a comprehensive plan for the park;

• the agency should have planning and land-use control powers over the private land in the park;

• local governments should have a role in planning and zoning in their jurisdictions, reflecting their legitimate interest in private land uses;

• the agency should coordinate its work with other state and regional agencies with planning interests in the park;

• the agency should have planning power consistent with the provisions of Article XIV of the state constitution (the "forever wild" article that protected forest preserve lands) over state-owned land within the park subject to mandatory consultation with the state's Department of Environmental Conservation;

• the administration of state-owned land within the park should remain with the Department of Environmental Conservation;

• and, pending the completion of a comprehensive land-use plan for the park, the agency should have interim powers over any new development within the park that was deemed to have parkwide signficance.

Throughout the country, the proposal was seen by government planners and academic experts as being a true breakthrough with powerful implications for preserving large landscape areas in other states. In the wooded villages of the Adirondacks, however, it was seen as a powerful invasion by state authorities of their sovereign local rights over a landscape that they believed belonged not to planners and conservationists but to those who sawed the trees, ran the motels, and built the second homes.

Since the proposed Adirondack Park Agency would greatly reduce the hegemony of local governments and scotch the plans of the big second-home developers, the opposition was fierce. Yet, despite enormous political pressure from Republican business interests which thought the Adirondack Park Agency idea anathema, Governor Rockefeller took the cause of the Adirondacks to heart. And he prevailed. In 1971 the Adirondack Park Agency Act was passed into law and a limited moratorium on further building was imposed, pending the creation of state-mandated land-use regulations. It was, many felt, Nelson Rockefeller's finest achievement in his long career in government.

In short order, the agency was a functioning body and began creating a plan that would severely limit future development in the park. The planning director was George D. Davis.

The plan Davis and the Park Agency created dealt with all the land within the blue line, but was most controversial in its provisions for limiting the development of the park's private holdings. After all the compromises had been made, it was settled that a limit of fifteen buildings per square mile would be imposed on "resource management lands" (53 percent of the private land), a limit of seventy-five buildings per square mile would be imposed in "rural-use" areas (34 percent of private land), with the rest (13 percent of the private land) given more liberal development limitations. In effect then, this meant that better than half the private land would be zoned for one dwelling per 42 acres, and for almost a third, one dwelling per 8.5 acres.

The only problem was that in haggling with the opposition, the agency found that to maintain a truly low development density in the resource areas of the park, largely commercial forest, the trade-off required was to relax restrictions on waterfront development and development in and around villages and hamlets. Indeed, the final regulations did not permit the agency to regulate the settled areas at all. As for waterfront restrictions, twenty-six buildings per shoreline mile in the "resource management" category were allowed, thirty-six per mile in "rural use" and on up to 106 per mile in hamlets—effectively a building every fifty feet.

The planners, including George Davis, were terribly worried that this trade-off of lakeshore and hamlet densities for the more rigorous limits in the remote sections would effectively make "sacrifice areas" of the most visible parts of the park. Still, they figured, at least the forest-resource and rural-use lands would be beyond the reach of developers. They were half-right. The lack of tough regulations did create some uglified sacrifice areas, especially around Lake George. They were wrong about chasing out the developers. In fact, during the 1980s developers found that they could actually market land profitably for recreational use even at what amounted to forty-two-acre zoning. The most notorious example was the sale of ninety-six thousand acres, sight unseen, acquired from a British corporate raider named James Goldsmith by Henry Lassiter, an Atlanta developer, for $17 million. This was the so-called "Diamond International-Lassiter Deal" into which the state of New York belatedly entered to buy some of the land back, at greatly inflated prices. The effect of the deal, along with a good many other real estate shenanigans, was galvanic—as galvanic as I-87 had been fifteen years before. Once again, it was time to act. Clearly a crash program was needed so that the Adirondacks, as New Yorkers had come to know and love them, would retain the character many thought had been insured by the original plan. Thus was the Commission on the Adirondacks in the Twenty-first Century created, and George Davis was asked to take on the job of executive director.

The new plan proposed by the commission was a complete tightening-up of the policies promulgated by the original Park Agency plan of the early 1970s. But there was more. Indeed, the Twenty-first Century recommendations added an entirely new dimension to the conservation policy debate about the park. The dimension, as George Davis described it to me, was that the new land-use regulations should reflect an "economic focus" that would be complementary to the environmental one. "In the Adirondacks," said Davis, "the region's economics are based on the forest products industry. But we're not talking about simply hauling away logs on flatbed trucks; we've also got to create an important secondary hardwood manufacturing capability." In addition, he would like to encourage the permanent settlement of people who can make a living as independent enterprisers or as telecommuters working from home, people who would contribute to the economy as well as strengthen the community, not just feed off it.

All in all, Davis's vision—and that of the Twenty-first Century commissioners—was, as he put it, of a "real landscape, not a tourist mecca, a place where the communities are honest communities, not just a bunch of chambermaids and waitressess working for resorts and restaurants, not a place where service people can't afford to live where they work. I want a real-people place as well as wilderness and biodiversity."

In this approach to planning, even though in an area of great natural beauty, tourism is well down on the list rather than at the top as an economic consideration, Davis said. The commission determined, no doubt correctly, that tourism and the second-home development that comes in its wake is a problem, not a solution, for the Adirondacks. For the woods to stay intact and the landscape to remain beautiful and the real communities to survive, the last thing you need is condos on hillsides and millionaire mansions on ridges or along the shores.

Despite this enlightened approach, the Twenty-first Century plan seems to be in for an even rougher trip than the earlier Park Agency plan, which was rough enough. When I visited the Adirondacks back then in 1973, some of the hot-headed back-woods types, incited by logging and development interests, among others whose economic ox was about to be gored (they thought), promised to "set fire to the woods" before they would allow any kind of restrictions on land use. Park Agency personnel were directed not to take official state vehicles into remote areas, lest they run into a nasty situation involving young indigenes with too many beers in their bellies. The week before I arrived, a truckload of horse manure had been dumped on the lawn outside the Park Agency's headquarters at Ray Brook, New York. A crudely printed sign was stuck into the steaming pile: "We've Taken Enough of Your Shit, Now Here's Some of Ours."

In time of course such reaction subsided and the Park Agency plan was grudgingly accepted—even by developers who, having brought scores of lawsuits on the "taking" issue, finally gave up, not having won a single one of them. The plan was rock solid and well buttressed by scientific fact and economic and sociological analysis.

It was hoped, therefore, that the new Twenty-first Century plan would not encounter the kind of awfulness experienced fifteen years before. But the hope was misplaced. Shortly after the unveiling, rowdies surrounded the house of a young executive of a local conservation group that had supported the new plan, shining lights and honking their horns. A swastika was painted on an office door, and out on the Northway, a group of pickups carrying protest signs drove abreast at twenty-five miles an hour, slowing Montreal–New York traffic for miles. For a spell George Davis, who was making audiovisual presentations of the plan in the town halls and school auditoriums in the region, had to have a state police escort.

Given all the antipathy, Governor Mario Cuomo, unlike his predecessor, Nelson Rockefeller, decided to distance himself from the recommendations, at least until the immediate reaction died down. (A year later, he would propose a much watered-down version.)

Many Adirondack conservationists believe, however, that this was not a spontaneous outburst of citizen displeasure, but part of a campaign financed largely by the real estate interests whose activities had led to the formation of the Twenty-first Century project in the first place. This was not just a bunch of good ol' boys in pickups. A quite sophisticated effort was mounted by means of a media blitz and sustained political pressure reminiscent of the National Rifle Association's approach to influencing public policy. It was the publicity and the organizing, rather than the redneck boisterousness, that has worried Adirondack conservationists the most. And so they remain: worried.

As for Davis himself, his work in the Adirondacks, along with other achievements that have characterized a brilliant career in conservation, earned him a MacArthur Foundation "genius grant"—a no-strings-attached stipend intended to give recipients the opportunity to follow their own star, at least for a while. For Davis, the star led to Siberia, where he is undertaking studies of forest ecology and conservation. This is getting away from it all with a vengeance. But he'll be back. People who love the North Country, as Davis does, always come back. And when he does the chances are good that he'll keep doing what he can so that this great living landscape will be all that he ever wished for it—or almost.

GREENLINING

The Santa Monica Mountains are a fragment of the Pacific Coast Range that runs close to the sea to the west of Los Angeles and comprises a forty-six-mile green wedge into the great urbanized basin itself. Griffith Park, the city's largest park, is in the range. Malibu, the famed seashore colony of filmdom, lies at the foot of the mountains. Mulholland Drive, a scenic roadway of some notoriety in the days when teenagers still went in for "parking," winds through the ridgelines and valleys.

A 1972 study of the Santa Monicas by the Bureau of Outdoor Recreation identified a 230,000-acre area of seashore, solitary canyon, and scenic vista, finding that 191,500 acres were as yet uncommitted to urban land uses. The study was the result of the Interior Department's focus on parks "where the people are," spurred by the "Gateway" national park projects in San Francisco and New York City. Civic leaders in Los Angeles, ever mindful of asserting their status as an important city, not just a big one, had been putting on the pressure since 1964 to make the Santa Monicas a unit of the national park system. The federal study did not, however, think the area would be an especially good candidate—not really national park material and too expensive to boot.

In 1974 Senator John V. Tunney, ignoring the report, introduced a bill to make the Santa Monica Mountains and seashore a "National Urban Park." The bill would have given broad authority to the secretary of the interior to secure specific areas of the mountains and seashore and to work with local and state government for the control of the remainder. It called for a two-year fund of $30 million per year, with other "necessary funds" to be appropriated thereafter to acquire about 100,000 acres—roughly half of a 202,000-acre designated area. The necessary funds were likely to be high. Back-country land was running to $2,000 per acre at the time, and shoreline property at

$2,000 a front *foot*. The Interior Department's report on the bill was negative, echoing the position taken in the 1972 BOR study. "Protection of the outdoor recreation, scenic, and historical values of all the Santa Monica Mountains," said Interior's statement, "can best be effected through a comprehensive effort in which the federal government's role is to provide technical reinforcement."

Two important questions were raised by the Tunney bill and the Interior Department's response. First, was the area "significant" enough nationally to be designated a national park? And second, where was the money to come from? The total cost had been estimated to be anywhere from $100 million to $1 billion. The lower estimate was suggested by proponents of national park status, the higher by those not so persuaded. In the face of an edict by a new president, Gerald Ford, that there would be "no new funding" for domestic programs, the outlook for the Santa Monicas looked grim.

In an effort to steer some kind of course between the Scylla of increasing demands to preserve such landscapes as the Santa Monicas, and the Charybdis of no-new-spending, Senator Bennett Johnston of Louisiana, chairman of the U.S. Senate's National Parks Subcommittee, introduced a different kind of park legislation calling for an absolute limit on federal money, some $50 million, rather than a "blank check," as he put it. A more significant difference, however, was that Johnston's bill called for the use of the whole battery of land-use controls to be the primary means to protect the landscape. The $50 million was for incidentals. The controls, in Johnston's words, would range from "simple zoning, to noncompensated and compensated easements, to easements of view, to easements of drain, to space limitations on buildings . . . just a whole lot of things that can and should be done, new frontiers."

To implement such a program, Johnston's bill required the establishment of a planning commission that was to be appointed by the governor of California and the chief executive officers of local units of government. The commission was to prepare a plan for the approval of the secretary of the interior whereupon it would be awarded the $50 million to get the ball rolling.

In reaction to this approach, California's secretary of natural resources declared that the state didn't need any lessons in how to create an organization for "managing a series of parks, reserves, and recreation units in the mountains," and that the real need was for "federal assistance in financing the acquisition and development of the units."

The problem with the response was not that it was ungrateful or unsupportive. It was that the Californians completely misunderstood the basic thrust of the Johnston bill. That California would be unable to undertake the task of park management was not an issue. Rather, the question was, would California be willing to use its land-use control powers to preserve the Santa Monica Mountains and seashore more or less *whole?*

More broadly, the misunderstanding made plain the philosophical differences between the hard-recreationists who would buy, develop, and operate pieces of land for various outdoor programs and activities, and the landscape conservationists who would preserve sizeable landscapes on the basis of their inherent landscape values.

In the case of the Santa Monicas, it was the *landscape* that counted. The need for urban recreational sites could scarcely be satisfied by this area, which was on the edges of the metropolis, not in the middle of it. The idea of buying it all up was neither socially necessary nor financially possible. And a partial purchase might prove to be ruinous. At the time of the debate of the Johnston bill, some forty thousand acres were owned by government agencies and public-interest organizations in the Santa Monica Mountains areas—about 20 percent of the total. Even if a *hundred* million dollars were appropriated for acquisition, it was doubtful that the preserved acreage could be increased much beyond 40 percent—not even that unless the federally purchased lands were augmented by gifts and state and local acquisitions. After the money was all gone, the preserved sites would still be discontinuous (as in the Adirondacks), and the unpreserved interstices—constituting the bulk of the land area—would, if uncontrolled, lead to the destruction of the values of what had been acquired at great civic effort and monetary cost. And, doubtless, development pressure would increase because of the éclat added by national park status. Who would not want to buy a homesite in a national park that was within commuting distance (albeit a long one) of L.A.? That was the problem the Johnston bill was trying to avoid.

It is the interstices between publicly owned sites that present the most difficult problem in the management of aesthetic, cultural, and recreational landscape areas—greater even than the money for land acquisition or for public-facility development. Johnston's approach presumed that there is a species of "public rights" in landscapes such as these that flows from the nature of the land's form and features, the kind of development it has historically sustained, and the traditional perceptions as to its value as a resource by its owners and users. And so it was the landscape itself that ought to be protected. This concept is the core of the Adirondack legislation, the Pine Barrens legislation, and Britain's National Parks and Access to the Countryside Act of 1949, which accepts the fact of continued private ownership (in the Lake District, only 25 percent of the land is owned by the quasi-public National Trust) and provides for paths and trails over private and public lands alike. Other than that, the private land is private, although strictly controlled to maintain recreational, historical, ecological, and scenic values.

In the mid-1970s, with Bennett Johnston's Santa Monica bill as a case in point, policy analysts drew on the Adirondack and the British experience, reaching for a concept (which would later be applied to the New Jersey Pine Barrens) that could protect outstanding landscapes wherever they might be without having to settle for the not-enough-money and interstices syndrome.

Based on the Adirondack history of the "blue line" and assuming a certain modern latitude in color choice, such areas began to be termed "greenline parks"—coherent landscape areas with outstanding public values that were (or could be) partially owned by public and quasi-public agencies, but for the most part would consist of unspoiled land still in private ownership. Such areas as these had routinely been proposed to Congress as potential National Recreation Areas to be administered by the National Park Service. But this was a kind of compromise, for most of them, like the Santa Monicas, were not cut out for intensive recreation, nor did they need to be owned and managed wholly by the federal government, nor did their indigenous populations and businesses have to be removed for them to retain their public values. And yet without federal participation, many such areas would be lost forever before the inexorable spreading of what Lewis Mumford once called "low-grade urban tissue"—whether from metropolitan expansion or recreational development.

And such landscapes are *everywhere:* the dramatic, unglaciated topography and old-timey villages of the "driftless area" in southwestern Wisconsin and northeastern Iowa, for example; the Oachita Mountains in Arkansas, celebrated by radio's Lum 'n Abner and their Jot-'Em-Down Store; the Laurel Highlands of Pennsylvania; the Big Horn Basin in Wyoming; the San Juan Islands in Washington's Puget Sound—a list might well go on for pages and even then miss a local treasure (as we shall see in the concluding essay of this chapter) uncharted on the policy analysts' maps.

For those who would prefer their scenic landscapes whole—a group that includes not only users, but owners who would not wish to be dispossessed of the land by having it turned into a traditional recreational park—the greenline concept offers a way to protect a landscape but use it too. As an exercise that is today only partly speculative—since the Adirondack experiment has succeeded (although not perfectly, as we have seen), as has the Pinelands National Reserve in New Jersey—it might be appropriate to describe how "greenlining" can work for other landscapes for which no similar legislation exists.

(Ironically, Johnston's idea was rejected for the Santa Monicas. Instead, at the insistence of local environmentalists and others who distrusted the greenline approach, Congress went ahead and established a "Santa Monica Mountains National Recreation Area," but with a limited amount of money for land acquisition. Some greenlining principles were introduced, but the "interstices problem" was not solved and the future of the mountains is still very much in doubt.)

———

Here, then, are the technical aspects of greenlining as it might now be applied.

To begin with, it is perhaps easier to identify a potential greenline park generally than it is to decide where to draw the green line. In the Adirondacks this was and had been a partly technical and partly political process, depending not only on geological and ecological landscape coherence, but also on local willingness to be included or excluded. In the Pine Barrens, the line could generally be determined by a soils analysis and by a long history of ecological research. The lesson to be drawn from the greenlining experience so far is that geomorphology is perhaps the best initial guide.

Another question: Who would administer such greenline areas? Here, the Adirondack experience is helpful (and indeed provided the model for the Pinelands): a special state commission, answerable to the state legislature, was established. (In the Pinelands, the commission has an ex officio seat for a representative of the Department of the Interior, since a major grant was made for planning and for some acquisition by Congress.) It drew its authority from, in part, an existing state-level department (Department of Environmental Conservation) and directly from the state constitution for its land-use control powers. Importantly, the Adirondack Park Agency was not a "council of governments" kind of planning body, although local government has retained an important policy-framing role as well as an administrative one. The same is generally true for the Pinelands Commission.

The critical issue in the matter of land-use regulation is to what extent the state governments—to which land-use control powers belong—can recapture the regulatory initiative they have delegated to localities. This was the crucial legislative issue in the Adirondack Park Agency Act. It was difficult to get state legislators, who spring from the political soil of local government, to vote away local land-use control hegemony, even in someone else's locality. Nevertheless, in the Adirondacks as well as the Pine Barrens the alternative was even less appealing—the potential destruction of a highly valued landscape resource.

The basic administrative organization for a greenline park would be a state level commission, established through legislative enactment and drawing its powers over land uses from those that inhere to state government in a federal system. If the federal government is to have a role in the enterprise, then it would be included on the commission but would in no way be given control. While local governments might be represented on such an administrative body, they probably should not be able to affect its decisions too easily since they are the most vulnerable of all officials to the blandishments of local development interests.

Given an authentic candidate for a greenline park and administrative body to plan and manage it for its public values, how would they go about it?

In Senator Johnston's discussion of his legislation, he described a full array of land-use management techniques that should be used in addition to the fee purchase of selected areas for intensive recreational use. The idea of using all available techniques in concert has long been a fixture in the literature of park, recreation, and open-space planning. It was emphasized, for example, in the landmark study *Outdoor Recreation for America*, the report of the Outdoor Recreation Resources Review Commission (ORRRC) established by Congress in 1958 which has been a standard reference ever since. Listed in this report, beyond the government's ability simply to buy land in fee simple (by eminent domain if necessary, by negotiated purchase if not), are "less-than-fee rights, leases, licenses, salebacks and leasebacks, zoning, mandatory land dedication, and cluster development."

There has been some sharpening of these concepts, and some new administrative wrinkles unanticipated by the ORRRC authors. But it is remarkable how conceptually sound their report remains after all these years.

_____

In planning for a greenline park, the easiest and most familiar of all the "tools" is fee-simple acquisition, which in greenlining is used primarily for the purchase of heavily used recreation areas or areas that must be managed strictly for ecological reasons. These purchases can and should be augmented by gifts of land, most typically for less intensive forms of recreation such as fishing, bird-watching, and hiking. The augmentation may consist of gifts of land to the administrative authority itself, or to quasi-public organizations set up for the purpose. In the United States, the Nature Conservancy, the Trust for Public Land, and a host of other organizations, many of them local "land trusts," serve this purpose. In England, where the government owns none of the national park land, the quasi-public National Trust fulfills the need for managing land for recreation and other public purposes. The trust works closely on a policy as well as management level with national and regional park authorities. Similarly, nonprofit organizations in the United States can focus their efforts within greenline areas, coordinating with the administrative body in a mutually supportive way. It is generally believed that some 50 percent of American parkland is acquired through donation. If the percentage holds for greenline parks, then the public dollar devoted to fee-simple acquisition can be doubled, or perhaps even better, since nonprofit organizations can be encouraged to concentrate their efforts within the greenline area.

Associated with fee acquisition, either through condemnation, negotiated purchase, or donation, is the acquisition of affirmative easements—positive rights in land for recreational use. State and federal agencies have long purchased recreational rights of land, most commonly fishing rights and trail rights-of-way. Within a greenline park these limited rights can powerfully augment the "chunks" of land acquired in fee by providing linkages via watercourses and trails—the so-called greenways. Moreover, such greenway access rights may be donated as well as purchased. Sometimes easements, or rights, may be acquired in perpetuity or sometimes limited to a number of years. In England, trail easements ("access agreements" under the terms of the National Parks and Access to the Countryside Act) that augment footpaths already in the public domain are negotiated with landowners, frequently on an annual basis. In New Jersey, the state has inaugurated a program to encourage trail access across private land by providing special management services and liability insurance to the owners. The trail rights are secured via an "access covenant" usually for a term of five years.

Besides affirmative easements that provide for trails and the like, there are also "negative easements" that do not permit public access but do restrict the owner of the land from undertaking any action that would degrade the public value the easement is intended to protect. Typically, in most public parks—national, state, and local—only a fraction of the land is intensively used, in many cases only 5 or 10 percent of it. The rest is ambiance or, as the ORRRC report put it, a "recreational environment." It would hardly be logical then for the public to deplete its treasury to buy land in fee simple within the greenline, or pay for public access, when physical public access is not really necessary.

To solve this problem, the ORRRC report and all studies since have recommended "scenic easements" (a form of negative easement) that are appurtenant to public roads, trails, and park sites, and "conservation easements" (also negative) to secure to the public the maintenance of natural processes that might not be sufficiently controllable through the ordinary exercise of the police power (that is, zoning and other land-use regulation). Such easements are often donated to public or quasi-public agencies. In the Adirondacks an easement on Elk Mountain, part of the vital visual backdrop of Blue Mountain Lake, was donated some years ago. In other areas, states and localities have secured conservation easements—sometimes called "development rights"—to protect wetlands, agricultural lands, and other valued resources. There are nongovernment easement programs as well, such as landowners banding together to convey conservation easements to a nonprofit land trust to insure in perpetuity the maintenance of a high-quality natural resource, such as a free-flowing stream. Frequently, nonprofit land conservation organizations will purchase land, place a conservation easement in the deed, and then resell it, as often as not recouping their original investment.

These negative easements, some appurtenant and some in gross (that is, not connected to a public land holding), do not permit public access. They do not preclude changes of land use within certain limits. They are not extinguished by conveyancing since they can "run with the land."

Of all the control techniques, the acquisition of some or all the deeded rights in land are the best understood and publicly accepted. Less common and therefore subject to misapprehension are the specialized control techniques that derive from what in land-use law is called the "police power"—which is the power vested in governments to regulate the uses of land for public health, safety, and welfare. The actualities of contemporary land regulation vary from state to state and from court to court, though the judicial trend since the "Earth Day" 1970s has seemed to be toward a liberal constitutional interpretation of the right of governments to use the police power to regulate land for environmental purposes. For this reason, the greenline concept may be an even more realistic option today than it was when the Adirondack Park Agency began its work in 1971, at least insofar as the lower courts are concerned. The Supreme Court may be another matter, in view of its radical turn to the right in the late 1980s and early 1990s.

In general, however, what the Adirondacks and other greenline areas have shown is that if land-use regulations are thoroughly grounded in sound ecological, economic, and social research, and are persuasive in terms of the public interest, there is a legal basis for them to be sustained even though they may seem economically disadvantageous to some private owners.

Even though rigorous controls, permit requirements, and other constraints on large-scale land-use changes may be a justifiable use of the police power, there is still the need to avoid a draconian exercise of it. For this reason as well as ecological and aesthetic ones, the Adirondack Park Agency Act permits the clustering of dwellings in all land classifications, and most other greenline areas encourage it. In the Adirondacks, the owner of a thousand-acre parcel in the "rural use" areas, where the minimum lot size is eight and a half acres, need not create 118 eight-and-a-half-acre lots with all the interior roads, powerlines, and other infrastructure this implies. Rather, these 118 dwellings can be clustered on the part of the site most suitable for development and not require expensive and destructive public-service infrastructures. Such a procedure preserves the rural-use potential of the property as well as its aesthetics, but allows an owner to undertake a development program appropriate for his or her land.

An extension of the clustering concept is the actual "transfer of development rights," not just within a single-ownership property as in clustering, but involving properties that are discontinuous and in different ownership. TDR, as it is called, has been an important tool for greenlining since it permits governments to bar development in critical areas but avoid a "taking" of property without compensation. Landowners within a restricted area can apply "lot credits," derived from preexisting zoning regulations, and apply them to properties outside the restricted area either directly or by selling them to a developer or a government development-rights "bank." TDR is the principal means by which the unique natural areas of the Pine Barrens are protected and in that context has worked well.

When the foregoing techniques are boiled down to their essentials, they are really only three: various forms of fee acquisition, various forms of "intermediate" preservation involving less-than-fee rights, and various forms of controls deriving from the police power. What is essential in their application in greenline areas is to use them comprehensively, flexibly, and fairly. Of utmost importance is to use them in ways that are appropriate to demonstrable public purposes. This means thoroughgoing research, using the most sophisticated land capability analysis possible. This procedure is precisely what has given the Adirondack Park Agency and the Pinelands Commission a sense of equanimity when faced with court challenges.

Most land-saving texts include a message on property taxes as a means to control inappropriate changes in land use. The tax approach—that is, differential assessment—is a murky subject at best. While tax abatement in return for not changing the use of land—from farmland to subdivision, for example—may buy a little time, such an inducement would work best in concert with a more permanent means of stabilizing land uses: through zoning, various development approaches such as TDR, or the use of architectural controls in historic districts. Nevertheless, in some cases private land within a greenline park might well be assessed at a lower level than surrounding areas as a means to encourage cooperation and compliance among private landowners in the overall plan for the protection of the area.

In addition, a fifth kind of land-saving technique, while extrastatutory, may still be effective. This is simply administrative jawboning. Within the green line, certain appropriate landownerships can be induced—such as low-impact commercial establishments that could produce design interest as well as employment, or fractional site coverage that would add to the open-space "feel" of the area or provide a service or focus of interest that would be appreciated by visitors and adjacent owners. Obviously such enterprises as plant nurseries might fall into a category like this, as would certain kinds of indigenous industries, such as the furniture and wood-products manufacturies envisioned by Adirondack planner George Davis. Country-house restaurants and inns would be appropriate too within the green line and would likely be a more salutary land use than another housing development. Though such park-enhancing land uses are difficult to produce legislatively, a greenline park authority might well set up institutions to encourage these kinds of enterprises. The long-term effect can add an important aesthetic and recreational dimension to the area. In the Adirondacks, for example, the first chairman of the Park Agency, Richard Lawrence, has been instrumental in preserving a rail line into the mountains, which helped to open up the park to non-car-owning users as well as reduce pressures to widen roads or construct new ones. In the Pine Barrens, the indigenous cranberry industry is encouraged by authorities. In the British national parks, commercial organizations are keen to preserve and enhance "park values," often recommending commercial regulations (on signage, for example) that individually might cause hardship but collectively help to increase the economic value of their enterprises.

A final point. A greenline park authority may have splendid powers devolved upon it by a state legislature and may even create a magnificent plan but have the whole business blow up in its face because of a public relations failure on the part of its staff. There is much to learn from the British experience in this regard. There, park officials are few and unobtrusive and enforce the regulations the same way. They prefer to let an irate landowner close a trail than to win a battle but lose the diplomatic war with all other owners. A keen sense of flexibility is required. In the Adirondacks, park managers are obliged to deal not only with outraged landowners when they must deny a building permit, but also with an outraged town government. This requires a personnel policy for the selection of middle-level professionals that goes well beyond training and experience and into quality of character. In regulating land uses from large subdivisions down to granting permission for an ancillary building in a restricted area, the Adirondack Park Agency staff learned the hard way that extraordinary self-restraint and courtesy is required, that imaginative solutions persuasively presented are a necessity. They learned, in short, that typical bureaucratic authoritarianism just doesn't work. Once this is understood, the staff for a greenline park can negotiate for the purchase of land, encourage land donations, secure trail and fishing easements, and mollify landowners and local officials regarding necessary restrictions so that complaints do not show up in the courts either as nuisance suits or as major constitutional challenges.

Perhaps the idea is well enough along so that we may try for a definition, in two parts:

1. Greenline parks are sizeable landscape areas, still in a relatively natural condition, that are designated by state legislation for planning and management on a comprehensive basis. Consisting of 25 percent or more of public or quasi-public land holdings (which tends to validate the public value of the area) in the form of state and local parks, nature sanctuaries, youth camping areas, and the like, greenline parks are a *mix* of public and private land controlled and managed to maintain their existing aesthetic, cultural, ecological, and recreational values. These values are ascertained and protective measures devised by rigorous landscape assessment research.

2. Authority to acquire land or right in land, to designate recreational uses for existing public land, to regulate uses of private land, and to implement comprehensive development plans consonant with public landscape values is lodged in a state agency, set up for the purposes by the state legislature and provided a regular budget to carry out its work. The planning and management agency would consist of individuals living within and without the park boundaries, and include as well ex officio members of appropriate state agencies and in special instances agencies of the federal government. County and city governments would, by legislative mandate, be consulted frequently on parkwide policy, and planning would have to be coordinated with local planning bodies.

For many the greenline approach as described above has seemed to be a kind of second-choice option, a way to protect areas that for one reason or another can't be protected through outright purchase by state government or the National Park Service. Such is not the case, however. Greenlining is meant to be applied to landscapes much too large and too culturally varied for any kind of single ownership or management philosophy. For such landscapes the idea of buying up the acreage and getting everyone to move out would not only be unaffordable, it would destroy the *life* of the land that in areas such as the Adirondacks and the Pine Barrens is as important as the topography and the natural features. This is why greenlining is thought by many to be the best, if not the only, means to preserve and manage our outstanding living landscapes. That only a handful have been identified and protected so far is a pity.

DIME COUNTRY

A friend of mine, David Plowden, who teaches at the Illinois Institute of Technology in Chicago, and I are crouched over several road maps of the Middle West. They are flattened out on Plowden's Winnetka, Illinois, coffee table. We are trying to decide where we can spend the next couple of days in a piece of authentic American landscape—not for any high professional purpose, just as tourists, though perhaps in an old-fashioned sense of the word. We have something more rigorous in mind than sightseeing.

Plowden is asking, "Well, where do you want to go?" He has a crackly, enthusiastic voice, vaguely British—which is logical since he is the son of an English actor, but a grandson of an American captain of industry, the lawyer who put together the Burlington Northern Railroad. Plowden is well into middle age, with a sweep of gray hair that touches his collar and the beginnings of a bay window, which on him looks prosperous in a nineteenth-century way. That figures too.

"I don't know," I answer. "Where do *you* want to go?"

"Well, you're the visitor. You decide."

"But it's your part of the country," I remind him.

"How about Indiana?" He points at it. "You want to go to Indiana?"

"What do you think?"

"Maybe downstate Illinois," Plowden suggests. "You like downstate Illinois?"

"Sure, whatever."

"Wisconsin?"

David Plowden knows that to see the land truly, to understand it, you have to get *into* the landscape. Into a real place. That's why I had called him on the telephone, long distance. I was benumbed by Washington's endless statistical analyses of land, including my own analyses. At the time I was writing about the annual loss of some three million acres of rural land in the U.S. to urbanization, a statistic with a vague sense of menace. I longed to take a look at a real place in rural America—the kind of place that represented the countryside we were so afraid of losing. So I asked Plowden to take me to some sunburnt slab of countryside that he particularly liked. We cut a deal; he wanted to get away for a couple of days too. A week later, I hopped a flight to Chicago. O'Hare. Busiest Airport in the World, according to the flight attendant, who announced the fact in capital letters just before landing.

Plowden, who has published nearly a score of books, documents the American land. But he is not a numbers man, an analyst of the statistics of urbanization or foreclosure or other current rural event. He is instead a respected landscape photographer, working mainly in black-and-white. He believes that the land is best expressed by letting it show you what it is. He believes that the surfaces of things can tell you more than you think they can. And the surfaces he likes best these days are those of the American Middle West, his adopted home.

The prospect of the trip had sounded terrific when we talked about it over the phone. But now on the ground, in suburban Chicago, I began to wonder if my idea wasn't just silly. We couldn't even decide on what state to go to, much less find some place that would be exemplary of a living landscape in these precincts. Maybe, I thought, I should just ask Plowden to take me back to O'Hare the next morning and forget the whole deal. Our polite conversation about it seemed endless. Plowden's wife Sandra had long since padded upstairs to bed. We had a couple of beers. We had a couple more. We were not getting any closer to choosing a place where we could "get into" the landscape.

I was beginning to fade. The hour was late and I was still on East Coast time. In desperation I backed up from the map-strewn coffee table, drew a coin from my pocket, and throwing it onto the map said: "Wherever that lands, that's where we're going."

And so it was that David Plowden and I discovered Dime Country.

———————————

The dime covered approximately twenty square miles—a 12,800-acre circle centered on Section 26 of the Town of Lowell, County of Dodge, State of Wisconsin. Dime Country is at the apex of a flattish isosceles triangle whose baseline contains Madison on the west and Milwaukee on the east. It is just a three-hour automobile drive from suburban Chicago (in our case via Plowden's somewhat nondescript liftback sedan, painted a cheery yellow), but Dime Country is as close to an ideal landscape as any you could encounter in the Middle West. "By God, Little," marveled David Plowden once we arrived, "something must have been guiding your hand when you threw that dime."

We were, I found out later, in the middle of the largest drumlin field in the United States, a drumlin being a long, low mound of glacial till. Here as elsewhere they are in a cluster, oriented by the flow of the ice, marking the margins of the ice sheets. They give the flattish landscape both topographical interest and order. But this is not the first thing that catches our attention. Soon after crossing the Dime Country border, we chose a sectionline road to explore which ran straight through the gently swelling landscape, with its hugely long vistas, given form by shelter belts and alternations of plowed and greening fields, the whole punctuated by (usually) gray concrete silos, white houses, red barns. We came to the first settlement, Richwood, at the intersection of County Road Q and County Road K and a single-track right-of-way belonging to the Milwaukee Railroad. Richwood is a cluster of no more than half a dozen structures. A few houses, storage buildings, and, to Plowden's enthusiastic approval, Casey's Saloon, whose modern sign advises that in the evening one can catch a "live music" appearance of none other than Von Ripper and his rock-and-roll band. I try to envision such a band whose lanky-haired members haul feed in flatbed trucks, work in the cannery, run big green John Deere tractors. In the parking area there is in fact a huge tractor tire, perhaps six feet across, placed thoughtfully over a jutting outcrop of striated granite, too big to move, too small to be noticed by careless drivers who at the end of an evening with Von Ripper might well rip open a crankcase or tear off a muffler if they forget the location of the rock. All of this has tremendous meaning for Plowden, who is a student of cultural juxtapositions which, here in downtown Richwood, are unselfconscious, authentic, soothing somehow, and in a way beautiful. "Look at it," he says, and he is to say these words more than once, "The American Rural Scene. I love it! This is the idea of America." We are in the landscape.

Plowden is hunched over his Hasselblad, which is permanently affixed to a tripod so that we can come to a screeching halt anywhere and swing into action without delay. He looks through the viewfinder, moves a few feet, impatiently moves a few more, takes a fast reading with the light meter, cranks and fires, cranks and fires, perhaps a whole roll of twelve exposures at the sign for Casey's Saloon and its setting—down the road, across the fields to a distant farmstead, framed by the solitary maple in the adjoining yard. It is the combination of nature and culture and working landscape that has so many meaningful variations for him. He can scarcely fire the Hasselblad fast enough. And so he does not notice a newish station wagon, rear deck loaded with cardboard boxes of liquor, crunching softly into the parking lot of Casey's Saloon where Plowden is running about, locating his tripod for just one more. The driver pulls up abreast of me. He is looking very serious. He has a companion in the front seat, also looking serious. The companion has lanky blond hair. Maybe it's Von Ripper! I think wildly. With a hay hook. "You boys need something?" asks the driver levelly.

Just taking some pictures, I tell him.

"Why are you doing that?" Driver wants to know. "This is my place."

Oh boy. It is Casey! Meanwhile Plowden is loading up his gear in the back of his yellow car. He is moving slowly and deliberately, seemingly oblivious to the conversation going on twenty feet away. Plowden is going to let me handle this. "Well, uh, you see, that fellow over there. He . . ." (I have an inspiration) "he teaches photography." I say this in a tone of voice meaning to convey a sense of harmless eccentricity.

As it turns out, Casey and Plowden have a long and learned conversation about black-and-white documentary photography, who the principal practitioners are these days, and where the major exhibits are showing in New York City, Chicago, and L.A. Once in a while Casey looks over at me as if I were some kind of idiot. Later, Plowden observes that they were "nice fellas" and that we probably gave them a bit of worry: "Coupla guys like us," says Plowden. "One with a beard and the other with a wild look in his eyes."

About a mile down County Route G, we turn right on Walton Road, off the asphalt and onto a graded dirt lane that runs northward along the ridgeline of a drumlin. To the right the fields slope gently to the east, bisected by the Milwaukee Railroad track, then bottom out, then rise again, over a horizontal distance of perhaps a mile, to the next drumlin over. To the left, westward, there is a fallow field, dipping more abruptly from the crest of the lane down to a marshy wetland populated by elegant red-winged blackbirds who swoop confidently back and forth from reed to reed, their bright red and yellow epaulets flashing, catching the sun when it is out, seeming luminescent when clouds dim the scene.

It is one of those spring days when alternating patches of light and shadow move across the sweep of the land, dappling its fields and folds as the high clouds move eastward, not yet ready to gather for a storm but thinking about it. The spot is too good to drive by, so we stop again and Plowden leaps out to set up. Just as he is beginning to shoot we hear a lonely whistle. It is a train coming up the Milwaukee tracks, and Plowden is overjoyed, blooded to the railroad as he is. Soon enough the train appears in the distance. As it comes toward us in a long, gentle curve, the clouds part, sending a bright shaft of Wisconsin sunlight into the vale below. It is truly a magical moment. But Plowden, I notice, is not taking pictures, even though the train is moving slowly. "Will you look at that," he murmurs, almost to himself. I realize that Plowden has made it into another realm, transcending the camera. He is not just *in* the landscape, he has *become* the landscape. And so have I, here on the ridge of a drumlin on a high cloudy Wisconsin afternoon in Dime Country.

———

I am pretty sure that we traversed all the through roads inside our magic circle of rural America, and saw a good percentage of the farms. Dairy mostly, though Dodge County is also known for sweet corn and peas, which are canned locally. It is a proud place too—self-conscious to that extent. Only a few farms are not tidy, unlike those of some other parts of the country. Rusted machinery and rutted farm roads, though in evidence, were not usual. And yet these were not gentleman farms either, but working places that perhaps gave a whole living to a majority of its families. What I liked best were the signs on the corner of a field: "The Greiders, Bill and Mary," or "Schmidt Farm." Nothing pretentious, no signs saying something like "Journey's End" at the beginning of a long driveway presumably leading to a mansion. This was a landscape where people know the worth of the land—as land, not real estate—and the worth of themselves.

Poking through this landscape on the morning of the second day we come upon a truss bridge crossing the Beaver Dam River, where Low Road, Ghost Hill Road, and Fairwood Road join together. It is, to Plowden's amazement, an *iron* bridge, dated, it would appear, at 1880 and manufactured by the Milwaukee Bridge & Iron Works. Plowden tells me that the iron bridges went out a few years after that, to be replaced by steel. This one, he says, is a Pratt truss, pin-connected bridge, and since he has written and photographed a definitive book on American bridges, I am inclined to believe him. While he takes pictures, I go to the center of the bridge, which moves gently upon each step, and look upstream at the deeply swirling river. The waters are backlit, for it is still early, and the sun catches the ripples, making them turn from pewter to bright silver and gold. Wrens dart about the nooks and crannies of the ironwork. I can watch them from above, through the openings in the wooden plank surface. Their song, a long liquid downward trilling, seems to imitate the river, brightly coursing downward under the bridge and through the land.

Outside of Reeseville—a country town whose population might reach into the low hundreds, rather than the low dozens, as in Richwood—we come across a newish Lutheran church, rebuilt no doubt on the site of the old, for alongside it is a churchyard with weathered stones also set upon the ridgeline of a drumlin. The churchyard overlooks another flattish valley of alternating plowed patches and green strips. The differing lenses of the plowed soil reveal light gray, brown, black, the mix of glacial till brought down from northern distances unimaginable during the age of ice. The farmsteads, each with a silo pointed heavenward, spread into the distance, the silos repeating the shapes of the gravestones themselves. One gravestone reads: "Eva Barbara Steinacker, 22 July 1834, 7 Sept 1874." Dead at forty. A tragedy, but she had lived in the early days, born before Dodge had become a county, which was in 1840, born in fact before Wisconsin was even a separate territory in 1836. In those days its western boundary went all the way to the Missouri River, where Lewis and Clark had explored on into the Montana wilderness. By midcentury 300,000 people had come to settle Wisconsin, a third of them from Germany. Eva lived during exciting times. Though she did not speak English, most likely she would know that in this state the Republican party was born, that in this state fugitive slave laws were judged unconstitutional, that 91,000 went to war for the Union, and that in 1860 the greatest wheat crop ever was harvested. The importance of such events is strongly suggested by churchyards such as these, where Eva Steinacker along with Johanna Steindorf, Jacob Knearr, and Caroline Schwanitz are at rest. "Hier ruht in Gott," reads a stone.

———————

It is time to leave. We can put it off no longer. Back to the city of broad shoulders. We find U.S. 16, still a country road despite its federal designation, and it runs straight and traffic-free along the section lines southward through Dime Country, toward that curved border that was penciled on a map two days before. We are moving fairly fast, for the World's Busiest Airport awaits my custom. Plowden is honking his horn every few minutes.

I ask him why he is honking the horn. He says that he is honking at the birds on the side of the road. I ask what he expects the birds to do about it. "I want them to move out of the way," Plowden gently explains.

So I have to tell him that birds don't pay any attention to noise. It's the motion of the car that makes them fly. "Nonsense," Plowden says, and to prove his point he starts to honk at birds sitting high above the road on the telephone wires. They do not, generally, pay any attention.

I say, "See?" He says nothing, but keeps honking at the birds all the same. And as we head toward the city I begin to laugh and laugh until the tears come. Just edging in, as they do sometimes when you're laughing. Only this is different. Perhaps, beneath the mirth, I am afraid I shall never see such a place again. Or perhaps it is a sense of relief that at least this piece of honest countryside can still endure. But what of the other places? comes the counterthought. They too are landscapes to "get into," with qualities the statistics do not reveal. More dimes are needed: that is my resolution. For I have been to Dime Country, in the landscape of it, and now it is in me.

Forever, and ever. Amen.

V

THE LAND ETHIC

In the world of "land use," as the Washington conservation-policy types call it, there are two kinds of people, I have decided. There are those who talk about the land ethic and there are those who make land-use policy. It isn't as though the twain never meet, but they don't exactly connect on a daily basis, either.

This chapter, with brief passages about my own once-rural California valley by way of an introduction and a conclusion, deals with the idea of making a connection between the philosophy and the action of land conservation—a matter that was a central concern to Aldo Leopold, the man who has informed so much of this book. The land ethic, his great intellectual contribution, is on the cusp at last. I hope.

A LANDSCAPE OF HOPE

The land ethic of the future—and there will be no good future without one—will have to be an ethic not to serve the political economy,
but to provide for the care of land whether it is economic or not: an
ethic that advances the *land's* reasons for being. This is what Aldo
Leopold has taught us, and I believe it. But it's hardly the case at
present. In fact, as far as land is concerned, the present is a flop. If you
do not believe this, go home again.

I did.

At the foot of the San Gabriels' talus slope, where the vineyards
(and orange groves and truck farms) fructified in the 1930s, there had
been a narrow, two-lane concrete highway. A canopy of fragrant euca-
lyptus trees had shaded the road as it meandered through the valley
and shaded, too, the long, strung-out column of tramps looking to do
chores for food in those days when there was no money. They came to
our settlement along California State Route 118, a wide place where
there was a grocery, and a post office, and Jack's gas station, and even
a tiny library. In springtime the tramps would come through the gate
of our bright-green picket fence to sit on the back steps of our old
house, a block off the highway, and eat a sandwich my mother had
prepared for them. I would watch them from my perch on a low limb
of the great pepper tree that shaded the yard, and they would say,
"Howdy boy," to me, like Woody Guthrie. And, "You some tow-
head, you are," in a thick drawl from Oklahoma or Arkansas or the
Texas Panhandle, and then they'd tip their hats and say, "Thank you
Ma'am," to my mother and wink at me and be on their way to the
next little town along the highway where produce trucks and flivvers
stuffed with furniture and children and hope chugged along in some
dance choreographed by the economics of the land in those years.

The hope was the amazing thing. And the faith: faith that new land could be found that would not wear out and turn to dust.

Eventually I found our old house. For I wanted hope too. But the bungalow's stucco was now mottled and flaky, the pepper tree gone, the picket fence with it. The house itself was standing precariously on the edge of a cliff—a cliff of concrete surmounting a freeway, a new six-laner which now cut through my valley.

I looked down on the three eastbound lanes where, I think, Mr. Lee's place was, a small chicken ranch now hovering in memory about twenty feet above the streaming traffic. I wondered where all this machinery was going and had a vision of the great river of cars disappearing at the edge of the earth after a million miles of shopping centers, eroded fields, pastures grown to brush, suburban-kitch office buildings, clear-felled forests, drive-in banks, dammed rivers, muddy lakes, festoons of high tension wires, and Wendy's and Hardie's and Arby's disappearing into a taupe-colored distance.

Mr. Lee had always told us not to put our finger through the chicken wire lest the Leghorn rooster, who was cranky, would come peck at it. And so we would put our finger through the chicken wire, and rooster would come and peck it, and we would yowl, and Mrs. Lee would give us a cookie.

Aldo Leopold wrote when I was two: "To build a better motor we tap the uttermost powers of the human brain; to build a better countryside we throw dice."

Zoom zoom zoom go the cars along the freeway. We put our fingers through the wire. We roll the dice. The land disappears. Mrs. Lee is no longer there to give us a cookie. And Mr. Leopold is dead.

IN SEARCH OF EDEN

At this late date in the millennium now ending we are embarked on an environmental search—a search for spiritual meaning as well as all manner of natural causes and effects. In the conduct of this enterprise it is essential that we get at the philosophical and literary roots of what we are about.

In this connection it has always seemed to me that the land-saving movement is, you might say, a movement of repressed Romantics. During the Lyndon Johnson Administration when I got my start as a full-time conservationist, the catch-phrase was "natural beauty," courtesy of Ladybird. It was astonishing how many of us tried to resist that kind of nomenclature even while embracing it, for our theoretical base was supposed to be utilitarian. This resulted in an approach to landscape preservation that relied on the quantity of recreational use rather than the quality of personal experience. User-days were counted, recreational needs were researched. The heretofore placid, synthetic science of ecology was rung in to demonstrate, for instance, that land-clearing causes erosion, erosion causes siltation, siltation causes disequilibrium in the hydrological system, which causes flooding, which causes excessive costs in the enterprise of flood control, to say nothing of the rather sticky problem of washing out downstream communities. Bulldozing this particular tract would not, therefore, produce the greatest good for the greatest number. So went the logic in service to a natural environment.

Soon economists were recruited to determine the real costs of environmental destruction. Computers hummed, clattered, printed out. Lawyers developed new rationales for land-use regulation, behavioral scientists measured the psychosocial impact of crowding in cities, ethologists studied animal behavior to give us clues to what *homo sapiens* would do when ultimately deprived of individual space. Into such hard-core conservation, intellectual, unemotional, comes a flower-lover from Texas with "natural beauty." Natural *beauty?* We thought we had left all that nonsense behind. This was the province of silly Wordsworth, as we had called him in college. We were involved with the complexities of land-use law, with ecology, with econometrics, with social effect, and Ladybird was calling our manly, rigorous enterprise "natural beauty." We tried to laugh it off. Once at a party in Washington, D.C., somebody handed me a guitar and we all sang a mocking song—"Do your duty by natural beauty"—country-style, straight out of Texas border Radio Station XELO, Juarez, whose sins against our urbane rationality included commercials for tulip bulbs along with Plastic Jesuses that Glow in the Dark and Last Supper Tablecloths. There was something similarly tasteless, we thought, about voicing a concept of "natural beauty" among the physical and social scientists, the planners and lawyers, the tough-minded administrators of government agencies and research organizations.

During that time I would take many walks with my son, who was and still is a lover of swamps. There was a particularly moist place we often visited, which in springtime produced, along with the musky swamp-smell he claimed to like, marsh marigolds peering out from the mould, glowing gold on a cloudy day of early spring, illuminating the rotted bark, the winter-worn grasses, the disintegrating leaves of other seasons. In one place there was a spring-rise, running cleanly through melting snow before it entered the stream below. But there amid the marigolds a stake with a plastic ribbon tied around its top had been driven into the yielding earth. My son wanted to know why somebody had put such a stake there and what it meant. I said it was probably surveyors, that the land would soon be subdivided, that houses would be built, that ditches would be dug to draw off the swamp water so basements would be dry. "They can't," he said. "How can they do that?" He was twelve. I told him about property rights. "Yes, but not this place." Why not, I wanted to know. "Well, they *can't!*" he explained, and put both his hands out as if to touch the scene, at once to enter it and to let it enter him.

Next Eastertime, go down to the drugstore and buy one of those frilly eggs with the little window embedded in one end. Put your eye to the peephole. You are now observing a version of the Edenic myth. There you are in the Garden and it is warm, and there are little lambs, and flowers, and a little cottage where you live, when you are not playing beneath the blue sky, watching the high white clouds.

All of us search for our own Edens. And some can find it in

landscapes that others find inhospitable. My son found it in a swamp. Joseph Wood Krutch believed the desert to be a garden, not a wilderness: its plants well spaced, the air peaceful and bright in most seasons, the animals varied, going calmly about their individual ways, integrated with their surroundings. That such were phenomena deriving from scant rainfall was immaterial. Krutch contrasted this peaceful scene against the summer growth of the Northeast: competitive, vinous, confusing layers upon layers of vegetation in constant battle for soil and sun. It reminded him of the argumentative clamor of cities.

The Edenic myth has dominated our public and private responses to landscape and is the tap that plunges down through the ages to the very beginnings of sentient beings. Throughout human history, from Sodom and Gomorrah to midtown Manhattan, we have attempted Edenic artifices to bring us relief from the necessity of society. In the broadest terms there seem to be three main historical Eden-substitutes as a compromise between our need for society and our need for seclusion: the garden, the pastoral landscape, and the wilderness.

"The garden is the perfect human habitat," Paul Shepard tells us in *Man in the Landscape.* "So far as there is one paradise for all men, all gardens in all times and places are alike; their peculiarities measure the unique experience of each society as it confronts nature."

One of the first peculiarities appeared in ancient Persian cities, where artificial mountains were covered by hanging gardens. The Greeks created hunting parks; Alexander devoted one quarter of Alexandria to that purpose. Baghdad, says Shepard, had "nearly a thousand little walled gardens with fountain, court, plants in boxes, mechanical trees and birds, and scented blooms." In later times there was the garden of the cloister and of course the ceremonial garden such as Versailles or the garden of the Governor's Palace in restored Williamsburg. In England the king's parks became public gardens. In the eighteenth century the English set about to make virtually their whole island a kind of natural garden—pastoral, as called for by Spenser, and before him, Virgil; not too wild, but natural. Thus a landscape sensibility emerged that transcended earlier, totally organized relationships with the out-of-doors, which had produced geometric rearrangements of nature's materials, as at Versailles. During the nineteenth century, gardens were created in American cities, most notably Central Park in New York. Frederick Law Olmsted used English landscape techniques. The park's topography was made, not preserved, as a close look at its construction will show. Its waterfalls are carefully designed and built, its ponds and plantings more the result of Olmsted's fertile imagination than of God's. The walls of this garden and others like it are the structures of the city—the high-rise apartment buildings that line the perimeter.

The second artifice of compromise between society and solitude is what Thomas Jefferson called the middle state. This is the rural landscape, replete with placid hoofed livestock, meadows, copses, sparkling brooks, and farmhouses with friendly smoke curling from the chimneys. The pastoral image was first implanted in Western consciousness by Virgil, whose *Eclogues*, says literary historian Leo Marx, are the "true fountainhead of the pastoral strain in our literature." Virgil's middle landscape was the rural band that separated the noisome city— Rome—from the fearful wilderness. One of Virgil's protagonists, Tityrus, returning from the wars, is granted a patch of rural land as a reward for his faithful service to the state (an event that can be compared to the GI Bill, which provided, for nothing down, suburban bungalows in the potato fields of Long Island). The pastoral life, then, is conferred by the government as the best life of all for the weary veteran.

"The good place," says Marx, "is the lovely green hollow. To arrive at this haven it is necessary to move away from Rome in the direction of nature. But the centrifugal motion stops far short of unimproved, raw nature. . . . It is located in a middle ground somewhere 'between,' yet in transcendent relation to, the opposing forces of civilization and nature."

This ideal pastoral landscape has been celebrated more in literature than in life. But upon discovery of the New World by Europeans, optimism that such a dream could come true produced not only a literary effusion, but a political imperative. One of those who took the ideal seriously, and tried to apply it, was Thomas Jefferson. Jefferson wished to forge a nation of free people whose gentle art was tillage, and who would live out the pastoral ideal. He believed that such a life would produce an enlightened and participating citizenry which would be very nearly self-governing and wholly democratic. Writes geographical essayist J. B. Jackson: "The key passage in Jefferson's denunciation of the city and praise of the country is undoubtedly the phrase: 'The country produces more virtuous citizens.' What he prefers to urban society is not rural solitude but rural society; the type of man he wishes to encourage as opposed to the urban citizen, oppressed by wealth and corruption, is not simply the rural inhabitant, it is the rural citizen, an active and effective participant in the political life of his community."

The thought that a whole nation could be comprised in its largest part of the middle landscape—of small, self-reliant communities of enlightened agrarians—dies hard in the United States. Only recently has the ideal of the "family farm" been called into question in our national political rhetoric as a life-style worthy of federal support. But the pastoral ideal has been picked up in modern times by utopian "back-to-the-land" youngsters who embrace agrarian self-sufficiency in rural communes. Unlike the family farmers, however, they are not liable to receive a government subsidy.

The third kind of compromise-Eden is what might be called the wilderness retreat. This too ranges back to our earliest history. Perhaps the best-known advocate was Jesus of Nazareth, who spent forty days and forty nights in the wilderness and returned to society the better for it. Retreat from the city was the answer for the English Romantics as well. Shelley described London as a Hell. (Actually the reverse: "Hell is a place very much like London.") Blake viewed it as a place of "mind-forg'd manacles," and so convinced was William Wordsworth that the city had nothing to offer that he rarely visited London. Wordsworth described the city as a "monstrous ant-hill" filled with a "deafening din," whose private courts were "gloomy as coffins" and whose lanes were "unsightly labyrinths." After the briefest of stays, he fled to his beloved lakes at the opposite end of England.

If the roots of modern environmentalism are to be found in the Romantic Movement generally, then our antecedent in the matter of the primacy of the natural landscape in the shaping of the human spirit is to be found in Wordsworth's robust response to the landscape of the Lake District. "I loved whatever I saw," he recalled in the *Prelude* of his childhood there,

> . . . nor lightly loved,
> But most intensely; never dreamt of aught
> More grand, more fair, more exquisitely framed
> Than those few nooks to which my happy feet
> Were limited [.]

In maturity he saw no limits to the power of the transforming landscapes:

For the discerning intellect of Man,
When wedded to this goodly universe
In love and holy passion, shall find these
A simple produce of the common day.

For Wordsworth nature was dynamic and vigorous, to be met frontally, with the imagination fully engaged. Approached in this way, senses alert, one could be led by nature *back* into a kind of primal God-awareness; or *down* into a sense of self; or *outward*, for, as he asserts, the love of nature leads to love of man. For Wordsworth it was not the natural environment as such that produced a sense of God, self, and love, but the man-nature relationship—a creative, dynamic act of will that seemingly came from both man *and* nature. In Tintern Abbey he wrote of the green earth—the mighty world of "eye and ear"—as being half created and half perceived. He was concerned not with nature, nor with man, but with the creative fit of nature and man. "How exquisitely," he wrote in *The Recluse,* "the individual Mind to the external World Is fitted," adding significantly, "and how exquisitely too The external World is fitted to the Mind."

As befits such a progenitor of environmental ideas, Wordsworth could be concrete on matters of land use and preservation. In 1835 he published a geography called *Guide to the Lakes,* a fourth revision of what had started out as an introductory text to a folio (1810) entitled "Select Views in Cumberland, Westmoreland, and Lancashire," containing drawings by one Reverend Joseph Wilkinson, whose artistic effort Wordsworth considered "intolerable" and whose intellect he described as "not superabundant in good sense." The pictures are long forgotten; the essay lives on as, in the estimate of many, still the best guidebook ever written. Wordsworth worked to create "a model of the manner in which topographical descriptions ought to be executed" and succeeded so well, according to Matthew Arnold, that a "naive ecclesiastic" once inquired of the poet if he had ever written anything else.

Ernest DeSelincourt, compiler of Wordsworth's works, observes in his introduction to a 1906 edition of the guide that "if the poems are the first-fruits of his labours, there are few pages of the *Guide* that do not bear eloquent witness to the same watchful eye always upon the object, the same reflective energy and penetrative imagination." While in his poetry Wordsworth sought, as he wrote in his Preface to the *Lyrical Ballads,* not "individual, local truth but general, operative truth," he felt no such lofty inhibitions in the *Guide*. Indeed, he was not above mundane—but important—conservation concepts. "In the economy of Nature," he suggests in a description of tarns, "these are useful, as auxiliars to Lakes; for if the whole quantity of water which falls upon the mountains in time of storm were poured down upon the plains without intervention, in some quarters, of such receptacles, the habitable grounds would be much more subject than they are to inundation."

Elsewhere Wordsworth decried the plantations of larch, a nonindigenous tree, and observed that letting nature alone can produce a "wild and irregular boundary . . . graceful in its outline, and never contemplated without some feeling, more or less distinct, of the powers of nature by which it is imposed."

It can be said, perhaps, that the Lake District gave us Wordsworth, much as Wordsworth has given us the Lake District, and through it a key to the Edenic secret. He lived there for all but three years of his life, and his affection for the area led him to propose, as I pointed out in an earlier chapter, that it be preserved (accomplished finally in 1949) as a "sort of national property, in which every man has a right and interest who has an eye to perceive and a heart to enjoy."

And Henry David Thoreau gave us Concord, an exurb, twenty miles by rail from Boston, then and now. As environmental rootstock, Thoreau was close to the trunk of the American experience—even to the point of anticipating the wholesale landscape destruction that was to come to it in the twentieth century. By the time he was born—in 1817—Wordsworth, at forty-seven, had already published the greatest of his poetry, with the exception of the *Prelude*. Thoreau owed much to this poet of the lakes, and other British Romantics, but his references are scanty and often allusive. In *Walden* he calls the pond-studded landscape of Concord's environs "my lake country." In a "Walk to Wachussett," an essay written in 1843, Thoreau tells of reading Virgil and Wordsworth in his tent during a rainstorm. "Nor did the weather prevent our appreciating the simple truth and beauty of Peter Bell," he records, quoting a few lines of an oft-parodied poem that some Wordsworthians wish could be expunged from the poet's oeuvre altogether.

Thoreau's relationship with the natural environment has been described as part and parcel of the Romantic Movement of Germany, France, and England. To be sure, the Thoreauvian tendencies toward individualism, toward the idealism of Plato and Kant, as well as his passion for direct experience in wild nature as a creative act are basically Romantic. But to consider him simply as an American version of Wordsworth, a provincial imitation of a "lake poet," is to lose his utility for us in our search for those elusive environmental roots.

Emerson said of him: "No truer American existed than Thoreau." And this was so not only because of Thoreau's disdain of continental foppishness, as Emerson suggests, but because Thoreau's scorn was also directed at his own countrymen, who were even then choosing a path that would lead ultimately to the brink of ecological disaster and social disintegration. Thoreau demonstrated to his fellow citizens what he considered to be a better life, spending two years and two months in a hut near the shore of Walden Pond. Even then he saw emerging in America what a hundred years later would be called a society of "organization men."

Thoreau could also see industrial urbanization approaching. He heard it screeching out of Boston, defiling a pure countryside. "That devilish Iron Horse," he wrote,

> whose ear-rending neigh is heard throughout the town, has muddied the Boiling Spring with his foot, and he it is that has browsed off all the woods on Walden shore, that Trojan horse, with a thousand men in his belly, introduced by mercenary Greeks!

He knew that the ear-rending neigh spelled the end of the Jeffersonian middle state—that orderly agrarian landscape between city and wilderness which was to become the mythical setting for the American Dream, the pastoral community of enlightened yeomen of the new world. But Thoreau did not believe sentimental pastoralism to be the answer. He chose instead the landscape of wildwood.

> Our village life would stagnate if it were not for the unexplored forest and meadows which surround it. We need the tonic of wilderness, to wade sometimes in marshes where the bittern and the meadow hen lurk, and hear the booming of the snipe; to smell the whispering sedge where only some wilder and more solitary fowl builds her nest, and the mink crawls with its belly close to the ground. At the same time that we are earnest to explore and learn all things, we require that all things be mysterious and unexplorable, that land and

sea be infinitely wild, unsurveyed and unfathomed by us because unfathomable. We can never have enough of nature.

What should not be overlooked in this passage is that Thoreau did
not want the wilderness to be separated from the town by some fanta-
sized pastoral scene, but to share a common border with it. The town
should give way immediately to untrammeled, unmanaged nature: not
a linear sequence of town, country, wilderness, but town into wilderness—just like that. Agriculture, to Thoreau, was nothing but a form
of commerce, part of the economic system, not productive of a sublime landscape or even an ideal vocation leading to a life of civic
purity in thought and deed as Jefferson proposed. In fact Thoreau was
much embittered by the kind of farmer of his town who loved not
"the beauty of his fruits, whose fruits are not ripe for him till they are
turned to dollars."

Thoreau was not a simple rusticator, however. "I left the woods for
as good a reason as I went there," he wrote. "Perhaps it seemed to me
that I had several more lives to live, and could not spare any more
time for that one." He was in fact a man of the town, extraordinarily
learned, needful of the company of Emerson and his Concord circle, a
Harvard graduate so skilled in Latin and Greek that he translated the
verse of his favorite poets into English. Thoreau needed Boston as well
as Concord. Emerson relates how Thoreau once went to borrow books
from the Harvard library only to find that a library rule prohibited
loans to graduates living beyond a ten-mile radius. Incensed, he ap-
pealed to the president of the college, making a case that the railroads
had destroyed the old scale of distance, that the library was the only
good thing about Harvard to begin with, and that he needed a great
quantity of books. Wrote Emerson, "The President found the peti-
tioner so formidable, and the rules getting to look so ridiculous, that
he ended by giving him a privilege which in his hands proved unlim-
ited thereafter."

There has been a tendency to visualize Thoreau as some kind of
New England mountain man, an ascetic avatar of primitive America, a
virtual hermit of the deep wilderness, Daniel Boone, Lewis and Clark,
and Natty Bumppo all rolled into one, rather than the urbane man of
letters that he was. To be sure, Thoreau climbed the local hills and
gloried in them; he was until the last years of his life extraordinarily
healthy and vigorous; he could outwalk as well as outthink most of his
neighbors. But his view of the primitive fastness of the American

continent differed altogether from his view of the wildwood surrounding Concord. Historian Roderick Nash tells us that the wilderness of Maine "shocked" Thoreau. "Even more grim and wild than anticipated," Thoreau wrote, "a deep and intricate wilderness." Thoreau described Mount Katahdin as "a place for heathenism and superstitious rites—to be inhabited by men nearer of kin to the rocks and wild animals than we."

Indeed, Thoreau celebrated not those distant, uninhabited primitive areas that so entrance the wilderness lover of today, but the unmanaged landscape at the margins of towns such as Concord. Given the abutment of town and wildwood that Thoreau argued for, a town could raise "not only corn and potatoes, but poets and philosophers for the coming ages."

In a phrase, he wanted the best of both worlds: the town when he needed it for employment, for intellectual stimulus, for socializing, for the libraries and the lecture halls; and the wildwood when he needed it for reflection, for synthesis, for "fronting" the elemental facts of human existence and a dynamic relationship with nature.

The *modus vivendi* that Thoreau worked out may have meaning for us today. He called it the "border life." As he put it:

> I live . . . on the confines of a world into which I make occasional and transient forays only. . . . Unto a life which I call natural I would gladly follow even a will-o'-the-wisp through bogs and sloughs unimaginable, but no moon nor fire-fly has shown me the causeway to it.

It was clear to Thoreau, just as it is clear to today's office worker or factory employee, that a full-scale retreat into nature was neither practical nor possible. And while Thoreau might have wished it otherwise, he wasted little time in lament. As a realist he was obliged to accept, and make the best—which was very, very good—of what was given to him, and to promote his views to his fellow citizens. Unlike Wordsworth, Thoreau offered a resident of Concord (and by extension, everyone) not just a discussion of, but a prescription for, a full and creative life. Wordsworth, absorbed by his poetical reflections on nature (described as the "egotistical sublime" by Keats), had little time to relate his findings on the relationship of society as a whole to "the land" in a way that would lead to improving the prospects for both.

Yet, Wordsworth, as demonstrated in *Guide to the Lakes*, had the desire to do so. Indeed, his response to a scheme to extend a railway line from Kendal to the edge of Lake Windermere was to argue that the rude masses from the city untutored in the arts of nature appreciation could get nothing out of a sojourn to the Lake District, and would do better to stay at home. The Lake District, Wordsworth believed, was a suitable vacation spot, worthy of preservation, but only for those born with "pure taste" or those willing to acquire it.

This was not Thoreau's way. He was, if anything, a reverse snob, especially in matters of life-style, preferring those who approached life openly and with inquiry and honesty; he abhorred pretense and sham. He was a populist and a democrat, in contrast to Wordsworth's British liberalism. Thoreau preferred the company of poor farmers to that of rich ones; he did not believe that "pure taste" had anything to do with station or that its conscious acquisition was necessary. Instead, he prescribed woods and swamps for everyone, as a necessity. Indeed, he feared that private ownership of the woods and swamps might someday preclude the open, free use of a landscape by anyone who would wish to roam as freely as he did:

> At present, in this vicinity, the best part of the land is not private property; the landscape is not owned, and the walker enjoys comparative freedom. But possibly the day will come when it will be partitioned off into so-called pleasure grounds, in which a few will take a narrow and exclusive pleasure only,— when fences shall be multiplied, and man-traps and other engines invented to confine men to the public road, and walking over the surface of God's earth shall be construed to mean trespassing on some gentleman's grounds. To enjoy a thing exclusively is commonly to exclude yourself from the true enjoyment of it. Let us improve our opportunities, then, before the evil days come.

For Wordsworth, the Lake District was a geography that could produce poetic imagination and a deeper, individual sense of God, self, and human perfectibility. For Thoreau, Concord was a geography that could produce social good. In both cases, the landscape was a figurative one. Both men wished to encompass the whole of the human condition and show how this condition could be affected by a creative joining with nature. Their differences in approach and in their conclusions are, perhaps, less important than their consecutiveness.

Wordsworth told Thoreau: "One impulse from a vernal wood May teach you more of man, Of moral evil and of good, Than all the sages can." And Thoreau replied from the shore of the New World: "A town is saved, not more by the righteous men in it than by the woods and swamps that surround it."

———————

The book of Romantic nature—whether expressed in the urban gardens of Alexander or Olmsted, in the pastoral dreams of Virgil or Jefferson, in the retreat of Wordsworth or the wildwood border of Thoreau—was, by the middle of the nineteenth century, beginning to close. Neither Wordsworth nor Thoreau lived to see the velocity of change that industrialization produced. Romantic nature was without a voice. And the town was not going to be saved, at least not by woods and swamps.

The towns soon became industrialized. The simple yeomen of the middle landscape either "starved to death on a government claim," as the song goes, or went west to break the sod. After the brief flurry of urban park-making by Olmsted and other designers during the latter part of the nineteenth century and early part of the twentieth, the cities were not to be known by their parks but by their tenements. The wilderness gave way before axe and plowshare to such an extent that it was thought prudent to reserve some of the more outstanding areas as national parks, beginning with Yellowstone in 1876 (a stirring of Romanticism here). National forests were set aside in the 1890s, though not to save towns with their scenery but to build cities with their products. Under Gifford Pinchot, the father of American forestry, the basic idea was hardly Romantic, but utilitarian: "The greatest good for the greatest number for the longest time." New ways of apprehending woods and swamps emerged.

In 1859 Charles Darwin published *The Origin of Species*, describing nature in terms of impersonal evolutionary mechanisms and random mutability in conflict, it would seem, with the natural theology of Wordsworth and Thoreau. Karl Marx added his own kind of determinism with *Das Kapital* and dialectical materialism, which predicted the unavoidable struggle between the bourgeoisie and the masses. Sigmund Freud provided a *coup de grace* to any thought that a retreat to the vernal wood could be ennobling. Such an idea was, as Leo Marx points out, astonishing to Freud. "How has it come about," wondered the great psychoanalyst, "that so many people have adopted this strange attitude of hostility to civilization?" For him, leafy Eden-substitutes were a pathological avoidance of reality.

Such turnings in the history of ideas did not abolish the delights of gardens, meadows, or the wildwood, of course, but the efficacy of these surroundings in solving social problems—as proposed by those of a Romantic persuasion—was questioned. In the face of the abuses of industrialization and its great destructive powers, the search for a quasi-Eden was almost academic. The new imperative was to solve the immediate problem—the dehumanizing of society by the machine— not to suggest ways in which we could find a border life or be provided with gardens, rural landscapes, and a wilderness. And that, for the time being at least, was the end of it.

One cannot distinguish between what is cause and what is effect at this juncture. Did the rampant industrialism of the last half of the nineteenth century drive out the notion that a spiritual relationship with nature could ennoble humanity and preserve nature from decimation? Or did the new deterministic philosophies of Marx and Darwin and Freud convince our great-grandparents that our fall is permanent, and perfectibility a myth that only the fuzzy, the futile, and the fallacious would indulge in? "Things are in the saddle," Emerson said, "and ride mankind." Did we have a failure of imagination—or perhaps a failure of faith in the values of imagination—that began in the dark ferment of the century past, and whose products are natural processes that no longer work? What agent fouled the air and water and created a landscape inhumane not only for the blighted souls of city and mill town, but for everybody? Did the momentum of greed, of twisted utilitarianism begun a hundred years ago, lead then to the wars that have so preoccupied this century? Did the wars in turn perpetuate a historical aberration? Strong minds will grapple with such questions for centuries to come. Perhaps they will better understand why *we* have become an environmental "planetary disease."

In the war between the personally perceived natural environment— productive of truth, beauty, and ennoblement—and the application of the utilitarian philosophy to the "resource base," Romantic nature lost. Not only did it lose, it was banished and largely forgotten. In Charles Dickens's *Hard Times* (1854), a bitter satire on utilitarianism, the Gradgrind School, operated by Master McChoakumchild, is described as

all fact . . . the relations between master and man were all fact, and everything was fact between the lying-in hospital and the cemetery, and what you couldn't state in figures, or show to be purchasable in the cheapest market and salable in the dearest, was not, and never should be, world without end, Amen.

I can recall that some people looked at the television program *All in the Family* when it first appeared some twenty-five years ago and rooted for Archie Bunker, nodding their heads in approbation at the mean-spiritedness he represented, agreeing with his vision of the world, believing their own bigotry and stupidity to have been vindicated, wholly unaware that they were watching a satire. I can imagine that some laissez-faire industrialists may have read Dickens with the same obtuseness. There are in fact people like that. Some will cling to dangerous prejudices until they are finally made to see. Others are afflicted for life and rule the world in the bad times of our history. They control educational policy, manipulate the economic machinery, become elected to high political office by appeals to hatred and by organizing majorities whom they can persuade to accept their own paranoic views. At such times those who believe in ideas, imagination, truth, beauty, and the essential spirituality of nature and its creatures tend to keep their heads down and, without making a public point of it, try to co-opt the prevailing beliefs to support a more enlightened point of view.

By the late nineteenth century it was no longer possible to celebrate an individual relationship to nature as one which would produce "poets and philosophers." Rather, the relationship was to be one which would produce products and profit. Very well, if those are the rules of the game, said the nature lovers; then we will play by those rules rather than not at all. Thus a concept known as "resource conservation" arose, which drew its authority not from Virgil, or Wordsworth, or Thoreau, but from George Perkins Marsh.

Marsh suggested that "environmentalism"—in the traditional sense—was not the overriding factor in our relation to nature. Environmentalism held that nature's power was such that it molded the human species and its society, just as it molded other species, into a shape that was complementary to, rather than competitive with, its inherent processes. Not so, said Marsh. In the more advanced periods of human existence on earth we had learned how to "derange" nature's "original balances." Accordingly, he set about to describe the dangers of imprudence and the necessity of caution in all operations which on a large scale interfere with the spontaneous arrangements of the organic or the inorganic world; to suggest the possibility and the importance of the restoration of disturbed harmonics and the material improvement of waste and exhausted regions.

Marsh's book *Man and Nature* was originally published in 1864 and is still in print. It is important to emphasize that Marsh's purpose was not aesthetic; he was not interested in the ennobling aspects of natural balance. "My purpose," he wrote, "is ... to make practical suggestions."

Resource conservation became the art of reconciling a Romantic view of nature and all its implicit values with the requirements of a society that did not believe in those values: to show how the preservation of the woods and swamps would benefit the town in ways the townspeople would understand, such as reducing the costs of flood control. One dared not talk of natural beauty or of impulses from a vernal wood. One spoke of woods and swamps as "resources," thus implying economic comparability with, say, a coal mine. Once, some years ago, I met a young ecologist at a time when I was practically the sole employee of an outfit known as the Open Space Action Committee. I was, I thought, in the business of saving woods and swamps. I explained what we were trying to do and indeed he found it very interesting and worthwhile.

"How long have you been in resource work?" he asked.

Does such philosophic deception make any difference? It does. In the effort to co-opt the pragmatic modes of utilitarianism to justify woods and swamps, resource conservation can so miss the point that the effort tends to be short on logic, myopic, ad hoc, and without reference to historical roots or a genuine philosophical base. One sometimes wonders if the proponents of parks, open spaces, and wilderness have not been trained themselves at the Gradgrind School by Master McChoakumchild.

———

Now let us return to Aldo Leopold and revisit a quotation from *A Sand County Almanac* (1949). He wrote:

In our attempt to make conservation easy, we have made it trivial. . . . When the logic of history hungers for bread and

we hand out a stone, we are at pains to explain how much the
stone resembles bread.

The logic of history requires gardens in our cities, a pastoral landscape aesthetic in our suburbs, and unadulterated wilderness for retreat. We have precious few of these. Is that because we do not make a
particularly convincing case for them? Who is it who does not see?

In the city we have created open spaces that not only fail to improve the urban environment but actively increase its tensions. Some
of these are city parks, usually at greater distances from those who
need them most as opposed to those who need them least. Others are
in housing projects—a no-man's-land of greensward and chainlink
fence. The fruit of such gardens is broken glass, the flowers spray-can
graffiti.

A friend of mine once spoke with Sergio, a nine-year-old Puerto
Rican boy from the South Bronx, a place that makes the Upper West
Side of Manhattan, where I once lived as "an urban pioneer," look like
Beverly Hills. Sergio was asked if he had ever been to any large state
parks. He shook his head, no.

"Well, they're sort of like Central Park, but bigger."

"Never been to Central Park neither," said Sergio.

"Never? Have you been to any park?"

Sergio nodded slowly.

"Where?"

"Here," Sergio said. "On the block."

"What do you do, on the block?"

"Sometimes we open the hydrant," Sergio answered. "When it's
hot."

There was a wisdom in Sergio that had eluded those benefactors
who would provide fenced grass and here and there an asphalted
quadrangle called a park. Sergio understood *place*. His place and therefore his park was the street, but no one chose to understand that or to
make it a garden. They chose to make it a parking lot instead. The
practice persists for cities to subsidize the middle-income owners of
automobiles with free parking facilities along the curbs of streets—
public land that comprises anywhere from a quarter to a third of the
total land area of a city. A thousand gardens for Baghdad, but none
for the South Bronx. Affluence has a curious way of expressing itself
these days.

Those who can, desert the city, like Virgil's Tityrus, in search of the middle landscape, the Jeffersonian ideal. In the early suburbs, well-to-do families who wished to reestablish a meaningful relationship to the land could create their own pastoral landscape. For the rest of us, Frank Lloyd Wright proposed, seriously, a "broadacre city." Each American family would have a miniature family farm, the Jeffersonian dream achieved for those who might be so inclined. But the population doubled, and as the city could not sustain a dignified life all those who could wished to make the American dream come true—if not on rural estates, then on half-acre or quarter-acre lots.

To the amazement of practically everyone, the "lovely green hollows" could not always be subdivided. Tiny—or even sizeable—house lots, when laid side by side, tended to replicate that from which the people had fled, the city. Thus the concept of "open space" was created and sent in to do battle with the housing developers, beginning in the 1950s. The federal government on the one hand offered VA and FHA mortgages to encourage single-family lot subdivision, and on the other tried to mitigate their destructive effect by subsidizing comprehensive land-use planning and by offering to help suburban communities buy land away from the developers with open space grants. The result was, and is, a landscape of ticky-tacky punctuated by green blobs that are called parks. The parks are neither gardens nor natural areas, by and large, but lands often burdened with the trappings of the outdoor recreationist. There is no sense of a pastoral landscape—a landscape that might have been perfectly possible had narrowly construed resource conservation not led to fatal compromise. For it was in the 1950s, 1960s, and even the 1970s that the civic leadership of suburbia promoted large-lot zoning as a defense against "Bronxification," as it was called in suburban Westchester County. Open space advocacy as it was then practiced entailed prohibitions on land use rather than an opportunity, well within grasp in those suburban places not yet overdeveloped, to preserve the pastoral essence. Even now open space is by and large preserved only when its economic practicality can be demonstrated. The pastoral dream has been abolished by the theories of McChoakumchild.

Having failed to direct our energies toward the historic imperatives of an appropriate relationship with nature in the cities, which cry out for gardens, and in the metropolitan countryside and the exurban rural regions where a kind of modern pastoralism might have been achieved, it would seem that the third landscape imperative ought to have a chance for success. Wilderness retreat should not be too difficult for a nation once so rich in wilderness. And yet even this has eluded us. Protected wildernesses are still an extremely small percentage of our public lands, and around their perimeters, as around the national parks, the old forests are being felled at an astonishing rate as tourist development spreads its tawdry artifacts to the very borders of these sacred places and sometimes reaches within them.

And thus, thanks to McChoakumchild, modern environmentalism, looking about and finding nothing but bad news, became strident, hysterical, and apocalyptic. It is an understandable phenomenon, for no one really takes a nature lover seriously, even now. Accordingly, crisis mongering is the mode, and though the crisis is real the pejorative style dulls the effect. Paul Ehrlich has offered doomsday population projections for the past twenty years. Barry Commoner lays down ecological laws of environment which a world would disregard on pain of extinction. The late Rachel Carson, who perhaps more than any other of the new wave brought home the message of ecology to the living rooms of America, implied imminent collapse in the DDT-poisoned biosphere. Ian McHarg, a landscape architect and town planner turned ecologist, has constructed a complex system of restraints on development that makes Leviticus look like the bylaws for a bridge club. An ethologist, John Calhoun, experimented with rats that became disruptive and aggressive in overcrowded mazes and made analogies with the social breakdown in the teeming cities.

Predictions of extinction abound. Wilderness should be preserved because it contains "genetic stock," the unmanipulated result of four billion years of evolution. Open space is to be preserved in the countryside to save money by precluding a dysfunctional hydrological regime. Parks are proposed in the city so that its people-rats won't get madder than they already are. These rationales are based on the facts, the scientific facts. Facts, facts, nothing but facts, as McChoakumchild would say.

Yet listen to Aldo Leopold:

> Science contributes moral as well as material blessings to the world. Its great moral contribution is objectivity, or the scientific point of view. This means doubting everything except facts; it means hewing to the facts, let the chips fall where they may. . . . That the good life on any river may likewise depend on the perception of its music, and the preservation of some music to perceive, is a form of doubt not yet entertained by science.

Science, especially the science of ecology, provides us the reasons for disaster, but not a life-affirming motive for changing our ways. It is therefore an incomplete idea. A Romantic view of nature provides a life-affirming motive for a faithful stewardship of the ecosphere, but fails in these cynical times to make it seem imperative. It is therefore also an incomplete idea.

The philosopher Scott Buchanan observed: "One of the impressive functions of the cosmic idea is to preside over the birth of possible, new, and good worlds, and to incite new wills to make them actual." Such a cosmic idea is, I believe, to be found in the joining of these concepts—of the scientific facts of ecology with the Romantic spirit of a personal relationship with nature. And it was Aldo Leopold who was the first to sense this possible union.

Leopold wrote, necessarily, in terms of the situation in which he found himself—which was 1930s-style conservation. He rebelled against its economic foundation and, at a time when it was hardly fashionable to do so, celebrated the land as an aesthetic experience. Yet he also introduced, for all practical purposes, the concept of ecology as a basis for public policy. He was careful, though, not to confuse the servant (ecology) with the master (perception):

Let no man jump to the conclusion that Babbitt must take his Ph.D. in ecology before he can "see" his country. On the contrary, the Ph.D. may become as callous as an undertaker to the mysteries at which he officiates.

For Leopold it was an aesthetic view of natural surroundings, supported and informed by ecology, that led to the concept of the "land ethic," perhaps the most important environmental revelation of this century. His essay by this title, originally published in the *Journal of Forestry* in 1933 and later in *A Sand County Almanac* in 1949, is the manifesto, or should be, of all who love the land.

As I explained at the outset of this book, it was Leopold's view that ethics evolve in ever widening circles. The first perception of right and wrong was limited to immediate family. Through history the circle included a larger and larger universe—tribe, nation, race. Accordingly, Leopold believed that ethics would be extended to the land as well: "The land ethic simply enlarges the boundaries of the community to include soils, waters, plants, and animals, or collectively, the land."

In summarizing his concept, he wrote these now-familiar lines:

We abuse the land because we regard it as a commodity belonging to us. When we see land as a community to which we belong, we may begin to use it with love and respect. There is no other way for land to survive the impact of mechanized man, nor for us to reap from it the aesthetic harvest it is capable, under science, of contributing to culture. That land is a community is the basic concept of ecology, but that land is to be loved and respected is an extension of ethics. That land yields a cultural harvest is a fact long known, but latterly often forgotten.

I propose this: Those who would save the land must balance predictions of apocalypse with visions of a better life. When we predict disaster we do the safe thing; for if we are right we can say "I told you so," should there be anybody left to listen; and if we are wrong no one will care, or even remember much of what the hullabaloo was all about. But if the environmental movement seeks change and seeks to have a hand in the direction of change, then it will have to get into the vision business, into the music of rivers in Leopold's evocative metaphor. If indeed we do have a cosmic idea within our grasp—the permanent bonding of the science of ecology and the land love that Leopold described as the basis for an ethic—then perhaps visions are not beyond us.

LAND STEWARDSHIP

Is there a land ethic in heaven? I hope so for Leopold's sake, since he despaired of there ever being one on earth. He despaired in the first published version of his remarkable essay on the land ethic. And the despair was unallayed by the passage of years. In the final version, appearing in *Sand County Almanac,* written after the war and the atom bomb, Leopold bitterly concluded that "no important change in ethics was ever accomplished without an internal change in our intellectual emphasis, loyalties, affections, and convictions. The proof that conservation has not yet touched these foundations of conduct lies in the fact that philosophy and religion have not yet heard of it."

And that is our text for today: because the fact is that philosophy and religion *did,* eventually, hear of conservation and of the land ethic that is its philosophical cornerstone. In fact the land ethic is something of an intellectual growth industry these days. And therefore might *we* be justified in predicting a different future for the land than could Professor Leopold? Despite the blasted landscapes of the present, might not ethical considerations finally be set into the grain of our future public and private decisions about land use and conservation even so? Or shall we keep on tossing the dice, again and again, until the land craps out?

If you are looking for hope, please attend to the word of the U.S. Catholic bishops in their November 1984 pastoral letter, "Catholic Social Teaching and the U.S. Economy," a section of which warrants quoting in its entirety:

> 33. The biblical vision of creation has provided one of the most enduring legacies of church teaching, especially in the patristic period. We find a constant affirmation that the goods of this earth are common property and that men and women are summoned to faithful stewardship rather than to selfish

appropriation or exploitation of what was destined for all. Cyprian writes in the middle of the third century that "whatever belongs to God belongs to all," and Ambrose states "God has ordered all things to be produced so that there would be food in common for all, and that the earth should be a common possession of all." Clement of Alexandria grounds the communality of possession not only in creation but in the incarnation since "it is God himself who has brought our race to communion (*koinonia*) by sharing himself, first of all, and by sending his word to all alike and by making all things for all. Therefore everything is in common." Recent church teaching, as voiced by John Paul II, while reaffirming the right to private property, clearly states that Christian tradition "has always understood this right within the broader context of the right common to all to use the goods of the whole creation."

Applied to land, this is as clear an ethical pronouncement as one could wish. To some it is shockingly clear. At a meeting held to discuss the implications of the bishop's letter for managing land resources, a government economist confessed his dismay. "I have a Ph.D. in economics," he said. "And in all my studies, I have never seen as radical an economic document as this."

You see, we commonly take land to be, mainly, an economic "input": with labor and capital, a "factor of production." The Great Plains are an input into the agriculture industry. The timbered Northwest is an input to the forest-products industry. The wilderness fastness is an input to the recreation industry. And my valley, described at the beginning of this chapter, was an input to the real estate industry. Leopold made this curiosity familiar, describing it as a kind of resource Babbitry. I personally know people who go around muttering "land is a factor of production" all day long, without even realizing what they are saying, just as some of us say grace at dinner—

God is great, God is good
And we thank Him for this food—

without wondering who *really* owns the land that makes the food. And the table. And the china and silver and tablecloth too. At this level of inquiry, it's hard to understand landownership in any but the most transient and inconsequential sense. Ownership: this is the linchpin in the whole business of land ethics, of course, as the bishops so forthrightly assert.

A real philosopher I know (Sara Ebenreck, who has a Ph.D. in ethics from Fordham University in New York) tells of the young Chief of the Western Cayuses who in 1855 protested the selling of the tribal lands. "I wonder if the ground has anything to say," he asked the governor of the Washington Territory. "I wonder if the ground is listening to what is being said."

Owning land—in the monopolistic, exploitative sense, not in Thomas Jefferson's sense that all should be allowed "a little portion"—has always seemed a bit like owning the air through which we pass, or the waters that fall or flow or tidally undulate. Land *moves*, like air and water. And we move through it in our brief lives. It opens before us and it is well to wonder, after we have passed: Do other travelers and voyagers find it good? What does the ground say? I am often astonished when people talk about the need for a land ethic as if it were an argument about table manners. It is not. It is an argument about violence, as Leopold made plain in the very opening lines of his essay. The stewardship of land is a form of not raping it.

"How do you feel about not-raping," says the fellow next to us at the cocktail party, for he has somehow discovered that we are the holders of strange views.

"Well, I'm all for it," I guess we are supposed to say. "There ought to be a whole lot more not-raping going on. We got to get the word out."

"Still," says the fellow at the cocktail party, fingers glistening with chicken grease from the barbecued wings of a factory-made leghorn, "you can overdo the idea of not-raping. After all, we have to be practical. This is a free country. A man has his rights. I'm sick and tired of all those do-gooders running around complaining all the time. Let's stand up for America."

But are we not called to stand up for the land too?

Another, earlier statement by the Catholic bishops—those whose sees are in the American heartland, a holy place by any standard—asserted that the Bible and the tradition of the church make manifest these ten principles of land stewardship:

1. The land is God's.
2. People are God's stewards on the land.
3. The land's benefits are for everyone.

4. The land should be distributed equally.
5. The land should be conserved and restored.
6. Land-use planning must consider social and environmental impacts.
7. Land use should be appropriate to land quality.
8. The land should provide a moderate livelihood.
9. The land's workers should be able to become the land's owners.
10. The land's mineral wealth should be shared.

An ecumenical group of North Carolina religious leaders, called the Land Stewardship Council, has written in its "Ministry Statement" that

> we are all Creatures of God. We and the land are the work of God's creative love. The strong basis for the traditional Jewish-Christian concept of stewardship can be seen in numerous places in the Scriptures. The Bible describes the proper relationship that people should have with the land and with each other. This is expressed plainly, for example, in Psalms 24:1— "The earth is the Lord's and all that is in it, the world and all that dwell therein." In Leviticus 25:23, God says that no land should be sold in perpetuity "because the land is mine"; to me you are "aliens and settlers."

In Minnesota, an outfit called the Land Stewardship Project has created its own bible. Put together by Joe and Nancy Paddock and Carol Bly, poets and writers, the book, photocopied and bound in a plastic "comb" binder, is a compendium of long and short quotations by fellow poets and writers interspersed with the editors' own insights. Black Elk, the Oglala Sioux holy man, is here. And Isaiah. And E. F. Schumacher. And Walt Whitman. And scores more you haven't heard of.

Joe Paddock, in his poem, "Black Wind":

> This vast
> prairie, its hide of sod
> stripped back, black
> living flesh of earth
> exposed.

Our way
has made thieves
of the wind and rain.

Listen,
listen to the wind moan
through the bone-white dead
cottonwood limb: *Half gone!*

Half gone! Half gone! . . .

In all of it, though, there is the amazing hope.

———

We are, like the Chinese (from Confucius to Mao), a nation in love with axioms. Our homes and offices are littered with them: from "Be It Ever So Humble . . ." to "The Buck Stops Here." We wear them on our T-shirts ("A Woman's Place is in the House . . . and the Senate") and the bumpers of our automobiles ("Save the Bay"). My own grandfather, a printer, used one on a magazine he published to promote his business. Under a lithographed team of horses straining at the plow were the words, "Work, Son of Adam, and Forget It."

Axioms are not ethics. Ethics, it seems to me, requires work: the work of a society trying to live up to its beliefs. A land ethic proposes restraint in land use, deferred reward from exploitation of the resource base, concern for posterity so that future generations will get as much or more from the land as we. It is a social goal, this land ethic of Aldo Leopold, and it must be expressed in "policy." And not only the abstract, big-P Policy of Principle, but the workaday little-p policy of legislation, of statute, of government regulation and management practice.

While the land ethic has latterly laid claim to our consciousness to a degree that would have heartened Professor Leopold, there are other social goals that tend to complicate the effort to create and implement the legislation needed to make it actual. Some of these goals—individual liberty, social justice, scientific progress—are much on the lips of those whose economic ox would be gored by the actual application of a land ethic in policy. They insist that the goals they espouse are in conflict with a land ethic. In fact, so persuasive have the opponents of a land ethic been with this tactic that of all industrial democracies, the United States (which has the most to gain from it) has the least effective legislation to protect its land base.

Whether the arguments are opposing wilderness designation, establishing wild and scenic rivers, conserving soil and water resources, planning for urban development, or limiting the conversion of prime farmland, the exploiters of land are adroit at using the rhetoric of the social reformers of yesteryear.

John Locke (1632–1704), who gave us the outline for a liberal constitutional government, provides the most relevant example. Locke proposed the concept of "natural rights"—being life, liberty, and property. They are natural because they would inhere to mankind in a "state of nature." He said that government was valid only with the consent of the governed, and that it was the "natural right" of people to "dispose of their persons and possessions as they think fit." We now listen to modern-day philosophers of the political right asserting their own anarchic version of Lockean liberalism, as in, "It's my land and I can do with it what I want."

Locke, an urbane Londoner, was in effect the originator of "individualism"—of the kind that is now thought to be a uniquely American characteristic. In its most simplistic form the American individualist is contemporaneously embodied by the Marlboro Man who rides the plains alone and inhales deeply despite warnings by the Surgeon General. Only slightly more subtle are the landowners who believe that moral responsibility stops at the property lines. The individualist who insists on the unpopular view that this may not be quite the correct interpretation of individual liberty is less admired now than he, or she, might have been by Locke and Jefferson.

How does the Lockean individualist view, American-style, comport with the bishops' communitarian philosophy of land use? The answer is, not very well. And here is the first of several conundrums that arise when we wish to apply the land ethic to policy. It is deepened, at least so it would seem on the surface, by Thomas Jefferson's small-d democratic insistence on the individual right of landownership to provide for one's own welfare and subsistence.

Thus do we become caught in a trap of our own manufacture. By appealing to authority without sensitivity to the historical setting in which the reform-minded concepts to which we mindlessly cling were created, we allow the moral teachings of the past to be perverted by those who would use them cynically. According to Eugene C. Hargrove, a professor of philosophy at the University of New Mexico, landowners cannot honestly justify a position that they are absolved of social responsibility by asserting a natural right of landownership to do with the land whatever they might choose. This is a claim, says Hargrove, that neither Locke nor Jefferson would have been comfortable with, given present-day circumstances in which the perverse exploitation of land is exacerbated by limitations on its quantity. Both men thought of the American frontier as virtually endless.

Locke and (less often) Jefferson are not the only authorities patriotically invoked in defense of unethical land use. Jeremy Bentham (1748–1832), another reformer, proposed that the basis for all legislation was "the greatest happiness for the greatest number." At one time this radical thought stood in contrast to policies that benefited only the nobility in England. Today, in the United States, Benthamite utilitarianism is used to justify everything from ski lifts in national forests to governmental sponsorship of the use of poisons in agriculture. Another reformer, Adam Smith (1723–1790), hoped to benefit the masses with his theories expounded in the *Wealth of Nations*. Here it is written that if individuals undertake their "industry" primarily for their own gain, then they will benefit society by "an invisible hand" that frequently produces a better result in serving society's needs than would governmental intervention in order to improve the public welfare. Ever since, industrialists and others have taken the work of the great Scottish moralist as license for greed and antisocial behavior in general, and specifically to excuse a failure to think of land resources in terms other than immediate gain from exploitation.

These days the Free Market is having its best run since Calvin Coolidge, and "trickle down" is no longer a cause for sniggering by limousine liberals. Adam Smith, in an agrarian age, said that government could not do very much to effect the welfare of individuals in society. And if a twentieth-century John Maynard Keynes proved him wrong, and if a fifty-year history of just the opposite created the wealthiest and strongest as well as the most decent nation on earth, then so what? If it ain't trickle down, it ain't the American way.

If you want a course in selective Anglo-American intellectual history, all you need to do is attend a hearing—in Congress or at Town Hall—on any legislation or ordinance designed to protect the land resource base: on policies that would give substance to the *idea* of a land ethic, which while much on the lips is scarcely on the books.

In such sacred places as these you will hear Mr. Bentham, who wants to construct a theme park in the last remaining unspoiled marsh in the state's coastal zone, insisting: "Listen, I'm a *people* person." Or Mr. Locke, who wants to build a three-thousand-unit townhouse development on some prime farmland, complaining: "I don't need a bunch of interfering conservationists telling me what I can do with my land." Or Mr. Smith, whose nuclear power plant is to be sited atop the local fault line, crying: "Jobs, jobs, jobs!"

They are, each of them, historically right, having got hold of some solid philosophical precepts. But they are tragically wrong too. And the dilemma doesn't bode well for the future of the land ethic.

What do we build on then? Most important are the citizen-effort models of course: the heartening case histories of those who earnestly try to express the land ethic in terms of civic action in small as well as large ways. Perhaps the small ways are better for purposes of inspiration. It is one thing to fight hard for the highly visible conservation goal such as, say, the protection of the Alaskan wilderness. But it takes nothing away from that achievement to remember that smaller victories (albeit equivalently partial) may be even more expressive of the internal change of intellectual emphasis, loyalties, affections, and convictions that Aldo Leopold believed to be the sine qua non of a functioning land ethic.

For example, a land ethicist I know, Tom Lamm, who works out of Black Earth, Wisconsin, helps to organize small farmers to do, finally, what politicos from Franklin Delano Roosevelt on down have been afraid to do: make soil erosion against the law. An account of the work of the Soil Stewardship Task Force in the *Wisconsin State Journal* quoted the farmers who make up the task force as saying that "regulations must be set in place to control abusive soil eroders who have not, and will not, respond to technical assistance and financial incentives alone." It is the small farmers, Lamm believes, who have the largest sense of land stewardship and who must therefore take the lead in the making of laws about the care of the land. Otherwise the land's future is left to real estate investors and other absentee owners to whom land is mainly surface and not the magical thing that a real dirt farmer knows it to be.

There are a good many people like Tom Lamm who give us hope and inspiration. I have a Rolodex full of them. Eddie Albert continues to celebrate his "green acres" in soil erosion work. Ned Ames gives away money for a foundation to preserve natural areas. George Anthan writes articles for a major Des Moines newspaper on farmland preservation. Malcolm Baldwin, when a senior staff member of the President's Council on Environmental Quality, rescued the Agricultural Lands

Study, which alerted the nation to the loss of farmland, from certain oblivion. John Banta now handles the planning at the Adirondack Park Agency to protect this irreplaceable six-million-acre landscape in New York State. Others listed under B are land ethicists too: Baranyay, Bass, Batcher, Beale, Beamish, Beard, Beaton, Beaty, Becker, Berg, Berger, Bergland, Berrett, Berry, Blodgett, Bodovitz, Boon, Borgers, Borrelli, Boswell-Thomas, Bray, Brinkley, Brooks, Brown, Brown, Browne, Burch, Burr, Burwell, and Byrnes. And it goes on like that through Zinn, Zitzmann, and Zube. Zinn is a geographer who works for the Congressional Research Service and edits a newsletter on coastal zone resource management. Zitzmann is a land-use planner formerly with the Soil Conservation Service. Zube, at the University of Arizona, is a leading figure in landscape aesthetic analysis. Poets and planners, Pooh-Bahs and panjandrums. But land lovers all.

Why isn't this enough, these examples, to show that progress in land ethics is afoot and that eventually all will be well? We have, to be sure, a wilderness policy (although it operates only fitfully on the federally owned lands). We have a recreation policy (though emasculated by budgets and staff cuts at the federal level). We have a soil erosion policy (albeit weak and pusillanimously voluntary). We have wildlife policies, and historic preservation policies, and we have various state and federal policies to protect places of special significance such as the coastal zone. But, alas, there is no policy for *land*.

Leopold insisted on dealing with land whole: the system of soils, waters, animals, and plants that make up a community called "the land." But we insist on discriminating. We apply our money and our energy in behalf of protection on a selective basis. Not of land, but "natural areas." Not of land, but "prime farmland." Not of land, but "wilderness." Leopold briefly compares the evolution of the land ethic with the evolution of ethics concerning children in our society. Child labor laws are now applied to all children, and recently the rights of children not to be beaten by their parents have been asserted. Would we say, for example, that we have an ethic for the protection of children in our society but that it pertains only to some children—perhaps those whose noses do not run—and not others? The question this raises for land and its future is, If an ethic is selectively applied is it still an ethic? Or is it just a hobby?

———————

The idea of a hierarchy in land quality is nevertheless *the* basic tenet of the conservation and environmental movement. We do not see this as an ethical flaw in our thinking, but necessary to the organization of our actions. We preserve prime farmland because it is the most productive in terms of dollars flowing into the agriculture industry. Therefore we are casual about other lands. In the 1970s we plowed up great swaths of thin prairie soils in the High Plains, soils that should never have seen the sillion shine of the plowshare. Great center-pivot irrigation rigs now crawl over the land like weirdly articulated steel insects, sucking up the irreplaceable reserves of water in the Ogalalla aquifer, the great multistate underground lake that when exhausted will leave the land defenseless against the wind which even now piles the sandy soil against the fences, like dunes.

In urban areas, we commonly assume that we must ruin one landscape to preserve another. A beautiful apple orchard becomes uglified by tasteless development because we wish to save a marsh, and we assume—incorrectly I believe—that since all development is ugly, let ugliness reign except in the marsh. The skunk cabbage thrives, but do we? What hierarchical perversity has led to the tacky commercialization of the so-called gateway communities at the entrances to our national parks? How is it that the beautiful landscapes of national parks and national monuments can be framed by such greed and ugliness that it blasphemes the landscapes within? Do we put a neon tube with little bubbles around the Pietà?

In fact the "normative" landscape is unremarkable. Ethologists tell us that all animals have an instinctive habitat preference. *Homo sapiens* is an animal; therefore we have a habitat preference just as imbedded as that in, say, a meadow mouse. What is the preferred habitat for man? Well, look no farther than the place where hominids arose, where they emerged as a separate species: the Great Rift Valley in East Africa, a savanna with short grass and scattered trees. Food was abundant, the landscape provided safety, the climate was ideal (not as dry then as it is now). So most of the time was taken up with peaceable intellectual, social, and artistic pursuits. I have called this the normative landscape. It is of course the Garden of Eden, paradise (which in Persian means garden). Where is it today? Why, in our most sacred places: the landscaped estates of the wealthy, public parks, golf courses, and cemeteries—short grass and scattered trees in pseudo-savannas called "memorial parks."

Other ordinary landscapes are good too of course. What is better than a bustling city neighborhood, a tidy suburb, an apple orchard framing a white farmhouse, a sea pounded cliff, a deep hemlock forest, an unspurious fishing village, a desert where the cholla and saguaro give spiny protection to a community of strange creatures? Any place is a good place if it is allowed to be true to its nature.

I argued previously that in Leopold's land ethic we are in the presence of a cosmic idea. It can, and has, incited new wills to make its promise at least partially actual, in the words of Scott Buchanan. But I also argued that the great irony of the land ethic is that those who embrace it most fervently—those who love the land—are among those who most successfully obstruct its fulfillment. By and large, land lovers have copped out, plumping for the protection of the land on every socioeconomic basis they can think of in the manner of Smith and Bentham and Locke, save the ethical one. We try to frame our defense of the land to suit the cynics: those who, said Oscar Wilde, understand the price of everything and the value of nothing.

As the sun sinks in the West in more ways than one we search frantically for tiny evidences that a land ethic, at least a prelusive one, can really exist in America and that it can exist for reasons of producing a good life rather than just making a living.

The closest any place has ever come to actualizing what we might call a Level-I land ethic has been the state of Oregon, under the leadership of its late governor, Tom McCall. McCall died of cancer in January 1983. He was, in my view, the most effective political operative in behalf of American land since Teddy Roosevelt.

In the early 1970s, Oregon enacted a legislative package concerning land use in the state. It was designed to stop what McCall cheerfully described as the "grasping wastrels of the land," the "buffalo hunters and pelt skinners," those who presided over the "ravenous rampage of suburbia," and infectious "coastal condomania." He would expose, he said (and this is my favorite McCallism), "the sagebrush saboteurs." In a nutshell Oregon's legislation established an independent state-level body that promulgated statewide land-use "goals and guidelines" for application via local regulations. If regulations were not applied locally, then the state government would apply them itself. There were nineteen goals-and-guidelines statements, dealing with such matters as transportation, industrial siting, waste treatment, water supply, and farmland. The net was a broad one. Not many square feet of McCall's "beautiful Oregon country" were left uncovered by the legislation.

One goal, dealing with agricultural land, is especially instructive. It provides the basis for "exclusive farm use" zoning—EFU—on most existing and potential privately owned farmland in the state. Though the farmland zones are established locally, the permitted uses are defined by state statute, which provides that any new lot in an EFU has to be large enough to maintain a viable agricultural economy in the area so that families can continue to make a whole living from it. If, therefore, farms average one hundred acres in, say, a dairying district, then local governments cannot permit the subdivision of land into parcels substantially less than that amount. So where is the new development supposed to go? Why, inside the UGB—the Urban Growth Boundary—established under the legislation to confine urbanization to areas in and around existing settlements rather than letting it ooze all over the landscape.

In my view, the Oregon story is important not because of the technicalities of its legislation, but because in one state at least a government (which is to say, the people) was able to establish convincingly that "the land" is of *public* concern, not simply a matter that can be left substantially to private economic decision. If it seems like a truism that there are public rights to be considered as well as private ones in the management of the land resource base, please remember that only a handful of state and local governments of the United States has any kind of policy dealing with land in any category, much less comprehensively.

These days we are confronted with a growing trend toward the "privatization" of land-use decision-making, to employ an overused contemporary term, which together with a rather negative government role, especially at the national level, seeks to influence private decisions so timidly that it is scarcely worth anyone's time messing with it. We do not seem to be able to produce clear-cut statutory policies that provide, in the law of the land, laws *for* the land. For example, in one lukewarm piece of legislation enacted in the mid-1980s, the best we could do for the Barrier Islands, those magnificent shifting dunes with their fragile ecosystems that guard our coastline from Virginia to Florida, was to constrain the federal government—the *government*, mind you, which is supposed to be on our side—from not doing anything *itself* to degrade the islands further.

Tom McCall, God bless him, would have none of this pussyfooting around. His approach was Mosaic, with plenty of thou-shalt-nots deriving from a clearly conceived right of the ordinary citizen to have a landscape worth looking at and living in.

But at what a price! In the end, when he was dying of cancer, he had, because a referendum had been placed on the ballot to abolish his policies, to convince his fellow citizens once again that their land was precious to them. For his trouble he was told, not for the first time, that his idea was nothing but thinly veiled Marxism, that what our forebears fought for, our sacred heritage, was being abridged, that he was depriving his fellow citizens of their constitutional right to destroy the land of Oregon as they saw fit. In 1982 in the midst of this battle, I invited McCall to attend a meeting I had organized in Ohio, and he told he would come. But later he telephoned; he said that the cancer was kicking up again, sapping his strength, and he'd better stay home in Oregon to fight off "the grasping wastrels" once again. He did and he won: the voters sustained the legislation. But soon after, McCall was gone. We were never to see him again. And his like comes around rarely American politics.

———

By leaning on champions like McCall, we reveal a terrible flaw in our perception of how Leopold's cosmic idea is to be made actual, for it is plain to me that the future of land stewardship—if we are to get beyond Level I, even in a single state—cannot rest on the chance that a Tom McCall will meet history in just the right way to save the land. And have it stay saved.

Let us be honest. There is no real ethic present in the United States, no permanent system of values to which we Americans have given our general consent, when the laws expressing it are constantly challenged, vicious arguments are mounted, patriotism is called into question as it was even for McCall. The land ethic of the future will not be without its complications in application, but its basic premise must be accepted as being natural and obvious, made manifest simply by "listening to the ground," in the words of the chief of the western Cayuses. For this, we must look not to the brilliant political apologist and leader, but to the ordinary *users* of the land, the stewards, for they are most in touch with it.

Why should *they* not be the ones to insist on policies for the land's posterity? As indeed they do, as in the case of Tom Lamm's farmers, though sometimes we do not hear them, so engrossed are we in our hierarchical attitudes about land. But if I were a farmer I'd rather farm for posterity than for a bunch of bankers. If I were a sawyer I'd be pleased to scratch what Gifford Pinchot wrote into the housing of my chainsaw, that what America *still* needs to understand is that "trees could be cut and the forest preserved at one and the same time." If I were a herdsman, I would want pastures of plenty to the horizon of time as well as space. If I were a fisherman I would wish for the heavy-bodied salmon to run freely up free rivers forever, squirming into the far pools of ancient memory.

When Thomas Jefferson urged "a little portion" of land for every family, he meant to give actual landownership as wide a civic base as possible in the New World—as a democratic right, an expression of an agrarian ideal embodied by the yeomen-freeholders in England, and as an obligation before God. We may now be on the crest of a historical third wave in our stuttering technological advance as a society (although I have my suspicions), but the basic Jeffersonian concept still has its strength—to give access to the land to those who wish it and can make good on it, and to have them responsible also for the land's welfare. I have never understood the arguments of those who would save land by limiting access to its use and title, aggregating up larger and larger parcels of it in government and corporate ownership. I realize that this may seem a heretical view to some conservationists who wish to remove land from individual ownership and who would much prefer the problem of regulating large corporations than an unruly lot of small landowners. At the same time I would insist (as many neo-Jeffersonian libertarians would not) that there is no license that comes with the land's title to abridge the public's perpetual right to a productive, ecologically sound, and beautiful landscape.

To assume that individual, small-scale ownership of land leads to its destruction is to confuse a failure of policy with the function of stewardship of land by those to whom it has been entrusted for care. The late René Dubos wrote of his beloved Île-de-France country, northwest of Paris, as a landscape that was not only preserved, but improved. He quotes the poet Charles Peguy:

> Deux mille ans de labeur ont fait de cette terre
> Un reservoir sans fin pour les ages nouveaux.

Dubos translates this: "Two thousand years of human labor have made of this land an inexhaustible source of wealth for the times to come."

Jefferson had confidence in the American people not only as electors of political leaders, but as owners of land. There is an ecological analogy here, in that with the complexity of a broad, small-scale pattern of ownership comes the stability of a healthy functioning system.

When the system is simplified, into small numbers of larger owner-ships by governments and corporations, it becomes like an attenuated ecosystem, subject to degradation.

So it is that the small landowners, and those who would become small landowners, are the people who most validly may insist on morality in land use, in principle as well as policy. It is in their behalf, primarily, that the bishops have addressed themselves to the land ethic. It is they who can understand, and act upon what Aldo Leopold had in mind, in contrast to the large American corporation—a "hog with all four feet in the trough" as one of my Madison Avenue advertising mentors called it—whose flaccid muscles and larded body preclude any response other than grunts and slurps in the inevitable destruction of American land resources.

And yet the future of the land ethic depends no less on the rest of us. Not as instructors in land ethics, for this presumes an authority not all of us feel, but as the faithful supporters of stewardship wher-ever we can find it—in law and practice. I cannot imagine how else the land ethic will come about—the actualizing of this cosmic idea—but in vivid increments of individual choice and collective action.

FROM THE LOOKOUT

"I lift mine eyes unto the hills," the psalmist wrote, "from whence cometh my help." In my former California valley, I could still lift my eyes to the San Gabriels, despite the zooming traffic at my feet, those snakes of cars mindlessly writhing along the lanes beneath the memory-image of Mr. Lee's chicken ranch. The mountains rose abruptly from the settlement below just as they always had, and as I lifted my eyes new memories flooded my mind, for when I was a youngster my friends and I would climb the first range of these mountains to a place we called the "Lookout."

———

"Watch out for rattlers!" yelled the leader (and I could hear him plainly, despite the years). He was a wiry ten-year-old with carrot-colored hair cut close for summer, which was perhaps the summer of 1940. The clattering stones always reminded him of the sandy-brown snakes that liked to hide among the roots and in the crevices to keep cool.

"Rattlers don't worry me," someone shouted back. "It's the mountain lion."

"Mountain lion?"

"Yeah, mountain lion. You never seen a mountain lion?"

"I've seen Mr. Williams's yellow dog. I bet that's your old mountain lion."

"It wasn't no yellow dog that chased the coyotes away."

"Shoot."

"Well, shoot yourself."

We pushed ahead, grabbing at ironwood branches to hand ourselves up the slope, wending through the dead yucca spires that earlier in the year, in spring, had shot up six feet from the nest of swordlike leaves, each spire surmounted by panicles of creamy blossoms.

Finally, dusty-dark, with sweat rivers eroding through to flushed faces, we gained the lookout and our California valley was spread before us.

"Jeez, lookit everything," said the redhead.

"There's the mesa," said another. "See, we're looking *down* on the mesa." It always amazed us, to be above it.

"You mean where the mountain lion scared the coyotes away?"

"Can't you pipe down!"

We knew that if the coyotes were gone from the mesa for an evening or two they'd soon be back, the moonlight behind them, howling with their muzzles pointed skyward in the yip-yip-yip that covered the sounds of the brothers creeping up on the chicken coops below.

As we looked across our valley, the brightness made it seem all the closer, like a medieval triptych whose foreshortened perspectives could give a scene a holy quality. The vineyard rows cut into each other at crisp angles, the details of the vine-trunks and the interlacing runners almost visible, even from here. And beneath the gray-green leaves hid the heavy blue and green bunches, like prizes.

"Lookit Mr. Kraus. Lookit!" It was the redhead again, though only a couple of feet from the farthest ear.

Mr. Kraus was cranking up the tractor that had the bouncy metal seat, and the pops and clanks drifted up to us, out of sync with his actions because of the distance. A tiny speck of red appeared as Mr. Kraus straightened up and ran a bandanna across his flat German brow. He was constructed of planes and bands of bone and muscle. With his sons he would be cutting the grapes using hawk-beaked knives honed like razors. They would pile the dark bunches in wooden crates left at the end of each row, thence to be hefted onto the flatbed wagon, drawn by the tractor.

We watched for a while as Mr. Kraus messed with the spark, then we surveyed other quarters. "The school, the school," someone said, directing our attention to it. And there it lay, its Spanish tile roofs enclosing a yard of live oaks whose cantilevered branches could, when school was in session, support a line of children as a telegraph wire supports a line of swallows.

And so we went through the litany of places, freshly revealed by our superior angle of view: the olive trees along school street, the state highway below, the tomato patch—a huge field of ruby fruit—and the orange groves set into the scene like emerald rectangles spread across the middle distance.

To the northwest was the Tujunga Wash, and southeast the Devil's Gate, great arroyos that guided the waters out of the mountains during the brief season of rain. At other times the water for the houses and the groves and vegetable crops (vineyards were dry-farmed) came from catch basins fed by water mines, bored in the canyons by the earliest settlers, perhaps even the rancheros of the original haciendas.

In such canyons we would find smooth stones and, carrying them up the mountain, would send them humming aloft from the Lookout, into the brilliant air, with David's slings made of rawhide thongs knotted to leather pouches that were slit to cradle the missiles. We swung them round and round, faster and faster, and when we released them there was only sound, for the stones would fly more swiftly than the eye could follow, upward in a great arc—a fragment of our place flung into a distant land, perhaps another country whose people would marvel at the mysterious object falling at their feet.

It is from fragments such as these that a land ethic for the future will be created, the fragments of a sensibility and a hope whose origins are in the earth itself. The Kodak Carousels of our memory go round and round in the darkened livingrooms of America, where images of the land are cast upon lenticular screens. "Oooh. Aaah," say the neighbors. "Beautiful. Just beautiful."

And so it is.

ABOUT THE AUTHOR

Charles E. Little is a former New York City advertising executive and conservation activist who came to Washington, D.C., in the early 1970s to work on national land-use policy. Since then, his published books, papers, and magazine articles have led to many policy innovations, including legislation for farmland protection and new approaches to cooperative planning for outstanding landscape areas. In Washington he served as a senior associate at the Conservation Foundation, as head of natural resources policy research at the Congressional Research Service of the Library of Congress, and as founder and first president of the American Land Forum. Since 1986 he has been a full-time writer. Mr. Little is the author or co-author of eight previous books, contributes to many magazines and journals, and conducts a book review column for *Wilderness* magazine. A native Californian, he now lives in Kensington, Maryland, with his wife, Ila Dawson Little, a professor of English literature.